Keto COSORI Air Fryer Cookbook for Beginners

600 Wholesome Recipes You'll Want to Make Everyday (How I Dropped 50 Pounds-and You Can Too!)

Dr Janda Blardn

© Copyright 2020 Dr Janda Blardn- All Rights Reserved.

In no way is it legal to reproduce, duplicate, or transmit any part of this document by either electronic means or in printed format. Recording of this publication is strictly prohibited, and any storage of this material is not allowed unless with written permission from the publisher. All rights reserved.

The information provided herein is stated to be truthful and consistent, in that any liability, regarding inattention or otherwise, by any usage or abuse of any policies, processes, or directions contained within is the solitary and complete responsibility of the recipient reader. Under no circumstances will any legal liability or blame be held against the publisher for any reparation, damages, or monetary loss due to the information herein, either directly or indirectly.

Respective authors own all copyrights not held by the publisher.

Legal Notice:

This book is copyright protected. This is only for personal use. You cannot amend, distribute, sell, use, quote or paraphrase any part of the content within this book without the consent of the author or copyright owner. Legal action will be pursued if this is breached.

Disclaimer Notice:

Please note the information contained within this document is for educational and entertainment purposes only. Every attempt has been made to provide accurate, up-to-date and reliable, complete information. No warranties of any kind are expressed or implied. Readers acknowledge that the author is not engaging in the rendering of legal, financial, medical or professional advice.

By reading this document, the reader agrees that under no circumstances are we responsible for any losses, direct or indirect, which are incurred as a result of the use of information contained within this document, including, but not limited to, errors, omissions, or inaccuracies.

Table of contents

Introduction 8
Chapter 1: Understanding the Keto Cosori Air Fryer 9
    Cosori Air Fryer 9
    How to Use Your Cosori Air Fryer? 9
    Benefits of Cosori Air Fryer 10
    What Is A Keto Diet? 11
    Benefits of the Keto Diet 11
Chapter 2: Breakfast Recipes 13
    Egg Stuffed Peppers 13
    Cheese Vegetable Frittata 13
    Sausage Egg Scramble 13
    Cheese Egg Breakfast Muffins 14
    Breakfast Egg Bites 14
    Classic Sweet Potato Hash 14
    Easy Cheesy Breakfast Eggs 14
    Cheese Egg Frittata 15
    Cheese Ham Egg Cups 15
    Breakfast Avocado Eggs 15
    Healthy Spinach Omelette 16
    Cheese Mushroom Egg Bake 16
    Breakfast Radish Hash Browns 16
    Breakfast Cream Souffle 17
    Cheese Omelet 17
    Cheese Sausage Egg Muffins 17
    Spinach Baked Eggs 18
    Easy Breakfast Frittata 18
    Bell Pepper Broccoli Frittata 18
    Sausage Cheese Breakfast Frittata 19
    Sausage Spinach Egg Cups 19
    Spinach Garlic Egg Muffins 19
    Greek Egg Muffins 20
    Veggie Frittata 20
    Kale Egg Muffins 21
    Cheese Mushroom Frittata 21
    Blueberry Cheese Muffins 21
    Egg Cheese Mustard Bake 22
    Cottage Cheese Egg Cups 22
    Tasty Herb Egg Cups 22
    Tomato Basil Egg Muffins 23
    Bacon Egg Muffins 23
    Pepper Feta Egg Muffins 23
    Garlic Cheese Quiche 23
    Broccoli Fritters 24
    Spicy Brussels sprouts 24
    Zucchini Breakfast Patties 25
    Bacon Brussels Sprouts 25
    Broccoli Quiche 25
    Bacon Cheese Egg Bites 26
    Cheese Sausage Pepper Frittata 26
    Mushroom Frittata 26
    Broccoli Bell Pepper Frittata 27
    Spinach Tomato Frittata 27
    Basil Feta Egg Bite 27
    Sausage Swiss Cheese Egg Bite 28
    Gruyere Cheese Egg Bite 28
    Cheddar Cheese Broccoli Egg Bite 28
    Green Chilis Egg Bite 29
    Roasted Pepper Egg Bite 29
    Cheddar Cheese Omelet 29
    Spicy Chicken Wings 29
    Fajita Chicken 30
    Lemon Chicken Breasts 30
    Salmon Dill Patties 30
    Chicken Fritters 31
    Delicious Chicken Burger Patties 31
    Cheesy Chicken Fritters 32
    Tuna Patties 32
    Ham Egg Bites 32
Chapter 3: Poultry Recipes 34
    Delicious Chicken Fajita 34
    Parmesan Chicken Wings 34
    Western Chicken Wings 34
    Perfect Whole Chicken 35
    Juicy Chicken Breasts 35
    Flavors Dijon Chicken 36
    Crispy Crusted Chicken Tenders 36
    Tender & Juicy Cornish Hens 36
    Flavors & Crisp Chicken Thighs 37
    Perfect Chicken Thighs Dinner 37
    Perfectly Spiced Chicken Tenders 37
    Quick & Easy Lemon Pepper Chicken 38
    Delicious Chicken Nuggets 38
    Quick & Easy Chipotle Wings 38
    Spicy Jalapeno Hassel back Chicken . 39
    Healthy Greek Chicken 39
    Tasty Hassel back Chicken 40
    Delicious Chicken Meatballs 40
    Mexican Chicken Fajitas 40
    Fajita Hassel back Chicken 41
    Western Turkey Breast 41
    Easy Turkey Meatballs 42
    Cajun Chicken Thighs 42
    Flavorful Chicken Tenders 42
    Juicy Lemon Pepper Chicken Thighs . 43
    Creamy Pesto Chicken 43

Tasty Chicken Tikka Bites 43	Flavorful Beef Roast 62
Healthy Chicken & Broccoli 44	Cheese Butter Steak 62
Lemon Pepper Turkey Breast............. 44	Tasty Ginger Garlic Beef 62
Garlic Chicken Wings 45	Juicy Burger Patties 63
Crispy Bagel Chicken Tenders............ 45	Meatloaf.. 63
Italian Chicken Drumsticks 45	Meatballs 63
Asian Chicken Meatballs 46	Spiced Steak 64
Herb Marinated Chicken Thighs........ 46	Healthy Beef & Broccoli 64
Juicy Caribbean Chicken 46	Meatloaf.. 65
Chicken Broccoli Fritters 47	Tasty Kebab 65
Spicy Chicken Wings 47	Meatballs 65
Nutritious Chicken & Veggies 48	Easy Beef & Broccoli........................ 66
Chicken Spinach Meatballs 48	Meatballs 66
Tender Turkey Legs 48	Tender Steak 66
Greek Meatballs 49	Meatballs 67
Perfect Chicken Breasts 49	Cheesy Burger Patties 67
Turkey Spinach Patties....................... 49	Garlicky Beef & Broccoli 67
Tasty Turkey Fajitas 50	Lime Cumin Beef 68
Ranch Garlic Chicken Wings 50	Burger Patties 68
Ranch Chicken Thighs 50	Meatloaf.. 68
Taco Ranch Chicken Wings 51	Rib Eye Steak 69
Crisp Cilantro Lime Chicken Wings .. 51	Beef Berger Patties 69
Turkey Mushroom Patties.................. 51	Tasty Beef Satay................................ 69
Crispy Cajun Chicken Wings 52	Easy Kebab 70
Crispy & Juicy Chicken Wings........... 52	Beef Cheese Patties 70
Simple Cajun Chicken Wings 53	Stuffed Bell Peppers 70
Adobo Chicken Thighs 53	Juicy Beef Kabobs 71
Herbed Turkey Breast 53	Sirloin Steaks 71
Thanksgiving Turkey Breast............... 54	Tasty Steak Fajitas 72
Spice Herb Turkey Breast 54	Steak with Mushrooms 72
Turkey Zucchini Patties..................... 54	Flavors Burger Patties....................... 72
Greek Turkey Patties 55	Beef Fajitas 73
Flavorful Turkey Breast..................... 55	Stuffed Peppers 73
Moist & Juicy Turkey Breast 55	Steak Pepper Kebab.......................... 73
Chapter 4: Beef Recipes.....................57	Juicy & Tender Parmesan Steak 74
Quick & Easy Steak Tips 57	**Chapter 5: Pork Recipes 75**
Simple Sirloin Steaks 57	Spicy Pork Chops 75
Flavorful Steak.................................. 57	Meatballs 75
Italian Beef Roast 57	Meatballs 75
Rosemary Thyme Beef Roast 58	BBQ Pork Chops 76
Italian Meatballs 58	Pesto Pork Chops 76
Burgers Patties 58	Coconut Butter Pork Chops 76
Meatballs 59	Crispy Pork Chops 77
Tasty Beef Patties.............................. 59	Cheese Garlicky Pork Chops 77
Meatloaf.. 60	Garlic Lemon Pork Chops................ 77
Tender & Juicy Kebab....................... 60	Herb Cheese Pork Chops 78
Meatloaf.. 60	Creole Seasoned Pork Chops 78
Meatballs 61	Tender Pork Chops.......................... 78
Marinated Steak 61	Asian Pork Chops 79
Asian Beef... 61	Easy & Delicious Pork Chops 79

Dash Seasoned Pork Chops 79
Easy Pork Butt 80
Spicy Pork Steak 80
Simple Air Fryer Pork Chops 80
Tasty Onion Pork Chops 81
Juicy & Tasty Pork Chops 81
Delicious Ranch Pork Chops 81
Meatballs 81
Easy Pork Patties 82
Lemon Pepper Seasoned Pork Chops . 82
Flavorful Pork Chops 82
Crispy Crusted Pork Chops 83
Meatballs 83
Meatloaf 83
Herb Butter Pork Chops 84
Air Fried Pork Chops 84
Cheddar Cheese Pork Chops 84
Meatballs 85
Garlic Pork Chops 85
Mustard Pork Chops 85
Meatballs 85
Pork & Peppers 86
Simple Rosemary Pork Chops 86
Asian Pork ribs 86
Flavorful Pork Roast 87
Spicy Pork Shoulder 87
Meatballs 87
Cheesy Pork Chops 88
Paprika Pork Chops 88
Smoked Paprika Pork Chops 88
Delicious Pork & Mushrooms 88
Cheesy Pork Chops 89
Delicious Stuffed Pork Chops 89
Simple & Tasty Pork Bites 89
Pork Tenderloin 90
Pesto Pork Chops 90
Cheese Garlic Pork Chops 91
Balsamic Pork Chops 91
Tasty BBQ Ribs 91
Spicy Pork Shoulder 92
Balsamic Pork Chops 92
Meatballs 92
Herb Butter Pork Chops 93
Spicy Pork Patties 93
Herb Pork Loin 93
Herb Pepper Pork Tenderloin 94

Chapter 6: Lamb Recipes 95
Juicy & Savory Lamb Chops 95
Rosemary Lamb Chops 95
Dijon Garlic Lamb Chops 95
Flavorful Cumin Lamb 96
Juicy & Tender Lemon Mustard Lamb
Chops 96
Meatballs 96
Spicy Lamb Steak 97
Lamb Roast 97
Easy Greek Lamb Chops 97
Delicious Zaatar Lamb Chops 98
Quick & Easy Lamb Chops 98
Dried Herb Lamb Chops 98
Moist Lamb Roast 99
Thyme Lamb Chops 99
Baked Lamb Chops 99
Meatballs 100
Meatballs 100
Meatballs 100
Lamb Patties 100
Spicy Lamb Chops 101
Lemon Basil Lamb Chops 101
Lemon Pepper Lamb 102
Meatballs 102
Greek Lamb Cutlets 102
Herb Lamb Cutlets 103
Meatballs 103
Garlic Herb Lamb Cutlets 103
Spicy Lamb Chops 104
Greek Lamb Patties 104
Mustard Lamb Chops 104

Chapter 7: Snacks & Appetizers 105
Roasted Herb Olives 105
Cheesy Crab Dip 105
Roasted Walnuts 105
Cheese Stuffed Mushrooms 105
Parmesan Carrot Fries 106
Stuffed Jalapeno Poppers 106
Spicy Crab Dip 106
Crispy Zucchini Fries 107
Healthy Zucchini Chips 107
Chicken Stuffed Poblanos 107
Ranch Zucchini Chips 108
Crispy Tofu 108
Crispy Cauliflower Florets 108
Parmesan Asparagus 109
Tasty Buffalo Cauliflower Bites 109
Beetroot Chips 110
Parmesan Brussels sprouts 110
Spicy Crab Dip 110
Flavors Chicken Tandoori 110
Asian Chicken Wings 111
Chicken Kabab 111

Meatballs 112
Tasty Chicken Tenders 112
Meatballs 112
Easy Taro Fries 113
Broccoli Fritters 113
Crispy Brussels sprouts 113
Herb Roasted Carrots 114
Simple Air Fried Vegetables 114
Healthy Roasted Pecans 114
Meatballs 114
Sausage Meatballs 115
Cheesy Chicken Dip 115
Delicious Shrimp Dip 115
Quick & Easy Eggplant Fries 116
Lime Radish Chips 116
Tasty Carrot Fries 116
Flavorful Herb Mushrooms 117
Turkey Dip 117
Easy Zucchini Chips 117
Easy Sweet Potato Fries 118
Healthy Jicama Fries 118
Crispy Cauliflower Bites 118
Spicy Salmon Bites 118
Healthy Roasted Almonds 119
Flavorful Eggplant Slices 119
Easy Jalapeno Poppers 119
Easy Broccoli Nuggets 120
Crab Stuffed Mushrooms 120
Delicious Chicken Dip 120

Chapter 8: Seafood Recipes 122
Easy Cajun Shrimp 122
Tender & Juicy Salmon 122
Shrimp & Vegetable Dinner 122
Lemon Garlic Shrimp 122
Lemon Garlic White Fish 123
Easy Coconut Shrimp 123
Parmesan White Fish Fillets 123
Tasty Shrimp Fajitas 124
Ginger Garlic Salmon 124
Tasty Chipotle Shrimp 124
Quick & Easy Salmon 125
Healthy Salmon Patties 125
Garlic Yogurt Salmon Fillets 125
Lime Garlic Shrimp Kabobs 126
Healthy Crab Cakes 126
Crisp Bacon Wrapped Scallops 126
Parmesan Basil Salmon 127
Crisp & Juicy Cajun Shrimp 127
Flavorful Curry Cod Fillets 127
Delicious Buttery Shrimp 128

Mexican Shrimp Fajitas 128
Dukkah Crusted Salmon 128
Lemon Garlic Scallops 129
Lemon Caper Scallops 129
Cajun Scallops 129
Flavorful Crab Cakes 130
Herbed Salmon 130
Quick & Easy Salmon Patties 130
Shrimp with Vegetables 131
Nutritious Salmon Fillets 131
Onion Pepper Shrimp 131
Old Bay Shrimp 132
Crunchy Fish Sticks 132
Juicy & Tender Cod Fillets 132
Flavorful Parmesan Shrimp 133
Perfectly Tender Frozen Fish Fillets .. 133
Old Bay Seasoned Crab Cakes 133
Simple & Perfect Shrimp 134
Asian Salmon Steak 134
Delicious Fish Bites 135
Chili Lime Cod 135
Savory Fish Sticks 135
Garlic Herb Tilapia 136
Parmesan Salmon 136
Easy Bacon Wrapped Shrimp 136
Cajun Tilapia 137
Easy Tuna Steaks 137
Healthy Tuna Patties 137
Tuna Zucchini Cakes 138
Pesto Scallops 138
Pesto Shrimp Kebabs 138
Flavorful Horseradish Salmon 138
Lemon Garlic Herb Salmon 139
Spicy Scallops 139
Spicy & Tasty Shrimp 139
Thai Shrimp 140
Chili Garlic Shrimp 140
Creamy Shrimp 140
Simple Catfish Fillets 141
Salmon Avocado Patties 141

Chapter 9: Meatless Meals 142
Healthy Mixed Vegetables 142
=Easy Roasted Vegetables 142
Easy & Crisp Brussels Sprouts 142
Garlic Green Beans 143
Simple Vegan Broccoli 143
Sesame Carrots 143
Asparagus with Almonds 143
Easy Roasted Carrots 144
Asian Broccoli 144

Healthy Squash & Zucchini 144
Crunchy Fried Cabbage 145
Balsamic Brussels Sprouts 145
Quick Vegetable Kebabs 145
Easy Soy Garlic Mushrooms 146
Spicy Edamame 146
Balsamic Mushrooms 146
Mediterranean Vegetables 147
Simple Roasted Okra 147
Greek Vegetables 147
Lemon Garlic Cauliflower 147
Balsamic Brussels Sprouts 148
Flavorful Butternut Squash 148
Crispy Green Beans 148
Roasted Zucchini 149
Air Fried Carrots, Zucchini & Squash
.... 149
Crispy & Spicy Eggplant 149
Curried Eggplant Slices 150
Spiced Green Beans 150
Air Fryer Basil Tomatoes 150
Air Fryer Ratatouille 151
Garlicky Cauliflower Florets 151
Parmesan Brussels sprouts 151
Flavorful Tomatoes 152
Healthy Roasted Carrots 152
Curried Cauliflower with Pine Nuts .. 152
Thyme Sage Butternut Squash 153
Green Beans with Onion 153
Easy Wild Mushrooms 153
Delicious Lemon Cheese Asparagus .. 153
Garlic Butter Mushrooms 154

Chapter 10: Desserts 155
Cinnamon Pecan Muffins 155
Strawberry Almond Muffins 155
Cinnamon Cream Cheese Muffins ... 155
Moist Almond Muffins 156
Lemon Cheese Muffins 156

Easy Mug Brownie 156
Delicious Choco Cookies 157
Almond Butter Fudge Brownies 157
Vanilla Mug Cake 157
Moist Chocolate Brownies 158
Chocolate Brownies 158
Super Easy Keto Brownies 158
Moist Chocolate Cake 159
Delicious Chocolate Muffins 159
Choco Almond Butter Brownie 160
Yummy Brownie Muffins 160
Cheesecake Muffins 160
Blueberry Muffins 160
Butter Cookies 161
Almond Cookies 161
Cream Cheese Brownies 161
Chocolate Protein Brownie 162
Brownie Bites 162
Zucchini Brownies 162
Chocolate Almond Butter Brownies . 163
Choco Lava Cake 163
Delicious Coffee Cake 163
Vanilla Cake 164
Apple Chips 164
Spiced Apples 164
Delicious Pumpkin Muffins 165
Cheese Cake 165
Air Fried Pineapple Slices 165
Vanilla Custard 166
Mozzarella Cheese Butter Cookies 166
Vanilla Almond Cinnamon Mug Cake
.... 166
Choco Mug Brownie 167
Lemon Ricotta Cake 167
Cinnamon Cappuccino Muffins 167
Moist Pumpkin Muffins 168

Chapter 11: 30-Day Meal Plan 169
Conclusion 171

Introduction

Keto diet and Cosori air fryer are one of the unique combinations of healthy and nutritious diet plan and a modern healthy cooking appliance. Keto diet is one of the world-famous healthy diets which is low in carb and high in fat. Most of the peoples worldwide use this diet for rapid weight loss purpose. Keto diet has various health benefits, in this book we have seen various health benefits of the keto diet.

All the recipes written in this book are based on keto diet recipes. These recipes are made into Cosori air fryer. Cosori air fryer is one of the modern cooking appliances works on 360° hot air circulation technology. If you are one of the people who like fried French fries and disappointed due to lack of crispiness then Cosori air fryer is the best choice for you. It makes a bowl of French fries within a tablespoon of oil and makes your French fries crisp from outside and tender from inside. Cosori air fryer is faster, it takes less than a minute to reaches from room temperature to 300°F. The hot air circulation technology cooks your food faster with perfection.

The book contains healthy keto diet recipes like breakfast and brunch, poultry, beef, pork, lamb, snacks and appetizer, seafood, meatless meal, and desserts. All the recipes in this book are unique and written in an easily understandable form. The recipes written in this book are given its exact preparation and cooking time. My goal here is that to provides you a healthy recipe with a healthy cooking appliance. The book contains all the information about the keto diet and Cosori air fryer with its benefits. There are different types of books available in the market on this topic thanks for choosing my book. I hope the information given in this book will help you to achieve your diet goal and you have enjoyed all the recipes written in this book.

Chapter 1: Understanding the Keto Cosori Air Fryer

Cosori Air Fryer

Cosori air fryer is an innovative and modern portable kitchen appliance run and controlled by advanced microprocessor technology. The Cosori air fryer comes with a modern look with a large touch button display panel. Cosori air fryer basically runs on 360° hot air circulation technology. It blows very hot air into the cooking chamber with the help of a blower fan which is situated at the top of the cooking chamber, this will help to cook your food evenly from all the side within very less time.

Cosori air fryer is a multipurpose cooking appliance not just use to air fry purpose only it roasts, bake and grill your food. It comes with 11 preset functions like poultry, seafood, steak, bacon, French fries, vegetables, root vegetables, preheat, frozen food, bread, and desserts. All these functions make your cooking easy while using these functions you never need to worry about time and temperature setting. If you are one of the people who like fried food but worried about extra calories then Cosori air fryer is a perfect cooking appliance for you. Frying your food into Cosori air fryer requires very less oil, it just fries a bowl of French fries within a tablespoon of oil. It gives nice brown texture to your French fries and makes it crisp and crunchy from outside and tender from inside. Compare to any traditional cooking method Cosori air fryer requires 80 to 85 percent less oil to cook your food. This will ensure you to eat healthy and nutritious food without worrying extra calories.

How to Use Your Cosori Air Fryer?

A Cosori air fryer is very simple to use the following step by step instruction guides you the proper way to use your Cosori air fryer.

1. Recipe selection

    The first step before air frying food is chosen as an appropriate recipe that is suitable for the air fryer. Most of the recipes that you can prepare in the stovetop, microwave, or oven can easily prepare in the air fryer. In this book, you have found different types of healthy keto recipes that are suitable for your air fryer.

2. Food Preparation

    This is an important step before starting your cooking process. In this step you have to cut down your food and vegetables into even and small pieces and Marinate your food if needed this will ensure cook your food evenly from all the sides. If you want to add some spices then don't spread dry, add your spices in oil, and spread it over food.

3. Preheat Air fryer

    If needed you can preheat your cosori air fryer before starting the recipe. This function cooks your food evenly from all the sides and also save your cooking time. Under this function, your cosori air fryer takes 3 to 5 minutes to preheat.

4. Coat your food

    Coat your food with bread crumb as per your recipe requirements. Then spread little oil over your food this will help to stick crumb with your food and also gives nice crisp and crust to your food.

5. Place food into the cooking basket

Always use good quality nonstick spray to grease your cooking tray before placing food into it. Do not over crowed food into the cooking basket. Cook in batches if you want to cook a large quantity of food.

6. Place cooking basket into the air fryer and choose appropriate function

After filling basket into food place food basket into the air fryer and choose an appropriate cooking function from given presets or you can choose to set manually and start cooking process.

7. Remove food basket

After finishing cooking time carefully remove the food basket from the air fryer. Transfer food into serving bowl and food is ready for serve.

8. Cleaning

After finishing the cooking process clean your cosori air fryer each and every use for better results. For cleaning purpose follow the user manual cleaning instruction comes with your air fryer.

Benefits of Cosori Air Fryer

Cosori Air Fryer is an advanced cooking kitchen gadget cooks different types of healthy and nutritious food with various benefits these benefits are as follows:

1. Use less fat and oils for cooking

This is one of the topmost benefits to cook your food into cosori air fryer. As compared to traditional deep frying method cosori air fryer requires 85 percent less oil for air frying your food without compromising the taste and texture of food. Reducing fats and oils from daily cooking also helps to reduce the daily calorie intake.

2. Protect nutritional values in food

While using the traditional deep frying method most of the essential vitamins and minerals are destroyed. An air fryer cooks your food in very less oil by just blowing hot air into the cooking chamber this will help to protect essential vitamins and minerals into food. In the deep frying method, bad fats are added into food but in the air frying method, bad fats are never produced and never added into your food.

3. Easy to operate

Cosori air fryer is not required any special skill to operate. It comes with 11 preset functions such as Chicken, Bacon, Shrimp, steak, seafood, vegetables, root vegetables, French fries, frozen food, and deserts. You just put your food into the cooking basket and select the appropriate function. While using these functions you never worry about time and temperature settings. These settings are automatically saved under these functions.

4. Save time and energy

Cosori air fryer basically runs on 360° hot air circulation technology. It blows very hot air into the cooking chamber and the temperature increases from room temperature to 300 °F less than a minute. If you are one of the persons who never have time to cook your food due to a job or busy schedule then Cosori air fryer is made for those people. It not only saves your cooking time but also saves energy. Compare to other cooking appliances cosori air fryer requires very little energy to cook your food.

5. Versatile cooking appliance

Cosori Air fryer not just use for only frying purposes but also use to roast, bake, cook, and grill your food. It means that the cosori air fryer is capable to perform the 5 different appliance operations into a single appliance.

6. Safe to use

While the cooking process is going on your cosori air fryer is closed from all sides. This will ensure that there is no risk of splatter hot oil over your skin. Cosori air fryer never burns food if any issue happens it automatically shut down itself.

What Is A Keto Diet?

Keto is not just a diet plan it is the way of eating healthy and nutritious food. Keto diet is a low carb diet that is high in fats and allows a moderate amount of protein during the diet. The primary goal of the diet plan is to reduce the daily carb intake and increase fat intake. To perform daily activities our body needs energy this energy is coming from glucose (carbs).

Keto diet is carb restrictive diet due to this glucose level is decreased in the body. This will help to push your body into the state of ketosis. It is simply a metabolic process occurs due to a lack of glucose (carb) into our body. In this state, our body breaks down fats for energy instead of glucose. Most of the peoples follow a keto diet for weight loss purpose. Keto diet is very effective on rapid weight loss and also effective in various medical conditions like Parkinson's, Alzheimer's, type-2 diabetes, heart-related disease, and epilepsy conditions.

Benefits of the Keto Diet

Keto diet is one of the healthy diet plans having the ability to change your eating habits towards healthy and nutritious food. The diet has various health benefits some of the benefits are given as follows:

1. Rapid weight loss

Weight loss is one of the health benefits seen during a keto diet. This is happening due to carb restriction, the glucose level is decreased and our body breaks down fats for energy instead of glucose. When your body is in the state of ketosis you have notice rapid weight loss during a keto diet. Most of the scientific study and research proves that compare to other diet keto diet is very effective on rapid weight loss and it also gives long term weight loss benefits.

2. Control blood sugar level

Normally our body insulin needs glucose to transport into cell this will increase insulin sensitivity in our body. When you are on keto diet ketones are produce these ketones that don't require insulin to transport into body cells this indicates that keto prevents insulin resistance. Due to this reason your blood sugar level is maintained and stable during a keto diet.

3. Improve brain functions

During the keto diet, our body used ketones for energy instead of glucose. These ketones are one of the best energy sources in our brains. Ketones full fill near about 70 percent of our brain energy needs. Some of the research and study conducted on this topic shows that it not only improves brain functions but also very effective on the treatment of various mental conditions like Parkinson's, Alzheimer's, and epilepsy.

4. Reduce the risk of heart disease

Keto diet is a low carb diet it increases the good cholesterol level (HDL) and also helps to improve the bad cholesterol level (LDL) in the blood. Due to a low carb diet, it increases the size of bad cholesterol (LDL) and reduces the LDL particles in the bloodstream. Keto diet has antioxidant properties which are very helpful to protect the lining of blood vessels. The scientific research and study conducted over a keto diet prove that keto diet improves blood circulation by 75 percent and heart efficiency by 30 percent. This will help to reduce the risk of heart-related disease.

5. Effectively work of various medical conditions

Due to antioxidant and anti-inflammatory properties, the keto diet is very effective in treating various diseases like Alzheimer's, Parkinson's, type-2 diabetes, epilepsy, cancer, obesity, and heart-related disease.

6. Anti-aging properties

During keto diet ketones provides energy, these ketones are transported into body cells without insulin. So it means that a keto diet is insulin resistance and reduces the insulin level into your body. This will help to decrease the oxidative stress level and increase the lifespan. The scientific research and study show that the low calories diet is helpful to slow down the aging process.

Chapter 2: Breakfast Recipes

Egg Stuffed Peppers

Preparation Time: 10 minutes; Cooking Time: 13 minutes; Serve: 2

Ingredients:
- 4 eggs
- 1 bell pepper, halved and remove seeds
- Pinch of red pepper flakes
- Pepper
- Salt

Directions:
1. Crack two eggs into each bell pepper half.
2. Season with red pepper flakes, pepper, and salt.
3. Place bell pepper halves into the air fryer basket and cook at 390 F for 13 minutes.
4. Serve and enjoy.

Nutritional Value (Amount per Serving):
Calories 145; Fat 8.9 g; Carbohydrates 5.3 g; Sugar 3.7 g; Protein 11.7 g; Cholesterol 327 mg

Cheese Vegetable Frittata

Preparation Time: 10 minutes; Cooking Time: 10 minutes; Serve: 6

Ingredients:
- 4 eggs
- 3 tbsp heavy cream
- 1/2 cup cheddar cheese, shredded
- 1/4 cup leek, diced
- 1 cup spinach, diced
- 1 cup mushrooms, diced
- Pepper
- Salt

Directions:
1. Spray air fryer safe pan with cooking spray and set aside.
2. In a bowl, whisk together eggs, heavy cream, pepper, and salt.
3. Add cheese, leek, spinach, and mushrooms and stir well.
4. Pour egg mixture into the prepared pan.
5. Place pan in the air fryer basket and cook at 300 F for 10 minutes.
6. Serve and enjoy.

Nutritional Value (Amount per Serving):
Calories 112; Fat 8.9 g; Carbohydrates 1.7 g; Sugar 0.7 g; Protein 6.8 g; Cholesterol 129 mg

Sausage Egg Scramble

Preparation Time: 10 minutes; Cooking Time: 8 minutes; Serve: 4

Ingredients:
- 6 eggs
- 1 cup cheddar cheese, shredded
- 3/4 cup coconut milk
- 6 sausage, cooked and crumbled
- Pepper
- Salt

Directions:
1. Spray four air fryer safe ramekins with cooking spray and set aside.
2. In a mixing bowl, whisk eggs with coconut milk, cheese, pepper, and salt. Add sausage and stir well.
3. Pour egg mixture into the prepared ramekins.
4. Place ramekins into the air fryer basket and cook at 320 F for 8 minutes or until eggs are cooked.
5. Serve and enjoy.

Nutritional Value (Amount per Serving):
Calories 449; Fat 38.1 g; Carbohydrates 3.4 g; Sugar 2.2 g; Protein 24.2 g; Cholesterol 309 mg

Cheese Egg Breakfast Muffins

Preparation Time: 10 minutes; Cooking Time: 5 minutes; Serve: 4
Ingredients:
- 4 eggs
- 1/4 cup cheddar cheese, shredded
- 1/4 cup heavy cream
- Pepper
- Salt

Directions:
1. In a bowl, whisk eggs with heavy cream, cheese, pepper, and salt.
2. Pour egg mixture into the four silicone muffin molds.
3. Place muffin molds into the air fryer basket and cook at 350 F for 5 minutes.
4. Serve and enjoy.

Nutritional Value (Amount per Serving):
Calories 117; Fat 9.5 g; Carbohydrates 0.7 g; Sugar 0.4 g; Protein 7.5 g; Cholesterol 181 mg

Breakfast Egg Bites

Preparation Time: 10 minutes; Cooking Time: 5 minutes; Serve: 6
Ingredients:
- 4 eggs
- 1/4 cup cheddar cheese, shredded
- 4 tsp almond milk
- Pepper
- Salt

Directions:
1. Spray egg bite mold with cooking spray and set aside.
2. In a bowl, whisk eggs with cheese, milk, pepper, and salt.
3. Pour egg mixture into the prepared mold.
4. Place the mold into the air fryer basket and cook at 330 F for 5 minutes. Make sure eggs are lightly browned in color on top.
5. Serve and enjoy.

Nutritional Value (Amount per Serving):
Calories 69; Fat 5.3 g; Carbohydrates 0.5 g; Sugar 0.4 g; Protein 4.9 g; Cholesterol 114 mg

Classic Sweet Potato Hash

Preparation Time: 10 minutes; Cooking Time: 12 minutes; Serve; 4
Ingredients:
- 2 cups sweet potatoes, peeled and diced
- 1 tsp Italian seasoning
- 1 tsp paprika
- 3 tbsp olive oil
- 3 bacon slices, diced
- Pepper
- Salt

Directions:
1. In a mixing bowl, toss sweet potatoes with Italian seasoning, paprika, oil, bacon, pepper, and salt.
2. Add sweet potatoes into the air fryer basket and cook at 400 F for 12 minutes. Shake basket halfway through.
3. Serve and enjoy.

Nutritional Value (Amount per Serving):
Calories 141; Fat 9.9 g; Carbohydrates 7.3 g; Sugar 1.5 g; Protein 5.9 g; Cholesterol 17 mg

Easy Cheesy Breakfast Eggs

Preparation Time: 10 minutes; Cooking Time: 5 minutes; Serve: 1
Ingredients:
- 2 eggs
- 1 tsp parmesan cheese, grated

- 2 tbsp cheddar cheese, shredded
- 2 tbsp heavy cream
- Pepper
- Salt

Directions:
1. Spray ramekin dish with cooking spray and set aside.
2. In a small bowl, whisk eggs with parmesan cheese, cheddar cheese, heavy cream, pepper, and salt.
3. Pour egg mixture into the prepared ramekin dish.
4. Place ramekin dish into the air fryer basket and cook at 330 F for 5 minutes.
5. Serve and enjoy.

Nutritional Value (Amount per Serving):
Calories 332; Fat 27.5 g; Carbohydrates 2.3 g; Sugar 0.8 g; Protein 19.7 g; Cholesterol 393 mg

Cheese Egg Frittata

Preparation Time: 10 minutes; Cooking Time: 6 minutes; Serve: 2

Ingredients:
- 4 eggs
- 1/3 cup cheddar cheese, shredded
- 1/2 cup half and half
- Pepper
- Salt

Directions:
1. Spray air fryer safe pan with cooking spray and set aside.
2. In a small bowl, whisk eggs with cheese, half and half, pepper, and salt.
3. Pour egg mixture into the prepared pan.
4. Place pan in the air fryer basket and cook at 320 F for 6 minutes.
5. Serve and enjoy.

Nutritional Value (Amount per Serving):
Calories 281; Fat 22 g; Carbohydrates 3.6 g; Sugar 0.9 g; Protein 17.6 g; Cholesterol 370 mg

Cheese Ham Egg Cups

Preparation Time: 10 minutes; Cooking Time: 5 minutes; Serve: 4

Ingredients:
- 4 eggs
- 1/2 cup cheddar cheese, shredded
- 4 tbsp heavy cream
- 1/2 cup ham, diced
- Pepper
- Salt

Directions:
1. Spray four ramekins with cooking spray and set aside.
2. In a small bowl, whisk eggs with cheese, heavy cream, ham, pepper, and salt.
3. Pour egg mixture into the prepared ramekins.
4. Place ramekins into the air fryer basket and cook at 300 F for 5 minutes.
5. Serve and enjoy.

Nutritional Value (Amount per Serving):
Calories 199; Fat 16.1 g; Carbohydrates 1.6 g; Sugar 0.4 g; Protein 12.2 g; Cholesterol 209 mg

Breakfast Avocado Eggs

Preparation Time: 10 minutes; Cooking Time: 9 minutes; Serve: 2

Ingredients:
- 2 eggs
- 1 avocado, cut in half and remove the seed
- Pinch of red pepper flakes
- Pepper
- Sal

- t

Directions:
1. Break one egg into each avocado half. Season with red pepper flakes, pepper, and salt.
2. Place avocado halves into the air fryer basket and cook at 400 F for 5 minutes or until eggs are cooked. Check after 5 minutes.
3. Serve and enjoy.

Nutritional Value (Amount per Serving):
Calories 268; Fat 24 g; Carbohydrates 9.1 g; Sugar 0.9 g; Protein 7.5 g; Cholesterol 164 mg

Healthy Spinach Omelette

Preparation Time: 10 minutes; Cooking Time: 8 minutes; Serve: 2

Ingredients:
- 3 eggs
- 1/2 cup cheddar cheese, shredded
- 2 tbsp spinach, chopped
- Pepper
- Salt

Directions:
1. Spray air fryer safe pan with cooking spray and set aside.
2. In a bowl, whisk eggs with cheese, spinach, pepper, and salt.
3. Pour egg mixture into the prepared pan.
4. Place pan into the air fryer basket and cook at 390 F for 8 minutes.
5. Serve and enjoy.

Nutritional Value (Amount per Serving):
Calories 209; Fat 15.9 g; Carbohydrates 1 g; Sugar 0.7 g; Protein 15.4 g; Cholesterol 275 mg

Cheese Mushroom Egg Bake

Preparation Time: 10 minutes; Cooking Time: 8 minutes; Serve: 1

Ingredients:
- 2 eggs
- 1/2 cup ham, diced
- 1/4 cup cheddar cheese, shredded
- 1/4 cup coconut milk
- 2 mushrooms, sliced
- 1 tbsp green onion, chopped
- Pepper
- Salt

Directions:
1. Spray air fryer safe pan with cooking spray and set aside.
2. In a bowl, whisk eggs with cheese, milk, pepper, and salt. Add ham, mushrooms, and green onion and stir well.
3. Pour egg mixture into the prepared pan.
4. Place pan into the air fryer basket and cook at 330 F for 8 minutes.
5. Serve and enjoy.

Nutritional Value (Amount per Serving):
Calories 498; Fat 38.3 g; Carbohydrates 8.6 g; Sugar 3.6 g; Protein 31.9 g; Cholesterol 396 mg

Breakfast Radish Hash Browns

Preparation Time: 10 minutes; Cooking Time: 13 minutes; Serve: 2

Ingredients:
- 1 lb radishes, clean and sliced
- 1 onion, sliced
- 1 tbsp olive oil
- 1 tsp onion powder
- 1 tsp garlic powder
- 1/2 tsp paprika
- 1/4 tsp pepper
- 1/2 tsp salt

Directions:

1. Toss sliced radishes and onion with olive oil.
2. Spray air fryer basket with cooking spray.
3. Spray radish and onion mixture into the air fryer basket and cook at 360 F for 8 minutes.
4. Transfer radish and onion mixture into the mixing bowl. Add onion powder, garlic powder, paprika, pepper, and salt and toss well.
5. Return radish and onion mixture into the air fryer basket and cook for 5 minutes more.
6. Serve and enjoy.

Nutritional Value (Amount per Serving):
Calories 125; Fat 7.4 g; Carbohydrates 13.6 g; Sugar 3.2 g; Protein 3.6 g; Cholesterol 0 mg

Breakfast Cream Souffle

Preparation Time: 10 minutes; Cooking Time: 10 minutes; Serve: 4

Ingredients:
- 4 eggs
- 1/4 tsp red chili pepper
- 4 tbsp cream
- Pepper
- Salt

Directions:
1. Preheat the cosori air fryer to 390 F.
2. Spray four ramekins with cooking spray and set aside.
3. In a bowl, whisk eggs with red chili pepper, cream, pepper, and salt.
4. Pour egg mixture into the prepared ramekins.
5. Place ramekins into the air fryer basket and cook for 10 minutes.
6. Serve and enjoy.

Nutritional Value (Amount per Serving):
Calories 71; Fat 5 g; Carbohydrates 0.8 g; Sugar 0.6 g; Protein 5.7 g; Cholesterol 166 mg

Cheese Omelet

Preparation Time: 10 minutes; Cooking Time: 8 minutes; Serve: 2

Ingredients:
- 2 eggs
- 1/4 cup cheddar cheese, shredded
- 1/4 cup heavy cream
- Pepper
- Salt

Directions:
1. Spray air fryer safe pan with cooking spray and set aside.
2. In a bowl, whisk eggs with cream, pepper, and salt.
3. Pour egg mixture into the prepared pan. Place pan in the air fryer basket and cook at 350 F for 4 minutes.
4. Sprinkle cheese on top and cook for 4 minutes more.
5. Serve and enjoy.

Nutritional Value (Amount per Serving):
Calories 172; Fat 14.6 g; Carbohydrates 1 g; Sugar 0.4 g; Protein 9.4 g; Cholesterol 199 mg

Cheese Sausage Egg Muffins

Preparation Time: 10 minutes; Cooking Time: 5 minutes; Serve: 6

Ingredients:
- 4 eggs
- 4 tbsp cheddar cheese, shredded
- 2 tbsp heavy cream
- 1/2 cup cooked sausage
- Pepper
- Salt

Directions:
1. Spray egg mold with cooking spray and set aside.

2. In a bowl, beat eggs until frothy. Add remaining ingredients into the eggs and stir to mix.
3. Pour egg mixture into the prepared egg mold.
4. Place egg mold into the air fryer basket and cook at 330 F for 5 minutes.
5. Serve and enjoy.

Nutritional Value (Amount per Serving):
Calories 82; Fat 6.6 g; Carbohydrates 0.4 g; Sugar 0.3 g; Protein 5.2 g; Cholesterol 122 mg

Spinach Baked Eggs

Preparation Time: 10 minutes; Cooking Time: 8 minutes; Serve: 2

Ingredients:
- 2 eggs
- 1/4 tsp parsley, chopped
- 1/4 tsp thyme
- 1/4 tsp rosemary
- 1/4 onion, diced
- 1/4 cup spinach, chopped
- Pepper
- Salt

Directions:
1. Preheat the cosori air fryer to 350 F.
2. Spray two ramekins with cooking spray and set aside.
3. In a bowl, whisk eggs with remaining ingredients.
4. Pour egg mixture into the prepared ramekins.
5. Place ramekins into the air fryer basket and cook for 5-8 minutes.
6. Serve and enjoy.

Nutritional Value (Amount per Serving):
Calories 70; Fat 4.4 g; Carbohydrates 2 g; Sugar 0.9 g; Protein 5.8 g; Cholesterol 164 mg

Easy Breakfast Frittata

Preparation Time: 10 minutes; Cooking Time: 15 minutes; Serve: 2

Ingredients:
- 1 cup egg whites
- 1/4 cup mushrooms, sliced
- 1/4 cup tomato, sliced
- 2 tbsp coconut milk
- t
- 2 tbsp chives, chopped
- Pepper
- Sal

Directions:
1. Spray air fryer safe pan with cooking spray and set aside.
2. Preheat the cosori air fryer to 320 F.
3. In a bowl, whisk eggs with pepper and salt. Add remaining ingredients and mix well.
4. Pour egg mixture to the prepared.
5. Place pan in the air fryer basket and cook for 15 minutes.
6. Serve and enjoy.

Nutritional Value (Amount per Serving):
Calories 105; Fat 3.9 g; Carbohydrates 3.1 g; Sugar 2.2 g; Protein 14.2 g; Cholesterol 0 mg

Bell Pepper Broccoli Frittata

Preparation Time: 10 minutes; Cooking Time: 17 minutes; Serve: 2

Ingredients:
- 3 eggs
- 1/2 cup bell pepper, chopped
- 1/2 cup broccoli florets
- 2 tbsp parmesan cheese, grated
- 2 tbsp coconut milk
- Pepper
- Salt

Directions:

1. Spray air fryer safe pan with cooking spray and set aside.
2. Place bell peppers and broccoli in the prepared pan.
3. Cook broccoli and bell pepper at 350 F for 7 minutes.
4. In a bowl, whisk together eggs, milk, and seasoning.
5. Once the vegetable is cooked then pour egg mixture over vegetable and sprinkle cheese on top.
6. Return pan in the air fryer basket and cook for 10 minutes more.
7. Serve and enjoy.

Nutritional Value (Amount per Serving):
Calories 191; Fat 13.3 g; Carbohydrates 5.6 g; Sugar 2.9 g; Protein 14.1 g; Cholesterol 256 mg

Sausage Cheese Breakfast Frittata

Preparation Time: 10 minutes; Cooking Time: 10 minutes; Serve: 2
Ingredients:
- 2 eggs
- 1 tbsp spring onions, chopped
- 1 breakfast sausage patty, chopped
- 1 tbsp butter, melted
- lt
- 2 tbsp cheddar cheese
- 1 tbsp bell peppers, chopped
- Pepper
- Sa

Directions:
1. Spray air fryer safe pan with cooking spray and set aside.
2. Add chopped sausage patty in prepared pan and air fry at 350 F for 5 minutes.
3. Meanwhile, in a bowl whisk together eggs, pepper, and salt. Add bell peppers, spring onions, and mix well.
4. Once sausages are cooked then pour the egg mixture to the pan and mix well.
5. Sprinkle with cheese and air fry at 350 F for 5 minutes.
6. Serve and enjoy.

Nutritional Value (Amount per Serving):
Calories 202; Fat 14.1 g; Carbohydrates 6.7 g; Sugar 3.5 g; Protein 13 g; Cholesterol 186 mg

Sausage Spinach Egg Cups

Preparation Time: 10 minutes; Cooking Time: 10 minutes; Serve: 2
Ingredients:
- 1/4 cup egg beaters
- 4 tbsp sausage, cooked and crumbled
- 4 tsp jack cheese, shredded
- 4 tbsp spinach, chopped
- Pepper
- Salt

Directions:
1. Spray two ramekins with cooking spray and set aside.
2. In a mixing bowl, whisk together all ingredients until well combined.
3. Pour mixture into the prepared ramekins.
4. Place ramekins into the air fryer basket and cook at 330 F for 10 minutes.
5. Serve and enjoy.

Nutritional Value (Amount per Serving):
Calories 306; Fat 23.4 g; Carbohydrates 2.4 g; Sugar 0.2 g; Protein 20.9 g; Cholesterol 72 mg

Spinach Garlic Egg Muffins

Preparation Time: 10 minutes; Cooking Time: 15 minutes; Serve: 6
Ingredients:
- 5 eggs
- 1/4 tsp garlic powder

- 1/4 tsp onion powder
- 1 bacon slice, cooked and crumbled
- 1/2 cup mushrooms, chopped
- 1 cup spinach, chopped
- Pepper
- Salt

Directions:
1. In a mixing bowl, whisk eggs with garlic powder, onion powder, pepper, and salt. Stir in spinach, mushrooms, and bacon.
2. Pour egg mixture into the six silicone muffin molds.
3. Place molds into the air fryer basket and cook at 400 F for 15 minutes.
4. Serve and enjoy.

Nutritional Value (Amount per Serving):
Calories 73; Fat 5 g; Carbohydrates 0.9 g; Sugar 0.5 g; Protein 6.1 g; Cholesterol 140 mg

Greek Egg Muffins

Preparation Time: 10 minutes; Cooking Time: 15 minutes; Serve: 6
Ingredients:
- 2 eggs
- 1/4 cup tomatoes, diced
- 1/2 cup coconut milk
- 4 egg whites
- 1/4 cup feta cheese, crumbled
- 1 tbsp fresh parsley, chopped
- 1/4 cup olives, diced
- 1/4 cup onion, diced
- Pepper
- Salt

Directions:
1. In a mixing bowl, whisk eggs with milk, pepper, and salt. Add remaining ingredients and stir well.
2. Pour egg mixture into the six silicone muffin molds.
3. Place molds into the air fryer basket and cook at 350 F for 15 minutes.
4. Serve and enjoy.

Nutritional Value (Amount per Serving):
Calories 105; Fat 8.2 g; Carbohydrates 2.8 g; Sugar 1.6 g; Protein 5.8 g; Cholesterol 60 mg

Veggie Frittata

Preparation Time: 10 minutes; Cooking Time: 20 minutes; Serve: 2
Ingredients:
- 4 eggs
- 1 cup bell peppers, chopped
- 1 cup zucchini, chopped
- 1 cup mushrooms, sliced
- 2 tbsp coconut milk
- 1 tbsp olive oil
- 1 cup cheddar cheese
- 1/2 cup onion, chopped
- Pepper
- Salt

Directions:
1. Spray air fryer safe pan with cooking spray and set aside.
2. Heat oil in a medium pan over medium heat. Add onion, bell peppers, zucchini, and mushrooms, and sauté for 5 minutes.
3. Remove pan from heat and set aside to cool.
4. In a bowl, whisk eggs with milk, pepper, and salt.
5. Add sautéed vegetables and cheese and stir well.
6. Pour egg mixture into the prepared pan.
7. Place pan in the air fryer basket and cook at 350 F for 20 minutes.
8. Serve and enjoy.

Nutritional Value (Amount per Serving):
Calories 495; Fat 38.4 g; Carbohydrates 12.5 g; Sugar 7.3 g; Protein 28.2 g; Cholesterol 387 mg

Kale Egg Muffins

Preparation Time: 10 minutes; Cooking Time: 15 minutes; Serve: 4
Ingredients:
- 3 eggs
- 1/2 cup kale, chopped
- 1 tsp olive oil
- 1 tbsp onion, minced
- 1/4 cup Swiss cheese, shredded
- 1/2 cup mushrooms, diced
- Pepper
- Salt

Directions:
1. Heat oil in a medium pan over medium-high heat. Add mushrooms and sauté for 2-3 minutes.
2. Add onion and kale and sauté for 2 minutes. Remove pan from heat and set aside to cool.
3. In a bowl, whisk eggs with pepper and salt.
4. Add sautéed mushroom kale mixture and shredded cheese and stir well.
5. Pour egg mixture into the silicone muffin molds.
6. Place molds into the air fryer basket and cook at 350 F for 15 minutes.
7. Serve and enjoy.

Nutritional Value (Amount per Serving):
Calories 90; Fat 6.4 g; Carbohydrates 2 g; Sugar 0.6 g; Protein 6.5 g; Cholesterol 129 mg

Cheese Mushroom Frittata

Preparation Time: 10 minutes; Cooking Time: 6 minutes; Serve: 2
Ingredients:
- 3 eggs
- 2 mushrooms, chopped
- 2 tbsp onion, chopped
- 1/4 bell pepper, diced
- 2 tbsp cheddar cheese, shredded
- 2 tbsp coconut milk
- Pepper
- Salt

Directions:
1. Spray air fryer safe pan with cooking spray and set aside.
2. In a bowl, whisk eggs with milk, pepper, and salt. Add remaining ingredients and stir well.
3. Pour egg mixture into the prepared pan
4. Place pan in the air fryer basket and cook at 400 F for 6 minutes.
5. Serve and enjoy.

Nutritional Value (Amount per Serving):
Calories 170; Fat 12.6 g; Carbohydrates 4.1 g; Sugar 2.5 g; Protein 11.2 g; Cholesterol 253 mg

Blueberry Cheese Muffins

Preparation Time: 10 minutes; Cooking Time: 20 minutes; Serve: 6
Ingredients:
- 8 oz cream cheese
- 1/4 tsp vanilla
- 1 egg, lightly beaten
- 1/4 cup Swerve
- 2 tbsp almonds, sliced
- 2 tbsp blueberries

Directions:
1. Add the cream cheese in a mixing bowl and beat until smooth.
2. Add egg, vanilla, and sweetener and beat until well combined.
3. Add almonds and blueberries and fold well.
4. Spoon mixture into the silicone muffin molds.
5. Place molds into the air fryer basket and cook at 350 F for 20 minutes.
6. Serve and enjoy.

Nutritional Value (Amount per Serving):

Calories 156; Fat 14.9 g; Carbohydrates 2 g; Sugar 0.5 g; Protein 4.2 g; Cholesterol 69 mg

Egg Cheese Mustard Bake

Preparation Time: 10 minutes; Cooking Time: 25 minutes; Serve: 3

Ingredients:
- 6 eggs
- 1/4 tsp dry mustard
- 2 tbsp butter, melted
- 1/4 lb cheddar cheese, grated
- 1/2 cup coconut milk
- Pepper
- Salt

Directions:
1. Spray air fryer safe pan with cooking spray and set aside.
2. In a bowl, whisk eggs with milk, mustard, pepper, and salt. Stir in cheese.
3. Pour egg mixture into the prepared pan.
4. Place pan in the air fryer basket and cook at 350 F for 25 minutes.
5. Serve and enjoy.

Nutritional Value (Amount per Serving):
Calories 439; Fat 38.6 g; Carbohydrates 3.5 g; Sugar 2.3 g; Protein 21.6 g; Cholesterol 387 mg

Cottage Cheese Egg Cups

Preparation Time: 10 minutes; Cooking Time: 15 minutes; Serve: 6

Ingredients:
- 3 eggs, lightly beaten
- 2 tbsp green chilies, diced
- 2 tbsp cottage cheese
- 1 tbsp coconut milk
- 2 tbsp cheddar cheese, shredded
- Pepper
- Salt

Directions:
1. Spray egg mold with cooking spray and set aside.
2. In a bowl, whisk eggs with milk, pepper, and salt. Add cheddar cheese, green chilies, and cottage cheese and stir well.
3. Pour egg mixture in a prepared egg mold.
4. Place egg mold into the air fryer basket and cook at 350 F for 15 minutes.
5. Serve and enjoy.

Nutritional Value (Amount per Serving):
Calories 53; Fat 3.7 g; Carbohydrates 1.1 g; Sugar 0.6 g; Protein 4.2 g; Cholesterol 85 mg

Tasty Herb Egg Cups

Preparation Time: 10 minutes; Cooking Time: 20 minutes; Serve: 6

Ingredients:
- 6 eggs
- 1/2 tbsp chives, chopped
- 1/2 tbsp fresh dill, chopped
- 1 tbsp fresh parsley, chopped
- 1/2 tbsp fresh basil, chopped
- 1/4 cup mozzarella cheese, grated
- Pepper
- Salt

Directions:
1. In a bowl, whisk eggs with pepper and salt. Add remaining ingredients and stir well.
2. Pour egg mixture into the silicone muffin molds.
3. Place molds into the air fryer basket and cook at 350 F for 20 minutes.
4. Serve and enjoy.

Nutritional Value (Amount per Serving):
Calories 67; Fat 4.6 g; Carbohydrates 0.6 g; Sugar 0.4 g; Protein 6 g; Cholesterol 164 mg

Tomato Basil Egg Muffins

Preparation Time: 10 minutes; Cooking Time: 20 minutes; Serve: 6

Ingredients:
- 6 eggs
- 1 1/2 tbsp basil, chopped
- 2 tsp olive oil
- 1/2 cup feta cheese, crumbled
- 5 cherry tomatoes, chopped
- 4 sun-dried tomatoes, chopped
- Pepper
- Salt

Directions:
1. In a mixing bowl, whisk eggs with pepper and salt. Add remaining ingredients and stir well.
2. Pour egg mixture into the silicone muffin molds.
3. Place molds into the air fryer basket and cook at 400 F for 20 minutes.
4. Serve and enjoy.

Nutritional Value (Amount per Serving):
Calories 143; Fat 9 g; Carbohydrates 8.1 g; Sugar 5.7 g; Protein 9 g; Cholesterol 175 mg

Bacon Egg Muffins

Preparation Time: 10 minutes; Cooking Time: 12 minutes; Serve: 6

Ingredients:
- 4 eggs, lightly beaten
- 2 tbsp coconut milk
- 2 bacon slices, cooked and crumbled
- 2 tbsp cheddar cheese, shredded
- Pepper
- Salt

Directions:
1. In a bowl, whisk eggs with milk, pepper, and salt. Add bacon and cheese and stir well.
2. Pour egg mixture into the silicone muffin molds.
3. Place molds into the air fryer basket and cook at 350 F for 12 minutes.
4. Serve and enjoy.

Nutritional Value (Amount per Serving):
Calories 97; Fat 7.5 g; Carbohydrates 0.6 g; Sugar 0.4 g; Protein 6.7 g; Cholesterol 119 mg

Pepper Feta Egg Muffins

Preparation Time: 10 minutes; Cooking Time: 20 minutes; Serve: 6

Ingredients:
- 4 eggs
- 1/2 cup egg whites
- 1 red bell pepper, chopped
- 2 tbsp green onion, chopped
- 5 fresh basil leaves, chopped
- 1 tsp garlic powder
- 2 tbsp feta cheese, crumbled
- 1/4 cup of coconut milk
- Pepper
- Salt

Directions:
1. In a bowl, whisk eggs, egg whites, coconut milk, garlic powder, pepper, and salt.
2. Add cheese, bell pepper, green onion, and basil and stir well.
3. Pour egg mixture into the silicone muffin molds.
4. Place molds into the air fryer basket and cook at 350 F for 20 minutes.
5. Serve and enjoy.

Nutritional Value (Amount per Serving):
Calories 92; Fat 6.1 g; Carbohydrates 3.1 g; Sugar 2 g; Protein 6.9 g; Cholesterol 112 mg

Garlic Cheese Quiche

Preparation Time: 10 minutes; Cooking Time: 30 minutes; Serve: 4

Ingredients:

- 6 eggs
- 1/2 cup onion, chopped
- 1/8 tsp cayenne
- 1/8 tsp nutmeg
- 8 oz cheddar cheese, grated
- 4 bacon slice, cooked and chopped
- 3/4 cup coconut milk
- 1/2 tsp garlic, minced
- 1 tbsp olive oil
- Pepper
- Salt

Directions:
1. Spray air fryer safe pan with cooking spray and set aside.
2. Heat oil in a pan over medium heat. Add onion and sauté for 5 minutes.
3. Add garlic and sauté for 30 seconds. Remove pan from heat and set aside to cool.
4. In a mixing bowl, whisk eggs with milk, pepper, and salt. Stir in sautéed onion garlic, cayenne, nutmeg, bacon, and cheese.
5. Pour egg mixture into the prepared pan.
6. Place pan in the air fryer basket and cook at 350 F for 25 minutes.
7. Serve and enjoy.

Nutritional Value (Amount per Serving):
Calories 566; Fat 47.6 g; Carbohydrates 5.5 g; Sugar 2.9 g; Protein 30.7 g; Cholesterol 326 mg

Broccoli Fritters

Preparation Time: 10 minutes; Cooking Time: 15 minutes; Serve: 4
Ingredients:
- 3 cups broccoli florets, steam & chopped
- 2 cups cheddar cheese, shredded
- 1/4 cup almond flour
- 2 eggs, lightly beaten
- 2 garlic cloves, minced
- Pepper
- Salt

Directions:
1. Line air fryer basket with parchment paper.
2. Add all ingredients into the mixing bowl and mix until well combined.
3. Make patties from broccoli mixture and place in the air fryer basket.
4. Cook at 375 F for 15 minutes. Turn patties halfway through.
5. Serve and enjoy.

Nutritional Value (Amount per Serving):
Calories 285; Fat 22 g; Carbohydrates 6.3 g; Sugar 1.7 g; Protein 19.2 g; Cholesterol 141 mg

Spicy Brussels sprouts

Preparation Time: 10 minutes; Cooking Time: 14 minutes; Serve: 2
Ingredients:
- 1/2 lb Brussels sprouts, trimmed and halved
- 1 tbsp chives, chopped
- 1/4 tsp cayenne
- 1/2 tsp chili powder
- 1/2 tbsp olive oil
- Pepper
- Salt

Directions:
1. Add all ingredients into the large bowl and toss well.
2. Spread Brussels sprouts in the air fryer basket and cook at 370 F for 14 minutes. Shake basket halfway through.
3. Serve and enjoy.

Nutritional Value (Amount per Serving):
Calories 82; Fat 4.1 g; Carbohydrates 10.9 g; Sugar 2.6 g; Protein 4 g; Cholesterol 0 mg

Zucchini Breakfast Patties

Preparation Time: 10 minutes; Cooking Time: 15 minutes; Serve: 6
Ingredients:
- 1 cup zucchini, shredded and squeeze out all liquid
- 2 tbsp onion, minced
- 1 egg, lightly beaten
- 1/4 tsp red pepper flakes
- 1/4 cup parmesan cheese, grated
- 1/2 tbsp Dijon mustard
- 1/2 tbsp mayonnaise
- 1/2 cup almond flour
- Pepper
- Salt

Directions:
1. Line air fryer basket with parchment paper.
2. Add all ingredients into the bowl and mix until well combined.
3. Make small patties from the zucchini mixture and place it into the air fryer basket.
4. Cook at 400 F for 15 minutes.
5. Serve and enjoy.

Nutritional Value (Amount per Serving):
Calories 48; Fat 3.3 g; Carbohydrates 2.1 g; Sugar 0.7 g; Protein 3.1 g; Cholesterol 31 mg

Bacon Brussels Sprouts

Preparation Time: 10 minutes; Cooking Time: 30 minutes; Serve: 4
Ingredients:
- 1 lb brussels sprouts, cut into half
- 1/2 avocado, diced
- 1/4 cup onion, sliced
- 4 bacon slices, cut into pieces
- 1 tsp garlic powder
- 3 tbsp lemon juice
- 2 tbsp balsamic vinegar
- 3 tbsp olive oil
- Pepper
- Salt

Directions:
1. In a small bowl, whisk together oil, garlic powder, 2 tbsp lemon juice, and salt.
2. In a mixing bowl, toss brussels sprouts with 3 tablespoons of oil mixture.
3. Add brussels sprouts into the air fryer basket and cook at 370 F for 20 minutes. Toss halfway through.
4. Now top with bacon and onion and cook for 10 minutes more.
5. Transfer brussels sprouts mixture into the large bowl. Add basil, avocado, and remaining oil mixture, and lemon juice and toss well.
6. Serve and enjoy.

Nutritional Value (Amount per Serving):
Calories 248; Fat 16.8 g; Carbohydrates 15.5 g; Sugar 4.5 g; Protein 11.7 g; Cholesterol 21 mg

Broccoli Quiche

Preparation Time: 10 minutes; Cooking Time: 10 minutes; Serve: 1
Ingredients:
- 1 egg
- 1 tbsp cheddar cheese, grated
- 4 broccoli florets
- 3 tbsp heavy cream
- Pepper
- Salt

Directions:
1. Spray 5-inch quiche dish with cooking spray.
2. In a bowl, whisk the egg with cheese, cream, pepper, and salt. Add broccoli and stir well.
3. Pour egg mixture into the quiche dish.
4. Place dish into the air fryer basket and cook at 325 F for 10 minutes.

5. Serve and enjoy.

Nutritional Value (Amount per Serving):
Calories 173; Fat 13 g; Carbohydrates 6.5 g; Sugar 1.9 g; Protein 9.9 g; Cholesterol 191 mg

Bacon Cheese Egg Bites

Preparation Time: 10 minutes; Cooking Time: 13 minutes; Serve: 4

Ingredients:
- 4 eggs
- 1/4 cup cheddar cheese, shredded
- 4 bacon slices, cooked and crumbled
- 1/2 small bell pepper, diced
- 1/2 onion, diced
- 4 tsp coconut milk
- Pepper
- Salt

Directions:
1. Spray four ramekins with cooking spray.
2. Crack 1 egg into each ramekin then adds 1 tsp coconut milk into each one.
3. Top each one off with bacon, bell pepper, onion, and cheese. Season with pepper and salt.
4. Place ramekins into the air fryer basket and cook at 300 F for 10-13 minutes.
5. Serve and enjoy.

Nutritional Value (Amount per Serving):
Calories 216; Fat 15.9 g; Carbohydrates 3.4 g; Sugar 1.9 g; Protein 14.8 g; Cholesterol 192 mg

Cheese Sausage Pepper Frittata

Preparation Time: 10 minutes; Cooking Time: 20 minutes; Serve: 2

Ingredients:
- 4 eggs, lightly beaten
- 1 green onion, chopped
- 2 tbsp bell pepper, diced
- 1/2 cup Monterey jack cheese
- 1/4 lb breakfast sausage, cooked and crumbled
- Pepper
- Salt

Directions:
1. Preheat the cosori air fryer to 360 F.
2. Spray air fryer pan with cooking spray and set aside.
3. In a bowl, whisk eggs with remaining ingredients. Pour egg mixture into the prepared pan.
4. Place pan in the air fryer basket and cook for 18-20 minutes.
5. Serve and enjoy.

Nutritional Value (Amount per Serving):
Calories 411; Fat 29.6 g; Carbohydrates 10.7 g; Sugar 7.2 g; Protein 26.8 g; Cholesterol 390 mg

Mushroom Frittata

Preparation Time: 10 minutes; Cooking Time: 6 minutes; Serve: 2

Ingredients:
- 3 eggs
- 2 tbsp parmesan cheese, shredded
- 2 tbsp cream
- 2 cremini mushrooms, sliced
- 1/4 small onion, chopped
- 1/4 bell pepper, diced
- Pepper
- Salt

Directions:
1. Spray air fryer pan with cooking spray and set aside.
2. Preheat the cosori air fryer to 400 F.
3. In a bowl, whisk eggs with cream, mushrooms, onion, bell pepper, pepper, and salt.
4. Pour egg mixture into the prepared pan.

5. Place pan in the air fryer basket and cook for 5 minutes. Top with cheese and cook for 1 minute more.
6. Serve and enjoy.

Nutritional Value (Amount per Serving):
Calories 159; Fat 10.3 g; Carbohydrates 3.9 g; Sugar 2.1 g; Protein 13.5 g; Cholesterol 258 mg

Broccoli Bell Pepper Frittata

Preparation Time: 10 minutes; Cooking Time: 17 minutes; Serve: 2

Ingredients:
- 3 eggs
- 2 tbsp cheddar cheese, shredded
- 2 tbsp cream
- 1/2 cup bell pepper, chopped
- 1/2 cup broccoli florets, chopped
- 1/4 tsp garlic powder
- 1/4 tsp onion powder
- Pepper
- Salt

Directions:
1. Spray air fryer pan with cooking spray. Add bell peppers and broccoli into the pan.
2. Place pan in the air fryer basket and cook at 350 F for 7 minutes.
3. In a bowl, whisk eggs with cheese, cream, garlic powder, onion powder, pepper, and salt.
4. Pour egg mixture over broccoli and bell pepper and cook for 10 minutes more.
5. Serve and enjoy.

Nutritional Value (Amount per Serving):
Calories 150; Fat 9.7 g; Carbohydrates 5.3 g; Sugar 2.9 g; Protein 11.2 g; Cholesterol 255 mg

Spinach Tomato Frittata

Preparation Time: 10 minutes; Cooking Time: 7 minutes; Serve: 2

Ingredients:
- 2 eggs
- 1/4 cup fresh spinach, chopped
- 1/4 cup tomatoes, chopped
- 2 tbsp cream
- 1 tbsp cheddar cheese, grated
- Pepper
- Salt

Directions:
1. Spray air fryer pan with cooking spray and set aside.
2. In a bowl, whisk eggs with remaining ingredients.
3. Pour egg mixture into the prepared pan. Place pan in the air fryer basket and cook at 330 F for 7 minutes.
4. Serve and enjoy.

Nutritional Value (Amount per Serving):
Calories 90; Fat 6.3 g; Carbohydrates 1.8 g; Sugar 1.2 g; Protein 16.8 g; Cholesterol 170 mg

Basil Feta Egg Bite

Preparation Time: 10 minutes; Cooking Time: 5 minutes; Serve: 7

Ingredients:
- 4 eggs
- 1 tbsp fresh basil, chopped
- 1/4 cup sun-dried tomatoes, diced
- 1/4 cup feta cheese, crumbled
- 1/2 cup cottage cheese, crumbled

Directions:
1. Spray egg mold with cooking spray and set aside.
2. In a bowl, beat eggs until frothy. Add remaining ingredients into the eggs and stir to mix.
3. Pour egg mixture into the prepared egg mold.

4. Place egg mold into the air fryer basket and cook at 330 F for 5 minutes.
   5. Serve and enjoy.

Nutritional Value (Amount per Serving):
Calories 66; Fat 4 g; Carbohydrates 1.3 g; Sugar 0.6 g; Protein 6.2 g; Cholesterol 100 mg

Sausage Swiss Cheese Egg Bite

Preparation Time: 10 minutes; Cooking Time: 5 minutes; Serve: 7

Ingredients:
- 4 eggs
- 1 tbsp green onion, chopped
- 1/4 cup mushrooms, chopped
- 1/4 cup sausage, cooked and crumbled
- 1/2 cup cottage cheese, crumbled
- 1/2 cup Swiss cheese, shredded
- Pepper
- Salt

Directions:
1. Spray egg mold with cooking spray and set aside.
2. In a bowl, beat eggs until frothy. Add remaining ingredients into the eggs and stir to mix.
3. Pour egg mixture into the prepared egg mold.
4. Place egg mold into the air fryer basket and cook at 330 F for 5 minutes.
5. Serve and enjoy.

Nutritional Value (Amount per Serving):
Calories 82; Fat 5.1 g; Carbohydrates 1.3 g; Sugar 0.4 g; Protein 7.7 g; Cholesterol 102 mg

Gruyere Cheese Egg Bite

Preparation Time: 10 minutes; Cooking Time: 5 minutes; Serve: 7

Ingredients:
- 4 eggs
- 1/4 cup bacon, cooked and crumbled
- 1/2 cup cottage cheese, crumbled
- 1/2 cup gruyere cheese, shredded

Directions:
1. Spray egg mold with cooking spray and set aside.
2. In a bowl, beat eggs until frothy. Add remaining ingredients into the eggs and stir to mix.
3. Pour egg mixture into the prepared egg mold.
4. Place egg mold into the air fryer basket and cook at 330 F for 5 minutes.
5. Serve and enjoy.

Nutritional Value (Amount per Serving):
Calories 86; Fat 5.6 g; Carbohydrates 0.8 g; Sugar 0.3 g; Protein 7.9 g; Cholesterol 104 mg

Cheddar Cheese Broccoli Egg Bite

Preparation Time: 10 minutes; Cooking Time: 5 minutes; Serve: 7

Ingredients:
- 4 eggs
- 1/4 cup broccoli, cooked and chopped
- 1/2 cup cottage cheese, crumbled
- 1/2 cup cheddar cheese, shredded
- Pepper
- Salt

Directions:
1. Spray egg mold with cooking spray and set aside.
2. In a bowl, beat eggs until frothy. Add remaining ingredients into the eggs and stir to mix.
3. Pour egg mixture into the prepared egg mold.
4. Place egg mold into the air fryer basket and cook at 330 F for 5 minutes.
5. Serve and enjoy.

Nutritional Value (Amount per Serving):
Calories 84; Fat 5.5 g; Carbohydrates 1.1 g; Sugar 0.3 g; Protein 7.5 g; Cholesterol 103 mg

Green Chilis Egg Bite

Preparation Time: 10 minutes; Cooking Time: 5 minutes; Serve: 7
Ingredients:
- 4 eggs
- 1/4 cup green chilis, diced
- 1/2 cup cottage cheese, crumbled
- 1/2 cup pepper jack cheese, shredded
- Pepper
- Salt

Directions:
1. Spray egg mold with cooking spray and set aside.
2. In a bowl, beat eggs until frothy. Add remaining ingredients into the eggs and stir to mix.
3. Pour egg mixture into the prepared egg mold.
4. Place egg mold into the air fryer basket and cook at 330 F for 5 minutes.
5. Serve and enjoy.

Nutritional Value (Amount per Serving):
Calories 57; Fat 3.1 g; Carbohydrates 1.4 g; Sugar 0.5 g; Protein 5.5 g; Cholesterol 96 mg

Roasted Pepper Egg Bite

Preparation Time: 10 minutes; Cooking Time: 5 minutes; Serve: 7
Ingredients:
- 4 eggs
- 1/4 cup spinach, chopped
- 1/2 roasted red pepper, chopped
- 1 tbsp green onion, chopped
- 1/2 cup cottage cheese, crumbled
- 1/2 cup Monterey jack cheese, shredded
- Pepper
- Salt

Directions:
1. Spray egg mold with cooking spray and set aside.
2. In a bowl, beat eggs until frothy. Add remaining ingredients into the eggs and stir to mix.
3. Pour egg mixture into the prepared egg mold.
4. Place egg mold into the air fryer basket and cook at 330 F for 5 minutes.
5. Serve and enjoy.

Nutritional Value (Amount per Serving):
Calories 82; Fat 5.3 g; Carbohydrates 1.3 g; Sugar 0.5 g; Protein 7.5 g; Cholesterol 102 mg

Cheddar Cheese Omelet

Preparation Time: 10 minutes; Cooking Time: 7 minutes; Serve: 1
Ingredients:
- 3 eggs
- 1/2 tp soy sauce
- 2 tbsp cheddar cheese, grated
- 1 onion, chopped
- 1/4 tsp garlic powder
- 1/4 tsp onion powder
- Pepper
- Salt

Directions:
1. Spray air fryer pan with cooking spray and set aside.
2. In a bowl, whisk eggs with remaining ingredients. Pour egg mixture into the prepared pan.
3. Place pan in the air fryer basket and cook at 350 F for 6-7 minutes.
4. Serve and enjoy.

Nutritional Value (Amount per Serving):
Calories 127; Fat 4.9 g; Carbohydrates 12.4 g; Sugar 5.5 g; Protein 9 g; Cholesterol 15 mg

Spicy Chicken Wings

Preparation Time: 10 minutes; Cooking Time: 25 minutes; Serve: 4
Ingredients:

- 2 lbs chicken wings
- 1/2 tsp Worcestershire sauce
- 1/2 tsp Tabasco
- 6 tbsp butter, melted
- 12 oz hot sauce

Directions:
1. Spray air fryer basket with cooking spray.
2. Add chicken wings into the air fryer basket and cook at 380 F for 25 minutes. Shake basket after every 5 minutes.
3. Meanwhile, in a mixing bowl, mix together hot sauce, Worcestershire sauce, and melted butter. Set aside. Add chicken wings and toss well.
4. Serve and enjoy.

Nutritional Value (Amount per Serving):
Calories 594; Fat 34.4 g; Carbohydrates 1.6 g; Sugar 1.2 g; Protein 66.2 g; Cholesterol 248 mg

Fajita Chicken

Preparation Time: 10 minutes; Cooking Time: 17 minutes; Serve: 4
Ingredients:
- 4 chicken breasts, make horizontal cuts on each piece
- 1/2 red bell pepper, sliced
- 2 tbsp fajita seasoning
- 1/2 green bell pepper, sliced
- 2 tbsp olive oil
- 1/2 cup cheddar cheese, shredded
- 1 onion, sliced
- Pepper
- Salt

Directions:
1. Line air fryer basket with aluminum foil.
2. Preheat the cosori air fryer to 380 F.
3. Rub oil and seasoning all over the chicken breast.
4. Place chicken into the air fryer basket and top with peppers and onion.
5. Cook for 15 minutes. Top with cheese and cook for 1-2 minutes more.
6. Serve and enjoy.

Nutritional Value (Amount per Serving):
Calories 431; Fat 22.6 g; Carbohydrates 8.2 g; Sugar 2.7 g; Protein 46.4 g; Cholesterol 145 mg

Lemon Chicken Breasts

Preparation Time: 10 minutes; Cooking Time: 20 minutes; Serve: 4
Ingredients:
- 4 chicken breasts, skinless and boneless
- 1 preserved lemon
- 1 tbsp olive oil

Directions:
1. Add all ingredients into the bowl and mix well. Set aside for 10 minutes.
2. Spray air fryer basket with cooking spray.
3. Place chicken into the air fryer basket and cook at 400 F for 20 minutes.
4. Serve and enjoy.

Nutritional Value (Amount per Serving):
Calories 312; Fat 14.4 g; Carbohydrates 1.4 g; Sugar 0.4 g; Protein 42.4 g; Cholesterol 130 mg

Salmon Dill Patties

Preparation Time: 10 minutes; Cooking Time: 10 minutes; Serve: 2
Ingredients:

- 1 egg
- 14 oz salmon
- 1 tsp dill weed
- 1/2 cup almond flour
- 1/4 cup onion, diced
- Pepper
- Salt

Directions:
1. Line air fryer basket with parchment paper.
2. Add all ingredients into the mixing bowl and mix until well combined.
3. Make patties from mixture and place into the air fryer basket.
4. Cook at 370 F for 10 minutes. Turn patties halfway through.
5. Serve and enjoy.

Nutritional Value (Amount per Serving):
Calories 341; Fat 18 g; Carbohydrates 3.3 g; Sugar 1 g; Protein 43 g; Cholesterol 169 mg

Chicken Fritters

Preparation Time: 10 minutes; Cooking Time: 10 minutes; Serve: 4
Ingredients:
- 1 lb ground chicken
- 1/2 tsp onion powder
- 1/2 tsp garlic powder
- 1/2 cup parmesan cheese, shredded
- 1/2 tbsp dill, chopped
- 1/2 cup almond flour
- 2 tbsp green onions, chopped
- Pepper
- Salt

Directions:
1. Line air fryer basket with parchment paper.
2. Add all ingredients into the large bowl and mix until well combined.
3. Make patties from mixture and place into the air fryer basket.
4. Cook at 350 F for 10 minutes. Turn patties halfway through.
5. Serve and enjoy.

Nutritional Value (Amount per Serving):
Calories 280; Fat 12.9 g; Carbohydrates 2.2 g; Sugar 0.4 g; Protein 37.8 g; Cholesterol 110 mg

Delicious Chicken Burger Patties

Preparation Time: 10 minutes; Cooking Time: 25 minutes; Serve: 5
Ingredients:
- 1 lb ground chicken
- 1 egg, lightly beaten
- 1 cup Monterey jack cheese, grated
- 1 cup carrot, grated
- 1 cup cauliflower, grated
- 1/8 tsp red pepper flakes
- 2 garlic cloves, minced
- 1/2 cup onion, minced
- 3/4 cup almond flour
- Pepper
- Salt

Directions:
1. Line air fryer basket with parchment paper.
2. Add all ingredients into the mixing bowl and mix until well combined.
3. Make patties from mixture and place into the air fryer basket.
4. Cook at 400 F for 25 minutes. Turn patties halfway through.
5. Serve and enjoy.

Nutritional Value (Amount per Serving):
Calories 314; Fat 16.6 g; Carbohydrates 5.9 g; Sugar 2.4 g; Protein 34.6 g; Cholesterol 134 mg

Cheesy Chicken Fritters

Preparation Time: 10 minutes; Cooking Time: 25 minutes; Serve: 4
Ingredients:
- 1 lb ground chicken
- 3/4 cup almond flour
- 1 egg, lightly beaten
- 1 garlic clove, minced
- 1 1/2 cup mozzarella cheese, shredded
- 1/2 cup shallots, chopped
- 2 cups broccoli, chopped
- Pepper
- Salt

Directions:
1. Line air fryer basket with parchment paper.
2. Add all ingredients into the mixing bowl and mix until well combined.
3. Make patties from mixture and place into the air fryer basket.
4. Cook at 390 F for 15 minutes. Turn patties and cook for 10 minutes more.
5. Serve and enjoy.

Nutritional Value (Amount per Serving):
Calories 322; Fat 14.2 g; Carbohydrates 8.2 g; Sugar 1.1 g; Protein 40.1 g; Cholesterol 147 mg

Tuna Patties

Preparation Time: 10 minutes; Cooking Time: 10 minutes; Serve: 10
Ingredients:
- 15 oz can tuna, drained and flaked
- 1 celery stalk, chopped
- 3 tbsp parmesan cheese, grated
- 1/2 cup almond flour
- 1 tbsp lemon juice
- 2 eggs, lightly beaten
- 1/2 tsp dried herbs
- 1/2 tsp garlic powder
- 2 tbsp onion, minced
- Pepper
- Salt

Directions:
1. Line air fryer basket with parchment paper.
2. Add all ingredients into the large bowl and mix until well combined.
3. Make patties from mixture and place into the air fryer basket in batches.
4. Cook at 360 F for 10 minutes. Turn patties halfway through.
5. Serve and enjoy.

Nutritional Value (Amount per Serving):
Calories 86; Fat 2.9 g; Carbohydrates 0.9 g; Sugar 0.3 g; Protein 13.7 g; Cholesterol 49 mg

Ham Egg Bites

Preparation Time: 10 minutes; Cooking Time: 12 minutes; Serve: 8
Ingredients:
- 6 eggs
- 1/2 cup cheddar cheese, shredded
- 1 cup ham, diced
- 2 tbsp cream
- 1/4 tsp garlic powder
- 1/4 tsp onion powder
- Pepper
- Salt

Directions:
1. In a bowl, whisk eggs with remaining ingredients.
2. Pour egg mixture into the silicone muffin molds.
3. Place molds into the air fryer basket and cook at 300 F for 12-14 minutes or until eggs are cooked.
4. Serve and enjoy.

Nutritional Value (Amount per Serving):

Calories 106; Fat 7.2 g; Carbohydrates 1.2 g; Sugar 0.4 g; Protein 8.8 g; Cholesterol 140 mg

Chapter 3: Poultry Recipes

Delicious Chicken Fajita

Preparation Time: 10 minutes; Cooking Time: 18 minutes; Serve: 4

Ingredients:
- 1 lb chicken breast, boneless, skinless & sliced
- 1/8 tsp cayenne
- 1 tsp cumin
- 2 tsp chili powder
- 2 tsp olive oil
- 1 onion, sliced
- 2 bell peppers, sliced
- Pepper
- Salt

Directions:
1. Add chicken, onion, and sliced bell peppers into the mixing bowl. Add cayenne, cumin, chili powder, oil, pepper, and salt and toss well.
2. Add chicken mixture into the air fryer basket and slide the basket into the air fryer.
3. Cook at 360 F for 15-20 minutes. Stir halfway through.
4. Serve and enjoy.

Nutritional Value (Amount per Serving):
Calories 186; Fat 5.7 g; Carbohydrates 8.1 g; Sugar 4.3 g; Protein 25.2 g; Cholesterol 73 mg

Parmesan Chicken Wings

Preparation Time: 10 minutes; Cooking Time: 25 minutes; Serve: 4

Ingredients:
- 1 1/2 lbs chicken wings
- 3/4 tbsp garlic powder
- 1/4 cup parmesan cheese, grated
- 2 tbsp arrowroot powder
- Pepper
- Salt

Directions:
1. Preheat the cosori air fryer to 380 F.
2. In a large bowl, mix together garlic powder, parmesan cheese, arrowroot powder, pepper, and salt. Add chicken wings and toss until well coated.
3. Add chicken wings into the air fryer basket. Spray top of chicken wings with cooking spray.
4. Select chicken and press start. Shake air fryer basket halfway through.
5. Serve and enjoy.

Nutritional Value (Amount per Serving):
Calories 386; Fat 15.3 g; Carbohydrates 5.6 g; Sugar 0.4 g; Protein 53.5 g; Cholesterol 160 mg

Western Chicken Wings

Preparation Time: 10 minutes; Cooking Time: 15 minutes; Serve: 4

Ingredients:
- 2 lbs chicken wings
- 1 tsp Herb de Provence
- 1 tsp paprika
- 1/2 cup parmesan cheese, grated
- Pepper
- Salt

Directions:
1. Add cheese, paprika, herb de Provence, pepper, and salt into the large mixing bowl. Add chicken wings into the bowl and toss well to coat.
2. Preheat the cosori air fryer to 350 F.
3. Add chicken wings into the air fryer basket. Spray top of chicken wings with cooking spray.
4. Cook chicken wings for 15 minutes. Turn chicken wings halfway through.

5. Serve and enjoy.

Nutritional Value (Amount per Serving):
Calories 473; Fat 19.6 g; Carbohydrates 0.8 g; Sugar 0.1 g; Protein 69.7 g; Cholesterol 211 mg

Perfect Whole Chicken

Preparation Time: 10 minutes; Cooking Time: 50 minutes; Serve: 4

Ingredients:
- 3 lbs whole chicken, remove giblets & pat dry with a paper towel
- 1 tsp Italian seasoning
- 1/2 tsp dried rosemary
- 1/2 tsp dry thyme
- 1/2 tsp garlic powder
- 1/2 tsp onion powder
- 1/4 tsp paprika
- 1 tbsp olive oil
- Pepper
- Salt

Directions:
1. In a small bowl, mix together oil, Italian seasoning, rosemary, thyme, garlic powder, onion powder, paprika, pepper, and salt.
2. Rub oil and spice mixture all over the chicken.
3. Place chicken breast side down in the air fryer basket.
4. Roast chicken at 360 F for 30 minutes.
5. After 30 minutes flip chicken and roast for 20 minutes more.
6. Allow cooling chicken for 10 minutes.
7. Slice and serve.

Nutritional Value (Amount per Serving):
Calories 683; Fat 29.1 g; Carbohydrates 0.9 g; Sugar 0.3 g; Protein 98.6 g; Cholesterol 304 mg

Juicy Chicken Breasts

Preparation Time: 10 minutes; Cooking Time: 10 minutes; Serve: 4

Ingredients:
- 4 chicken breasts, boneless
- 1/8 tsp cayenne pepper
- 1/2 tsp paprika
- 1/2 tsp dried parsley
- 1/2 tsp onion powder
- 1/2 tsp garlic powder
- Pepper
- Salt

Directions:
1. Add 6 cups warm water and 1/4 cup kosher salt into the large bowl and stir until salt dissolve.
2. Add chicken breasts into the water and place a bowl in the refrigerator for 2 hours to brine.
3. After 2 hours remove water and pat dry chicken breasts with paper towels.
4. In a small bowl, mix together garlic powder, onion powder, dried parsley, paprika, cayenne pepper, and pepper.
5. Spray chicken breasts with cooking spray then rub with spice mixture.
6. Preheat the cosori air fryer to 380 F.
7. Place chicken breasts into the air fryer basket and cook for 10 minutes. Turn chicken breasts halfway through.
8. Serve and enjoy.

Nutritional Value (Amount per Serving):
Calories 281; Fat 10.9 g; Carbohydrates 0.7 g; Sugar 0.2 g; Protein 42.4 g; Cholesterol 130 mg

Flavors Dijon Chicken

Preparation Time: 10 minutes; Cooking Time: 14 minutes; Serve: 6
Ingredients:
- 1 1/2 lbs chicken breasts, boneless
- 1/4 tsp cayenne
- 1 tsp Italian seasoning
- 1 tbsp coconut aminos
- 1 tbsp fresh lemon juice
- 1 tbsp Dijon mustard
- 1/2 cup mayonnaise
- 1/2 tsp pepper
- 1 tsp sea salt

Directions:
1. In a small bowl, mix together mayonnaise, cayenne, Italian seasoning, coconut amino, lemon juice, mustard, pepper, and salt.
2. Add chicken into the zip-lock bag. Pour mayonnaise mixture over chicken and mix well.
3. Seal ziplock bag and place in the refrigerator overnight.
4. Preheat the cosori air fryer to 400 F.
5. Place marinated chicken in the air fryer basket and cook for 14 minutes. Turn chicken halfway through.
6. Serve and enjoy.

Nutritional Value (Amount per Serving):
Calories 300; Fat 15.3 g; Carbohydrates 5.6 g; Sugar 1.4 g; Protein 33.2 g; Cholesterol 107 mg

Crispy Crusted Chicken Tenders

Preparation Time: 10 minutes; Cooking Time: 10 minutes; Serve: 6
Ingredients:
- 2 eggs, lightly beaten
- 6 chicken tenders
- 1/2 tsp onion powder
- 1/2 tsp garlic powder
- 1 tsp paprika
- 1 cup pork rinds, crushed
- 1 tsp salt

Directions:
1. In a shallow bowl, mix together crushed pork rinds, paprika, garlic powder, onion powder, and salt.
2. In a separate shallow bowl, add beaten eggs.
3. Dip chicken tenders in eggs then coat with crushed pork rind mixture.
4. Place coated chicken tenders in the air fryer basket and cook at 400 F for 10 minutes. Turn chicken tenders halfway through.
5. Serve and enjoy.

Nutritional Value (Amount per Serving):
Calories 66; Fat 3.5 g; Carbohydrates 0.6 g; Sugar 0.3 g; Protein 7.9 g; Cholesterol 72 mg

Tender & Juicy Cornish Hens

Preparation Time: 10 minutes; Cooking Time: 45 minutes; Serve: 4
Ingredients:
- 2 Cornish game hens
- 1/2 tsp dried thyme
- 1/2 tsp dried oregano
- 1/2 tsp dried basil
- 1 tsp paprika
- 1 tsp garlic powder
- 1 tsp pepper
- 2 tbsp olive oil
- 1 tbsp kosher salt

Directions:
1. In a small bowl, mix together oil, garlic powder, paprika, basil, oregano, thyme, pepper, and salt.

2. Rub oil spice mixture all over hens.
3. Place hens in the air fryer basket breast side down and cook for 35 minutes at 360 F.
4. Turn the hens and cook for 10 minutes more.
5. Serve and enjoy.

Nutritional Value (Amount per Serving):
Calories 400; Fat 30.5 g; Carbohydrates 1.4 g; Sugar 0.2 g; Protein 28.9 g; Cholesterol 168 mg

Flavors & Crisp Chicken Thighs

Preparation Time: 10 minutes; Cooking Time: 22 minutes; Serve: 4
Ingredients:
- 4 chicken thighs, bone-in, skin-on, & remove excess fat
- 3/4 tsp onion powder
- 1/2 tsp oregano
- 3/4 tsp garlic powder
- 1 tsp paprika
- 1 tbsp olive oil
- 1/2 tsp kosher salt

Directions:
1. Preheat the cosori air fryer to 380 F.
2. Add chicken thighs into the large zip-lock bag. Add spices and oil over chicken.
3. Seal zip-lock bag and shake well to coat.
4. Place chicken thighs in the air fryer basket skin side down and cook for 12 minutes.
5. Turn chicken thighs and cook for 10 minutes more.
6. Serve and enjoy.

Nutritional Value (Amount per Serving):
Calories 313; Fat 14.3 g; Carbohydrates 1.2 g; Sugar 0.4 g; Protein 42.5 g; Cholesterol 130 mg

Perfect Chicken Thighs Dinner

Preparation Time: 10 minutes; Cooking Time: 15 minutes; Serve: 4
Ingredients:
- 4 chicken thighs, bone-in & skinless
- 1/4 tsp ground ginger
- 2 tsp paprika
- 2 tsp garlic powder
- 1/4 tsp pepper
- 1 tsp salt

Directions:
1. Preheat the cosori air fryer to 400 F.
2. In a small bowl, mix together ginger, paprika, garlic powder, pepper, and salt and rub all over chicken thighs.
3. Spray chicken thighs with cooking spray.
4. Place chicken thighs into the air fryer basket and cook for 10 minutes.
5. Turn chicken thighs and cook for 5 minutes more.
6. Serve and enjoy.

Nutritional Value (Amount per Serving):
Calories 286; Fat 11 g; Carbohydrates 1.8 g; Sugar 0.5 g; Protein 42.7 g; Cholesterol 130 mg

Perfectly Spiced Chicken Tenders

Preparation Time: 10 minutes; Cooking Time: 13 minutes; Serve: 4
Ingredients:
- 6 chicken tenders
- 1 tsp onion powder
- 1 tsp oregano
- 1 tsp garlic powder
- 1 tsp paprika
- 1 tsp kosher salt

Directions:

1. Preheat the cosori air fryer to 380 F.
2. In a small bowl, mix together onion powder, oregano, garlic powder, paprika, and salt and rub all over chicken tenders.
3. Spray chicken tenders with cooking spray.
4. Place chicken tenders into the air fryer basket and cook for 13 minutes.
5. Serve and enjoy.

Nutritional Value (Amount per Serving):
Calories 423; Fat 16.4 g; Carbohydrates 1.5 g; Sugar 0.5 g; Protein 63.7 g; Cholesterol 195 mg

Quick & Easy Lemon Pepper Chicken

Preparation Time: 10 minutes; Cooking Time: 30 minutes; Serve: 4
Ingredients:
- 4 chicken breasts, boneless & skinless
- 1 1/2 tsp granulated garlic
- 1 tbsp lemon pepper seasoning
- 1 tsp salt

Directions:
1. Preheat the cosori air fryer to 360 F.
2. Season chicken breasts with lemon pepper seasoning, granulated garlic, and salt.
3. Place chicken into the air fryer basket and cook for 30 minutes. Turn chicken halfway through.
4. Serve and enjoy.

Nutritional Value (Amount per Serving):
Calories 285; Fat 10.9 g; Carbohydrates 1.8 g; Sugar 0.3 g; Protein 42.6 g; Cholesterol 130 mg

Delicious Chicken Nuggets

Preparation Time: 10 minutes; Cooking Time: 12 minutes; Serve: 2
Ingredients:
- 1 lb chicken breasts, boneless, skinless, & cut into 1-inch pieces
- 1 tsp chili powder
- 1 tsp garlic powder
- 1 tsp paprika
- 1 cup almond flour
- 1 egg, lightly beaten
- 2 tsp sea salt

Directions:
1. Add lightly beaten egg in a shallow bowl.
2. In a separate shallow bowl, mix together almond flour, paprika, garlic powder, chili powder, and salt.
3. Preheat the cosori air fryer to 400 F.
4. Dip chicken pieces in egg then coat with almond flour mixture.
5. Place coated chicken pieces into the air fryer basket and spray with cooking spray.
6. Cook nuggets for 10-12 minutes or until done. Turn halfway through.
7. Serve and enjoy.

Nutritional Value (Amount per Serving):
Calories 554; Fat 26.4 g; Carbohydrates 5.5 g; Sugar 1.2 g; Protein 71.9 g; Cholesterol 284 mg

Quick & Easy Chipotle Wings

Preparation Time: 10 minutes; Cooking Time: 10 minutes; Serve: 6
Ingredients:
- 2 lbs chicken wings
- 1/2 cup ketchup, sugar-free
- 2 chipotle peppers in adobo sauce
- 1/2 tsp dried thyme

- 1/2 tsp oregano
- 1/2 tsp garlic powder
- 1/2 tsp chili powder
- 1/2 tsp dry mustard
- 1 tsp paprika
- 1 tsp salt

Directions:
1. In a large mixing bowl, mix paprika, mustard, chili powder, garlic powder, oregano, thyme, and salt.
2. Add chicken wings and toss well to coat.
3. Preheat the cosori air fryer to 400 F.
4. Lightly spray chicken wings with cooking spray and place in the air fryer basket.
5. Cook chicken wings for 10 minutes.
6. In a mixing bowl, stir together ketchup and chipotle peppers. Add chicken wings and toss to coat.
7. Serve and enjoy.

Nutritional Value (Amount per Serving):
Calories 315; Fat 11.8 g; Carbohydrates 6.1 g; Sugar 4.7 g; Protein 44.6 g; Cholesterol 136 mg

Spicy Jalapeno Hassel back Chicken

Preparation Time: 10 minutes; Cooking Time: 15 minutes; Serve: 2
Ingredients:
- 2 chicken breasts, boneless and skinless
- 1/2 cup cheddar cheese, shredded
- 4 tbsp pickled jalapenos, chopped
- 2 oz cream cheese, softened
- 4 bacon slices, cooked and crumbled

Directions:
1. Make five to six slits on top of chicken breasts.
2. In a bowl, mix together 1/2 cheddar cheese, pickled jalapenos, cream cheese, and bacon.
3. Stuff cheddar cheese mixture into the slits.
4. Place chicken into the air fryer basket and cook at 350 F for 14 minutes.
5. Sprinkle remaining cheese on top of the chicken and air fry for 1 minute more.
6. Serve and enjoy.

Nutritional Value (Amount per Serving):
Calories 736; Fat 49 g; Carbohydrates 3.7 g; Sugar 0.2 g; Protein 65.5 g; Cholesterol 233 mg

Healthy Greek Chicken

Preparation Time: 10 minutes; Cooking Time: 12 minutes; Serve: 2
Ingredients:
- 10 oz chicken breast, boneless, skinless, & cut into 1-inch pieces
- 2 tbsp feta cheese, crumbled
- 1 1/2 tbsp olive oil
- 1/4 tsp dried thyme
- 1/2 tsp garlic powder
- 1/2 tsp dried parsley
- 1 tsp dried oregano
- 1/2 zucchini, chopped
- 1/2 bell pepper, chopped
- 1/2 onion, chopped
- Pepper
- Salt

Directions:
1. In a mixing bowl, toss together chicken, oil, thyme, garlic powder, parsley, oregano, zucchini, bell pepper, onion, pepper, and salt.
2. Add chicken mixture into the air fryer basket and cook at 380 F for 12 minutes. Shake basket halfway through.
3. Add crumbled feta cheese and toss well.
4. Serve and enjoy.

Nutritional Value (Amount per Serving):
Calories 310; Fat 16.3 g; Carbohydrates 8 g; Sugar 4.1 g; Protein 32.8 g; Cholesterol 99 mg

Tasty Hassel back Chicken

Preparation Time: 10 minutes; Cooking Time: 18 minutes; Serve: 2
Ingredients:
- 2 chicken breasts, boneless and skinless
- 1/2 cup sauerkraut, squeezed and remove excess liquid
- 5 thin Swiss cheese slices, tear into pieces
- 4 thin deli corned beef slices, tear into pieces
- Pepper
- Salt

Directions:
1. Make five slits on top of chicken breasts. Season chicken with pepper and salt.
2. Stuff each slit with beef, sauerkraut, and cheese.
3. Spray chicken with cooking spray and place in the air fryer basket.
4. Cook chicken at 350 F for 18 minutes.
5. Serve and enjoy.

Nutritional Value (Amount per Serving):
Calories 724; Fat 39.9 g; Carbohydrates 3.6 g; Sugar 2.6 g; Protein 83.6 g; Cholesterol 260 mg

Delicious Chicken Meatballs

Preparation Time: 10 minutes; Cooking Time: 12 minutes; Serve: 4
Ingredients:
- 1/2 lb ground chicken
- 1 egg, lightly beaten
- 2 garlic cloves, minced
- 1/2 cup swiss cheese, shredded
- 1/3 cup onion, diced
- 1/2 lb ham, diced
- Pepper
- Salt

Directions:
1. Add all ingredients into the mixing bowl and mix until well combined. Place in refrigerator for 30 minutes.
2. Preheat the cosori air fryer to 390 F.
3. Remove meatball mixture from refrigerator and make 12 meatballs.
4. Spray meatballs with cooking spray and place in the air fryer basket.
5. Cook meatballs for 12-15 minutes.
6. Serve and enjoy.

Nutritional Value (Amount per Serving):
Calories 273; Fat 13.9 g; Carbohydrates 4.4 g; Sugar 0.7 g; Protein 31 g; Cholesterol 136 mg

Mexican Chicken Fajitas

Preparation Time: 10 minutes; Cooking Time: 15 minutes; Serve: 2
Ingredients:
- 10 oz chicken breast, boneless, skinless, & sliced
- 1/4 tsp dried oregano
- 1/2 tsp onion powder
- 1/2 tsp garlic powder
- 1/2 tsp paprika
- 1 tsp cumin
- 2 tsp chili powder
- 1 1/2 tbsp olive oil
- 1/2 red bell pepper, sliced
- 1/2 green bell pepper, sliced
- 1/2 onion, sliced
- 1/2 tsp salt

Directions:
1. Add chicken, bell peppers, and onion in a mixing bowl.
2. Drizzle with oil and season with chili powder, cumin, paprika, garlic powder, onion powder, oregano, and salt. Toss well to coat.
3. Add chicken mixture into the air fryer basket and cook at 350 F for 15 minutes. Shake basket halfway through.
4. Serve and enjoy.

Nutritional Value (Amount per Serving):
Calories 291; Fat 14.9 g; Carbohydrates 8.1 g; Sugar 3.3 g; Protein 31.4 g; Cholesterol 91 mg

Fajita Hassel back Chicken

Preparation Time: 10 minutes; Cooking Time: 15 minutes; Serve: 4
Ingredients:
- 4 chicken breasts, boneless and skinless
- 1/4 cup cheddar cheese, shredded
- 1/4 cup Colby jack cheese, shredded
- 1 onion, sliced
- 1/2 red bell pepper, sliced
- 1/2 yellow bell pepper, sliced
- 1/2 green bell pepper, sliced
- 2 tbsp fajita seasoning
- 2 tbsp olive oil

Directions:
1. Preheat the cosori air fryer to 380 F.
2. Make five to six slits on top of chicken breasts. Rub with fajita seasoning and oil.
3. Stuff sliced onion and bell peppers into each slit.
4. Place chicken into the air fryer basket and cook for 15 minutes.
5. Remove chicken from the air fryer and place on a baking pan.
6. Sprinkle shredded cheddar cheese and Colby jack cheese over chicken and broil chicken until cheese is melted.
7. Serve and enjoy.

Nutritional Value (Amount per Serving):
Calories 425; Fat 22.5 g; Carbohydrates 7.2 g; Sugar 2 g; Protein 46 g; Cholesterol 144 mg

Western Turkey Breast

Preparation Time: 10 minutes; Cooking Time: 60 minutes; Serve: 8
Ingredients:
- 4 lbs turkey breast, boneless
- 1 tbsp olive oil
- 1/2 tsp ground cinnamon
- 1 1/2 tsp paprika
- 1 1/2 tsp garlic powder
- 1/2 tsp pepper
- 2 tsp salt

Directions:
1. Preheat the cosori air fryer to 350 F.
2. In a small bowl, mix together cinnamon, paprika, garlic powder, pepper, and salt.
3. Rub oil and spice mixture all over turkey breast.
4. Place turkey breast skin side down in the air fryer basket and cook for 25 minutes.
5. Turn turkey breast and cover with foil and cook for 35-45 minutes more or until the internal temperature of the turkey reaches 160 F.
6. Remove turkey breast from the air fryer and allow it to cool for 10 minutes.
7. Slice and serve.

Nutritional Value (Amount per Serving):
Calories 254; Fat 5.6 g; Carbohydrates 10.4 g; Sugar 8.1 g; Protein 38.9 g; Cholesterol 98 mg

Easy Turkey Meatballs

Preparation Time: 10 minutes; Cooking Time: 10 minutes; Serve: 4
Ingredients:
- 1 egg, lightly beaten
- 1 tbsp fresh cilantro, minced
- 4 tbsp fresh parsley, chopped
- 1 bell pepper, chopped
- 1 1/2 lbs ground turkey
- Pepper
- Salt

Directions:
1. Preheat the cosori air fryer to 400 F.
2. Add all ingredients into the mixing bowl and mix until well combined.
3. Make small meatballs from mixture and place into the air fryer basket.
4. Cook meatballs for 10 minutes or until lightly browned. Shake basket halfway through.
5. Serve and enjoy.

Nutritional Value (Amount per Serving):
Calories 359; Fat 19.9 g; Carbohydrates 2.6 g; Sugar 1.6 g; Protein 48.3 g; Cholesterol 239 mg

Cajun Chicken Thighs

Preparation Time: 10 minutes; Cooking Time: 15 minutes; Serve: 4
Ingredients:
- 4 chicken thighs, boneless
- 1/2 tsp cajun seasoning
- 1 tsp dried mixed herbs
- 1 tsp paprika
- 3 tbsp parmesan cheese, grated
- 1/3 cup almond flour

Directions:
1. Preheat the cosori air fryer to 400 F.
2. In a medium bowl, mix together almond flour, parmesan cheese, paprika, dried mixed herbs, and Cajun seasoning.
3. Spray chicken thighs with cooking spray and coat with almond flour mixture.
4. Place coated chicken thighs into the air fryer basket and cook for 12-15 minutes.
5. Serve and enjoy.

Nutritional Value (Amount per Serving):
Calories 326; Fat 14.3 g; Carbohydrates 1.3 g; Sugar 0.1 g; Protein 46.2 g; Cholesterol 137 mg

Flavorful Chicken Tenders

Preparation Time: 10 minutes; Cooking Time: 12 minutes; Serve: 4
Ingredients:
- 1 lb chicken tenders
- 1/4 tsp oregano
- 1/4 tsp ground mustard
- 1/4 tsp onion powder
- 1/2 tsp garlic powder
- 1/2 tsp paprika
- 1 cup almond flour
- 2 eggs, lightly beaten
- 1/2 tsp pepper
- 1/2 tsp celery salt
- 1/2 tsp salt

Directions:
1. Preheat the cosori air fryer to 400 F.
2. Add eggs into the shallow bowl and set aside.
3. In a separate shallow bowl, mix together almond flour, oregano, mustard, onion powder, garlic powder, paprika, pepper, celery salt, and salt.
4. Dip chicken tenders into the egg wash then coat with almond flour mixture.

5. Place coated chicken tenders into the air fryer basket. Spray top of chicken tenders with cooking spray.
6. Cook chicken tenders for 12 minutes. Turn halfway through.
7. Serve and enjoy.

Nutritional Value (Amount per Serving):
Calories 291; Fat 14.2 g; Carbohydrates 2.5 g; Sugar 0.6 g; Protein 37.3 g; Cholesterol 183 mg

Juicy Lemon Pepper Chicken Thighs

Preparation Time: 10 minutes; Cooking Time: 12 minutes; Serve: 4

Ingredients:
- 6 chicken thighs, boneless and skinless
- 1 tbsp lemon zest
- 1/2 tsp dried oregano
- 1 tsp garlic powder
- 1 tsp paprika
- 2 1/2 tbsp fresh lemon juice
- 1 1/2 tsp pepper
- Salt

Directions:
1. Add chicken thighs into the large mixing bowl.
2. Add oregano, garlic powder, paprika, lemon juice, pepper, and salt over chicken and coat well. Place in refrigerator for 30 minutes.
3. Place marinated chicken thighs into the air fryer basket and cook for 12 minutes. Turn halfway through.
4. Garnish with lemon zest and serve.

Nutritional Value (Amount per Serving):
Calories 426; Fat 16.5 g; Carbohydrates 2 g; Sugar 0.5 g; Protein 63.8 g; Cholesterol 195 mg

Creamy Pesto Chicken

Preparation Time: 10 minutes; Cooking Time: 15 minutes; Serve: 4

Ingredients:
- 1 lb chicken thighs, boneless, skinless, & cut into halves
- 1/2 tsp red pepper flakes
- 1/4 cup parmesan cheese, shredded
- 1/4 cup half and half
- 1/2 cup pesto
- 1/2 cup cherry tomatoes, cut in half
- 1/2 cup bell peppers, sliced
- 1/2 cup onion, sliced

Directions:
1. Spray 6*3 heat-safe pan with cooking spray and set aside.
2. In a mixing bowl, mix together pesto, red pepper flakes, half and half, and parmesan cheese.
3. Add chicken into the pesto mixture and coat well.
4. Pour chicken pesto mixture into the prepared pan and top with tomatoes, bell peppers, and onions.
5. Place pan in the air fryer basket and cook at 360 F for 15 minutes.
6. Serve and enjoy.

Nutritional Value (Amount per Serving):
Calories 406; Fat 24.6 g; Carbohydrates 6.4 g; Sugar 4 g; Protein 38.8 g; Cholesterol 118 mg

Tasty Chicken Tikka Bites

Preparation Time: 10 minutes; Cooking Time: 12 minutes; Serve: 4

Ingredients:
- 1 lb chicken breast, boneless, skinless, & cut into bite-size pieces
- 1 lemon juice
- 1/4 tsp cayenne pepper

- 1/2 tsp paprika
- 1/2 tsp coriander powder
- 1/2 tsp ground cumin
- 1 tsp garam masala
- 1/4 cup fresh cilantro, chopped
- 1 tbsp ginger garlic paste
- 1/2 cup Greek yogurt
- 1 tsp kosher salt

Directions:
1. In a mixing bowl, mix together chicken, cayenne, paprika, coriander powder, ground cumin, garam masala, cilantro, ginger garlic paste, yogurt, and salt. Place in refrigerator overnight.
2. Place marinated chicken pieces into the air fryer basket and spray the top of chicken with cooking spray.
3. Cook at 400 F for 12 minutes. Turn chicken halfway through.
4. Drizzle lemon juice over the chicken bites and serve.

Nutritional Value (Amount per Serving):
Calories 158; Fat 3.7 g; Carbohydrates 1.8 g; Sugar 1.6 g; Protein 27.4 g; Cholesterol 74 mg

Healthy Chicken & Broccoli

Preparation Time: 10 minutes; Cooking Time: 20 minutes; Serve: 4
Ingredients:
- 1 lb chicken breast, boneless, skinless, & cut into bite-size pieces
- 1/2 onion, sliced
- 2 cups broccoli florets
- 2 tsp rice vinegar
- 1 tsp sesame oil
- 1 tbsp soy sauce
- 1 tsp garlic, minced
- 2 tbsp olive oil
- Pepper
- Salt

Directions:
1. In a mixing bowl, mix together olive oil, garlic, soy sauce, sesame oil, rice, vinegar, pepper, and salt.
2. Add chicken, onion, and broccoli into the bowl and mix well and marinate for 1 hour.
3. Place marinated chicken and vegetables into the air fryer basket and cook for 380 F for 20 minutes. Shake air fryer basket 2-3 times.
4. Serve and enjoy.

Nutritional Value (Amount per Serving):
Calories 217; Fat 11.1 g; Carbohydrates 3.3 g; Sugar 1 g; Protein 25.1 g; Cholesterol 73 mg

Lemon Pepper Turkey Breast

Preparation Time: 10 minutes; Cooking Time: 60 minutes; Serve: 6
Ingredients:
- 3 lbs turkey breast, de-boned
- 1 tsp lemon pepper seasoning
- 1 tbsp Worcestershire sauce
- 2 tbsp olive oil
- 1/2 tsp salt

Directions:
1. Add olive oil, Worcestershire sauce, lemon pepper seasoning, and salt into the zip-lock bag. Add turkey breast to the marinade and coat well and marinate for 1-2 hours.
2. Remove turkey breast from marinade and place it into the air fryer basket.
3. Cook at 350 F for 25 minutes. Turn turkey breast and cook for 35 minutes more or until the internal temperature of turkey breast reaches 165 F.
4. Slice and serve.

Nutritional Value (Amount per Serving):
Calories 279; Fat 8.4 g; Carbohydrates 10.3 g; Sugar 8.5 g; Protein 38.8 g; Cholesterol 98 mg

Garlic Chicken Wings

Preparation Time: 10 minutes; Cooking Time: 20 minutes; Serve: 6

Ingredients:
- 2 lbs chicken wings
- 2 tsp garlic, minced
- 2 tsp fresh parsley, chopped
- 1 cup parmesan cheese, grated
- Pepper
- Salt

Directions:
1. Preheat the cosori air fryer to 400 F.
2. In a mixing bowl, mix together cheese, garlic, parsley, pepper, and salt. Add chicken wings and toss until well coated.
3. Place chicken wings into the air fryer basket and cook for 20 minutes. Turn wings halfway through.
4. Serve and enjoy.

Nutritional Value (Amount per Serving):
Calories 342; Fat 14.8 g; Carbohydrates 1 g; Sugar 0 g; Protein 49.2 g; Cholesterol 146 mg

Crispy Bagel Chicken Tenders

Preparation Time: 10 minutes; Cooking Time: 12 minutes; Serve: 4

Ingredients:
- 1 egg, lightly beaten
- 1 lb chicken tenders
- 1 tsp paprika
- 2 tbsp ground flax seed
- 1/4 cup everything bagel seasoning
- 1/2 cup almond flour
- 1 tbsp ghee, melted
- 2 tbsp almond milk

Directions:
1. Preheat the cosori air fryer to 390 F.
2. In a shallow bowl, whisk together egg, ghee, and milk and set aside.
3. In a separate shallow bowl, mix together almond flour, bagel seasoning, ground flaxseed, and paprika.
4. Spray air fryer basket with cooking spray.
5. Dip chicken tenders in egg mixture then coat with almond flour mixture.
6. Place coated chicken tenders into the air fryer basket and cook for 12 minutes. Turn chicken tenders halfway through.
7. Serve and enjoy.

Nutritional Value (Amount per Serving):
Calories 331; Fat 17.4 g; Carbohydrates 5.6 g; Sugar 0.8 g; Protein 36.4 g; Cholesterol 150 mg

Italian Chicken Drumsticks

Preparation Time: 10 minutes; Cooking Time: 30 minutes; Serve: 4

Ingredients:
- 2 lbs chicken drumsticks
- 2 tbsp olive oil
- 1 1/2 tbsp garlic powder
- 1/4 tsp paprika
- 2 tsp Italian seasoning
- Pepper
- Salt

Directions:
1. Place chicken drumsticks into the large bowl. Pour oil, garlic powder, paprika, Italian seasoning, pepper, and salt over chicken and coat well.
2. Place chicken in the refrigerator for 2 hours.
3. Preheat the cosori air fryer to 400 F.

4. Place marinated chicken drumsticks into the air fryer basket and cook for 30 minutes. Turn chicken drumsticks halfway through.
5. Serve and enjoy.

Nutritional Value (Amount per Serving):
Calories 461; Fat 20.7 g; Carbohydrates 2.6 g; Sugar 1 g; Protein 62.9 g; Cholesterol 201 m

Asian Chicken Meatballs

Preparation Time: 10 minutes; Cooking Time: 10 minutes; Serve: 4
Ingredients:
- 1 lb ground chicken
- 4 tbsp unsweetened shredded coconut
- 1 tsp sesame oil
- 1 tsp sriracha sauce
- 1 tbsp soy sauce
- 1 tbsp Hoisin sauce
- 2 tbsp green onion, chopped
- 1/4 cup fresh cilantro, chopped
- Pepper
- Salt

Directions:
1. Add ground chicken and remaining ingredients into the mixing bowl and mix until well combined.
2. Make small balls from mixture and place into the air fryer basket and cook at 350 F for 10 minutes. Turn meatballs halfway through.
3. Serve and enjoy.

Nutritional Value (Amount per Serving):
Calories 291; Fat 14.5 g; Carbohydrates 3.9 g; Sugar 1.8 g; Protein 33.8 g; Cholesterol 102 mg

Herb Marinated Chicken Thighs

Preparation Time: 10 minutes; Cooking Time: 14 minutes; Serve: 8
Ingredients:
- 8 chicken thighs, bone-in & skin-on
- 1/2 tsp dried sage
- 1/2 tsp onion powder
- 1/2 tsp dried oregano
- 1 tsp dried basil
- 1 tsp spike seasoning
- 1 1/2 tsp garlic powder
- 2 tbsp fresh lemon juice
- 1/4 cup olive oil
- 1/4 tsp pepper

Directions:
1. In a small bowl, mix together oil, lemon juice, garlic powder, spike seasoning, basil, oregano, onion powder, sage, and pepper.
2. Add chicken thighs into the zip-lock bag then pour oil mixture over chicken. Coat well and marinate the chicken in the refrigerator for 6 hours.
3. Preheat the cosori air fryer to 360 F.
4. Remove chicken from marinade and place into the air fryer basket.
5. Cook chicken for 8 minutes. Turn chicken and cook for 6 minutes more or until the internal temperature of chicken reaches 165 F.
6. Serve and enjoy.

Nutritional Value (Amount per Serving):
Calories 335; Fat 17.2 g; Carbohydrates 0.7 g; Sugar 0.3 g; Protein 42.4 g; Cholesterol 130 mg

Juicy Caribbean Chicken

Preparation Time: 10 minutes; Cooking Time: 10 minutes; Serve: 8
Ingredients:

- 3 lbs chicken thighs, boneless and skinless
- 3 tbsp coconut oil, melted
- 1 1/2 tsp ground nutmeg
- 1 1/2 tsp ground ginger
- 1 tbsp cayenne pepper
- 1 tbsp ground cinnamon
- 1 tbsp ground coriander
- Pepper
- Salt

Directions:
1. In a medium bowl, mix together nutmeg, ginger, cayenne, cinnamon, coriander, pepper, and salt.
2. Coat chicken thighs with spice mixture and brush with melted coconut oil.
3. Place chicken thighs into the air fryer basket and cook at 390 F for 10 minutes.
4. Serve and enjoy.

Nutritional Value (Amount per Serving):
Calories 375; Fat 18 g; Carbohydrates 1.5 g; Sugar 0.2 g; Protein 49.4 g; Cholesterol 151 mg

Chicken Broccoli Fritters

Preparation Time: 10 minutes; Cooking Time: 10 minutes; Serve: 8
Ingredients:
- 1 lb chicken thighs, boneless, skinless cut into small pieces
- 2 cups broccoli florets, steamed and chopped
- 1 cup cheddar cheese, shredded
- 1/2 cup almond flour
- 1/2 tsp garlic powder
- 2 eggs, lightly beaten
- Pepper
- Salt

Directions:
1. Spray air fryer basket with cooking spray.
2. Add chicken and remaining ingredients into the mixing bowl and mix until well combined.
3. Make small fritters from the chicken mixture and place it into the air fryer basket.
4. Cook chicken fritters at 400 F for 8 minutes. Turn chicken fritters and cook for 2 minutes more.
5. Serve and enjoy.

Nutritional Value (Amount per Serving):
Calories 199; Fat 10.9 g; Carbohydrates 2.3 g; Sugar 0.6 g; Protein 22.4 g; Cholesterol 106 mg

Spicy Chicken Wings

Preparation Time: 10 minutes; Cooking Time: 30 minutes; Serve: 4
Ingredients:
- 2 lbs chicken wings
- 2 tsp garlic powder
- 4 tsp chili powder
- 3 tbsp olive oil
- Pepper
- Salt

Directions:
1. Add chicken wings and remaining ingredients into the zip-lock bag and shake well to coat.
2. Place chicken wings into the air fryer basket and cook at 380 F for 30 minutes. Toss chicken wings every 5 minutes.
3. Serve and enjoy.

Nutritional Value (Amount per Serving):
Calories 534; Fat 27.8 g; Carbohydrates 2.5 g; Sugar 0.5 g; Protein 66.2 g; Cholesterol 202 mg

Nutritious Chicken & Veggies

Preparation Time: 10 minutes; Cooking Time: 10 minutes; Serve: 4

Ingredients:
- 1 lb chicken breast, boneless & cut into bite-size pieces
- 1 tbsp Italian seasoning
- 1/2 tsp garlic powder
- 1/2 tsp chili powder
- 2 tbsp olive oil
- 2 garlic cloves, minced
- 1/2 onion, chopped
- 1 cup bell pepper, chopped
- 1 zucchini, chopped
- 1 cup broccoli florets
- Pepper
- Salt

Directions:
1. Preheat the cosori air fryer to 400 F.
2. Add chicken and remaining ingredients into the large mixing bowl and toss well.
3. Add chicken and veggies mixture into the air fryer basket and cook for 10 minutes or until chicken is cooked. Shake air fryer basket halfway through.
4. Serve and enjoy.

Nutritional Value (Amount per Serving):
Calories 235; Fat 11.2 g; Carbohydrates 8 g; Sugar 3.8 g; Protein 25.9 g; Cholesterol 75 mg

Chicken Spinach Meatballs

Preparation Time: 10 minutes; Cooking Time: 10 minutes; Serve: 4

Ingredients:
- 1 lb ground chicken
- 3/4 cup almond flour
- 1/4 cup feta cheese, crumbled
- 2 tbsp parmesan cheese, grated
- 1/4 cup sun-dried tomatoes, drained
- 2 tsp garlic
- 3 cups baby spinach
- Pepper
- Salt

Directions:
1. Add spinach, sun-dried tomatoes, and 1 tsp garlic into the food processor and process until a paste is formed.
2. Add spinach mixture into the large mixing bowl. Add remaining ingredients into the bowl and mix until well combined.
3. Spray air fryer basket with cooking spray.
4. Make small meatballs from mixture and place into the air fryer basket.
5. Cook meatballs at 400 F for 10 minutes.
6. Serve and enjoy.

Nutritional Value (Amount per Serving):
Calories 303; Fat 14.7 g; Carbohydrates 3.5 g; Sugar 1 g; Protein 38.4 g; Cholesterol 114 mg

Tender Turkey Legs

Preparation Time: 10 minutes; Cooking Time: 27 minutes; Serve: 4

Ingredients:
- 4 turkey legs
- 1/4 tsp thyme
- 1/4 tsp oregano
- 1/4 tsp rosemary
- 1 tbsp butter
- Pepper
- Salt

Directions:
1. Season turkey legs with pepper and salt.
2. In a small bowl, mix together butter, thyme, oregano, and rosemary.
3. Rub the butter mixture all over turkey legs.

4. Preheat the cosori air fryer to 350 F.
5. Place turkey legs into the air fryer basket and cook for 27 minutes.
6. Serve and enjoy.

Nutritional Value (Amount per Serving):
Calories 182; Fat 9.9 g; Carbohydrates 1.9 g; Sugar 0.1 g; Protein 20.2 g; Cholesterol 68 mg

Greek Meatballs

Preparation Time: 10 minutes; Cooking Time: 10 minutes; Serve: 4

Ingredients:
- 1 lb ground chicken
- 1 egg, lightly beaten
- 1 tsp onion powder
- 1 tsp lemon zest
- 1 tbsp dried oregano
- 1 1/2 tsp garlic paste
- Pepper
- Salt

Directions:
1. Add all ingredients into the mixing bowl and mix until well combined.
2. Preheat the cosori air fryer to 390 F.
3. Make small meatballs from mixture and place into the air fryer basket and cook for 8-10 minutes.
4. Serve and enjoy.

Nutritional Value (Amount per Serving):
Calories 239; Fat 9.6 g; Carbohydrates 1.8 g; Sugar 0.4 g; Protein 34.5 g; Cholesterol 142 mg

Perfect Chicken Breasts

Preparation Time: 10 minutes; Cooking Time: 15 minutes; Serve: 4

Ingredients:
- 1 lb chicken breasts, skinless and boneless
- 1 tsp poultry seasoning
- 2 tsp olive oil
- 1 tsp salt

Directions:
1. Rub chicken breasts with oil and season with poultry seasoning and salt.
2. Place chicken breasts into the air fryer basket and cook at 360 F for 10 minutes. Flip chicken and cook for 5 minutes more.
3. Serve and enjoy.

Nutritional Value (Amount per Serving):
Calories 237; Fat 10.8 g; Carbohydrates 0.3 g; Sugar 0 g; Protein 32.9 g; Cholesterol 101 mg

Turkey Spinach Patties

Preparation Time: 10 minutes; Cooking Time: 20 minutes; Serve: 4

Ingredients:
- 1 lb ground turkey
- 1 1/2 cups fresh spinach, chopped
- 1 tsp Italian seasoning
- 1 tbsp olive oil
- 1 tbsp garlic, minced
- 4 oz feta cheese, crumbled
- Pepper
- Salt

Directions:
1. Add ground turkey and remaining ingredients into the mixing bowl and mix until well combined.
2. Make four equal shapes of patties from turkey mixture and place it into the air fryer basket.
3. Cook turkey patties for 20 minutes.
4. Serve and enjoy.

Nutritional Value (Amount per Serving):
Calories 336; Fat 22.4 g; Carbohydrates 2.4 g; Sugar 1.3 g; Protein 35.5 g; Cholesterol 142 mg

Tasty Turkey Fajitas

Preparation Time: 10 minutes; Cooking Time: 20 minutes; Serve: 4
Ingredients:
- 1 lb turkey breast, boneless, skinless, and cut into 1/2-inch slices
- 1/4 cup fresh cilantro, chopped
- 1 jalapeno pepper, chopped
- 1 onion, sliced
- 2 bell pepper, sliced into strips
- 1 1/2 tbsp olive oil
- 2 lime juice
- 1/2 tsp onion powder
- 1 tsp garlic powder
- 1/2 tbsp oregano
- 1/2 tsp paprika
- 1 tbsp chili powder

Directions:
1. In a small bowl, mix together onion powder, garlic powder, oregano, paprika, cumin, chili powder, and pepper.
2. Squeeze one lime juice over turkey breast then sprinkle spice mixture over turkey breast.
3. Brush turkey breast with 1 tbsp olive oil and set aside.
4. Add onion and bell peppers into the medium bowl and toss with remaining oil.
5. Preheat the cosori air fryer to 375 F.
6. Add onion and bell peppers into the air fryer basket and cook for 8 minutes. Shake basket and cook for 5 minutes more.
7. Add jalapenos and cook for 5 minutes. Shake basket and add sliced turkey over vegetables and cook for 8 minutes.
8. Garnish fajitas with cilantro and serve.

Nutritional Value (Amount per Serving):
Calories 211; Fat 7.8 g; Carbohydrates 16.2 g; Sugar 9.1 g; Protein 20.9 g; Cholesterol 49 mg

Ranch Garlic Chicken Wings

Preparation Time: 10 minutes; Cooking Time: 25 minutes; Serve: 4
Ingredients:
- 2 lbs chicken wings
- 5 garlic cloves, minced
- 1/4 cup butter, melted
- 3 tbsp ranch seasoning mix

Directions:
1. Add chicken wings into the zip-lock bag.
2. Mix together butter, garlic, and ranch seasoning and pour over chicken wings. Seal bag shakes well and places in the refrigerator overnight.
3. Place marinated chicken wings into the air fryer basket and cook at 360 F for 20 minutes. Shake air fryer basket twice.
4. Turn temperature to 390 F and cook chicken wings for 5 minutes more.
5. Serve and enjoy.

Nutritional Value (Amount per Serving):
Calories 552; Fat 28.3 g; Carbohydrates 1.3 g; Sugar 0.1 g; Protein 66 g; Cholesterol 232 mg

Ranch Chicken Thighs

Preparation Time: 10 minutes; Cooking Time: 23 minutes; Serve: 4
Ingredients:
- 8 chicken thighs, bone-in & skin-on
- 2 1/2 tbsp ranch dressing mix

Directions:

1. Add chicken thighs into the mixing bowl and sprinkle with ranch dressing mix. Toss well to coat.
2. Spray chicken thighs with cooking spray and place into the air fryer basket.
3. Cook at 380 F for 23 minutes. Turn chicken halfway through.
4. Serve and enjoy.

Nutritional Value (Amount per Serving):
Calories 558; Fat 21.7 g; Carbohydrates 0.5 g; Sugar 0.3 g; Protein 84.6 g; Cholesterol 260 mg

Taco Ranch Chicken Wings

Preparation Time: 10 minutes; Cooking Time: 30 minutes; Serve: 4
Ingredients:
- 2 lbs chicken wings
- 1 tsp ranch seasoning
- 1 1/2 tsp taco seasoning
- 1 tsp olive oil

Directions:
1. Preheat the cosori air fryer to 400 F.
2. In a mixing bowl, add chicken wings, ranch seasoning, taco seasoning, and oil and toss well to coat.
3. Place chicken wings into the air fryer basket and cook for 15 minutes.
4. Turn chicken wings to another side and cook for 15 minutes more.
5. Serve and enjoy.

Nutritional Value (Amount per Serving):
Calories 444; Fat 18 g; Carbohydrates 0 g; Sugar 0 g; Protein 65.6 g; Cholesterol 202 mg

Crisp Cilantro Lime Chicken Wings

Preparation Time: 10 minutes; Cooking Time: 30 minutes; Serve: 4
Ingredients:
- 1 1/2 lbs chicken wings
- 1/2 tsp garlic powder
- 1/4 tsp cumin
- 1/2 tsp oregano
- 1/4 cup cilantro
- 1 tbsp olive oil
- 1 tbsp fresh lime juice
- 1/2 tsp pepper
- 1 tsp salt

Directions:
1. Preheat the cosori air fryer to 400 F.
2. Add all ingredients except chicken wings into the mixing bowl and mix well. Add chicken wings into the bowl and coat well.
3. Place chicken wings into the air fryer basket and cook for 30 minutes. Turn chicken wings halfway through.
4. Serve and enjoy.

Nutritional Value (Amount per Serving):
Calories 358; Fat 16.2 g; Carbohydrates 1.4 g; Sugar 0.3 g; Protein 49.4 g; Cholesterol 151 mg

Turkey Mushroom Patties

Preparation Time: 10 minutes; Cooking Time: 10 minutes; Serve: 4
Ingredients:
- 1 lb ground turkey
- 1/4 cup almond flour
- 1 tsp grainy mustard
- 1 tbsp Worcestershire sauce
- 1 tbsp fresh parsley, chopped
- 2 garlic cloves, minced
- 1 small onion, chopped
- 4 oz mushrooms, clean, dry and trim

- Pepper
- Salt

Directions:
1. Add mushrooms into the food processor and process until a chunky mixture is formed.
2. In a mixing bowl, mix together ground turkey, chunky mushroom mixture, and remaining ingredients until well combined.
3. Make patties from mixture and place into the refrigerator for 30 minutes.
4. Spray air fryer basket. Place patties into the air fryer basket and cook at 330 F for 10 minutes.
5. Serve and enjoy.

Nutritional Value (Amount per Serving):
Calories 252; Fat 13.5 g; Carbohydrates 4.4 g; Sugar 2.1 g; Protein 32.6 g; Cholesterol 116 mg

Crispy Cajun Chicken Wings

Preparation Time: 10 minutes; Cooking Time: 40 minutes; Serve: 4

Ingredients:
- 2 1/2 lbs chicken wings
- 1 tsp chili powder
- 1/2 tbsp oregano
- 1/2 tbsp ground thyme
- 1/2 tbsp onion powder
- 1 tbsp paprika
- 1 tbsp garlic powder
- 1/4 tsp pepper
- 1/2 tbsp salt

For Cajun sauce:
- 1 tsp parsley flakes
- 2 tbsp parmesan cheese
- 1 tsp Cajun seasoning
- 2 tsp garlic, minced
- 1/2 cup butter, melted

Directions:
1. In a small bowl, mix together all sauce ingredients and set aside.
2. Preheat the cosori air fryer to 400 F.
3. In a mixing bowl, add chicken wings, chili powder, oregano, thyme, onion powder, paprika, garlic powder, pepper, and salt and toss to coat.
4. Place chicken wings into the air fryer basket and cook for 30 minutes. Turn chicken wings halfway through.
5. Brush chicken wings with cajun sauce and cook for 10 minutes more.
6. Serve and enjoy.

Nutritional Value (Amount per Serving):
Calories 787; Fat 46 g; Carbohydrates 5 g; Sugar 1.1 g; Protein 85.5 g; Cholesterol 318 mg

Crispy & Juicy Chicken Wings

Preparation Time: 10 minutes; Cooking Time: 20 minutes; Serve: 4

Ingredients:
- 2 lbs chicken wings
- 1/2 tsp cayenne pepper
- 1 tsp white pepper
- 1 tsp smoked paprika
- 2 tsp garlic powder
- 2 tsp onion powder
- 1/2 tbsp thyme

Directions:
1. Preheat the cosori air fryer to 400 F.
2. Spray air fryer basket with cooking spray.
3. In a small bowl, mix together cayenne pepper, white pepper, paprika, garlic powder, onion powder, and thyme.
4. Rub chicken wings with spice mixture and place into the air fryer basket.

5. Cook chicken wings for 10 minutes. Turn chicken wings and cook for 10 minutes more.
6. Serve and enjoy.

Nutritional Value (Amount per Serving):
Calories 444; Fat 17 g; Carbohydrates 3 g; Sugar 0.9 g; Protein 66.2 g; Cholesterol 202 mg

Simple Cajun Chicken Wings

Preparation Time: 10 minutes; Cooking Time: 25 minutes; Serve: 4

Ingredients:
- 2 lbs chicken wings
- 1/3 cup ranch dressing
- 1 tbsp + 1/2 tsp Cajun seasoning

Directions:
1. Rub 1 tablespoon Cajun seasoning all over chicken wings.
2. Place chicken wings into the air fryer basket and cook at 400 F for 25 minutes. Turn chicken wings halfway through.
3. Meanwhile, in a small bowl, mix together ranch dressing and 1 teaspoon cajun seasoning.
4. Serve chicken wings with Cajun ranch dressing.

Nutritional Value (Amount per Serving):
Calories 437; Fat 16.9 g; Carbohydrates 1.1 g; Sugar 0.5 g; Protein 65.9 g; Cholesterol 202 mg

Adobo Chicken Thighs

Preparation Time: 10 minutes; Cooking Time: 20 minutes; Serve: 4

Ingredients:
- 4 chicken thighs
- 1 tbsp olive oil
- 2 tbsp Adobo seasoning

Directions:
1. Rub chicken thighs with oil and adobo seasoning.
2. Place chicken thighs into the air fryer basket and cook at 350 F for 20 minutes. Turn chicken halfway through.
3. Serve and enjoy.

Nutritional Value (Amount per Serving):
Calories 307; Fat 14.3 g; Carbohydrates 0 g; Sugar 0 g; Protein 42.2 g; Cholesterol 130 mg

Herbed Turkey Breast

Preparation Time: 10 minutes; Cooking Time: 60 minutes; Serve: 8

Ingredients:
- 2 1/2 lbs turkey breast, bone-in & skin-on
- 1/2 tsp fresh sage, chopped
- 1/2 tsp fresh thyme, chopped
- 1 tbsp butter, softened
- 1/4 tsp pepper
- 1 tsp salt

Directions:
1. In a small bowl, mix together butter, sage, thyme, pepper, and salt.
2. Rub the butter mixture all over turkey breast.
3. Place turkey breast into the air fryer basket and cook at 325 F for 30 minutes.
4. Turn turkey breast to another side and cook for 30 minutes more or until the internal temperature of turkey breast reaches 165 F.
5. Slice and serve.

Nutritional Value (Amount per Serving):
Calories 161; Fat 3.8 g; Carbohydrates 6.1 g; Sugar 5 g; Protein 24.2 g; Cholesterol 65 mg

Thanksgiving Turkey Breast

Preparation Time: 10 minutes; Cooking Time: 40 minutes; Serve: 6

Ingredients:
- 2 lbs turkey breast
- 1 tsp fresh rosemary, chopped
- 1 tsp fresh thyme, chopped
- 3 garlic cloves, minced
- 4 tbsp butter, melted
- Pepper
- Salt

Directions:
1. Season turkey breast with pepper and salt.
2. In a small bowl, mix together butter, rosemary, thyme, and garlic. Brush butter mixture all over turkey breast.
3. Place turkey breast into the air fryer basket and cook at 375 F for 40 minutes or until the internal temperature of turkey breast reaches 160 F.
4. Slice and serve.

Nutritional Value (Amount per Serving):
Calories 229; Fat 10.2 g; Carbohydrates 7.1 g; Sugar 5.3 g; Protein 26 g; Cholesterol 85 mg

Spice Herb Turkey Breast

Preparation Time: 10 minutes; Cooking Time: 35 minutes; Serve: 4

Ingredients:
- 2 1/2 lbs turkey breast, bone-in & skin-on
- 1/2 tsp paprika
- 1/2 tsp garlic powder
- 1/2 tsp dried sage
- 1 tsp ground rosemary
- 1 tsp dried thyme
- 1 tbsp olive oil
- 1/2 tsp pepper
- 1 tsp kosher salt

Directions:
1. In a small bowl, mix together paprika, garlic powder, sage, rosemary, thyme, pepper, and salt.
2. Brush turkey breast with olive oil and rub with dry spice herb mixture.
3. Place turkey breast skin side down into the air fryer basket and cook at 360 F for 20 minutes.
4. Turn turkey breast and cook for 15 minutes more or until the internal temperature of turkey breast reaches 165 F.
5. Slice and serve.

Nutritional Value (Amount per Serving):
Calories 329; Fat 8.3 g; Carbohydrates 12.9 g; Sugar 10.1 g; Protein 48.6 g; Cholesterol 122 mg

Turkey Zucchini Patties

Preparation Time: 10 minutes; Cooking Time: 10 minutes; Serve: 5

Ingredients:
- 1 lb ground turkey
- 1 tbsp onion, grated
- 1 garlic clove, grated
- 1/4 cup almond flour
- 6 oz zucchini, grated and squeezed out all liquid
- Pepper
- Salt

Directions:
1. Add ground turkey and remaining ingredients into the mixing bowl and mix until well combined.
2. Preheat the cosori air fryer to 370 F.

3. Make patties from mixture and place into the air fryer basket and cook for 10 minutes. Turn patties halfway through.
4. Serve and enjoy.

Nutritional Value (Amount per Serving):
Calories 192; Fat 10.7 g; Carbohydrates 1.8 g; Sugar 0.7 g; Protein 25.6 g; Cholesterol 93 mg

Greek Turkey Patties

Preparation Time: 10 minutes; Cooking Time: 14 minutes; Serve: 2
Ingredients:
- 8 oz ground turkey breast
- 1/2 tsp red pepper, crushed
- 2 tsp fresh oregano, chopped
- 1 1/2 tbsp olive oil
- 2 garlic cloves, minced
- 1/4 tsp salt

Directions:
1. Add ground turkey and remaining ingredients into the mixing bowl and mix until well combined.
2. Make 2 patties from mixture and place into the air fryer basket and cook at 360 F for 14 minutes. Turn patties halfway through.
3. Serve and enjoy.

Nutritional Value (Amount per Serving):
Calories 323; Fat 19.2 g; Carbohydrates 4.2 g; Sugar 1.6 g; Protein 33.2 g; Cholesterol 84 mg

Flavorful Turkey Breast

Preparation Time: 10 minutes; Cooking Time: 40 minutes; Serve: 6
Ingredients:
- 2 3/4 lbs turkey breast, skin-on & bone-in
- 2 tbsp butter
- 1 tsp garlic, minced
- 1 tsp fresh chives, chopped
- 1 tbsp fresh rosemary, chopped
- Pepper
- Salt

Directions:
1. Preheat the cosori air fryer to 350 F.
2. In a small bowl, mix together butter, garlic, chives, rosemary, pepper, and salt.
3. Rub the butter mixture all over the turkey breast.
4. Place turkey breast into the air fryer basket and cook for 20 minutes.
5. Turn turkey breast and cook for 20 minutes more or until the internal temperature of turkey breast reaches 165 F.
6. Slice and serve.

Nutritional Value (Amount per Serving):
Calories 253; Fat 7.4 g; Carbohydrates 9.3 g; Sugar 7.3 g; Protein 35.6 g; Cholesterol 100 mg

Moist & Juicy Turkey Breast

Preparation Time: 10 minutes; Cooking Time: 60 minutes; Serve: 10
Ingredients:
- 4 lbs turkey breast, ribs removed
- 1/2 tbsp poultry seasoning
- 1 tbsp olive oil
- 2 tsp kosher salt

Directions:
1. Brush turkey breast with oil and rub with poultry seasoning.
2. Preheat the cosori air fryer to 350 F.
3. Place turkey breast into the air fryer basket and cook for 20 minutes.
4. Turn turkey breast and cook for 30-40 minutes more or until the internal temperature of turkey breast reaches 165 F.

5. Slice and serve.

Nutritional Value (Amount per Serving):
Calories 201; Fat 4.4 g; Carbohydrates 7.8 g; Sugar 6.4 g; Protein 31 g; Cholesterol 78 mg

Chapter 4: Beef Recipes

Quick & Easy Steak Tips

Preparation Time: 10 minutes; Cooking Time: 6 minutes; Serve: 3
Ingredients:
- 1 1/2 lbs steak, cut into 3/4-inch cubes
- 1/8 tsp cayenne
- 1 tsp Montreal steak seasoning
- 1/2 tsp garlic powder
- 1 tsp olive oil
- Pepper
- Salt

Directions:
1. Spray air fryer basket with cooking spray.
2. Preheat the cosori air fryer to 400 F.
3. Toss steak cubes with oil, cayenne, steak seasoning, garlic powder, pepper, and salt.
4. Add steak cubes into the air fryer basket and cook for 4-6 minutes.
5. Serve and enjoy.

Nutritional Value (Amount per Serving):
Calories 469; Fat 12.9 g; Carbohydrates 0.4 g; Sugar 0.1 g; Protein 82 g; Cholesterol 204 mg

Simple Sirloin Steaks

Preparation Time: 10 minutes; Cooking Time: 12 minutes; Serve: 2
Ingredients:
- 2 sirloin steaks
- 2 tbsp steak seasoning

Directions:
1. Spray steaks with cooking spray and season with steak seasoning.
2. Place steaks into the air fryer basket and cook at 400 F for 12 minutes. Turn steaks halfway through.
3. Serve and enjoy.

Nutritional Value (Amount per Serving):
Calories 334; Fat 11.2 g; Carbohydrates 0 g; Sugar 0 g; Protein 54.6 g; Cholesterol 161 mg

Flavorful Steak

Preparation Time: 10 minutes; Cooking Time: 18 minutes; Serve: 2
Ingredients:
- 2 steaks, rinsed and pat dry with a paper towel
- 1 tsp olive oil
- 1/2 tsp garlic powder
- 1/4 tsp onion powder
- Pepper
- Salt

Directions:
1. Rub steaks with oil and season with garlic powder, onion powder, pepper, and salt.
2. Place steaks into the air fryer basket and cook at 400 F for 18 minutes. Turn steaks halfway through.
3. Serve and enjoy.

Nutritional Value (Amount per Serving):
Calories 252; Fat 8.1 g; Carbohydrates 0.8 g; Sugar 0.3 g; Protein 41.7 g; Cholesterol 104 mg

Italian Beef Roast

Preparation Time: 10 minutes; Cooking Time: 45 minutes; Serve: 6
Ingredients:

- 2 1/2 lbs beef roast
- 2 tbsp Italian seasoning
- 1 tsp olive oil
- Pepper
- Salt

Directions:
1. Rub beef roast with oil and season with Italian seasoning, pepper, and salt.
2. Place the beef roast into the air fryer basket and cook at 350 F for 45 minutes.
3. Slice and serve.

Nutritional Value (Amount per Serving):
Calories 372; Fat 13.9 g; Carbohydrates 0.5 g; Sugar 0.4 g; Protein 57.4 g; Cholesterol 172 mg

Rosemary Thyme Beef Roast

Preparation Time: 10 minutes; Cooking Time: 15 minutes; Serve: 4
Ingredients:
- 2 lbs beef roast
- 1 tsp dried rosemary
- 1 tsp dried thyme
- 1/4 tsp onion powder
- 1 tsp olive oil
- Pepper
- Salt

Directions:
1. Rub beef roast with oil and season with rosemary, thyme, onion powder, pepper, and salt.
2. Place the beef roast into the air fryer basket and cook at 390 F for 15 minutes. Turn roast after 10 minutes.
3. Slice and serve.

Nutritional Value (Amount per Serving):
Calories 434; Fat 15.4 g; Carbohydrates 0.5 g; Sugar 0.1 g; Protein 68.9 g; Cholesterol 203 mg

Italian Meatballs

Preparation Time: 10 minutes; Cooking Time: 11 minutes; Serve: 4
Ingredients:
- 1 egg
- 1 lb ground beef
- 1 tsp Italian seasoning
- 1 tbsp onion, minced
- 1/4 cup marinara sauce, sugar-free
- 1/3 cup parmesan cheese, shredded
- 1 tsp garlic, minced
- Pepper
- Salt

Directions:
1. Spray air fryer basket with cooking spray.
2. Add all ingredients into the mixing bowl and mix until well combined.
3. Make meatballs from mixture and place into the air fryer basket and cook at 350 F for 12 minutes.
4. Serve and enjoy.

Nutritional Value (Amount per Serving):
Calories 274; Fat 10.8 g; Carbohydrates 3.2 g; Sugar 1.7 g; Protein 38.9 g; Cholesterol 150 mg

Burgers Patties

Preparation Time: 10 minutes; Cooking Time: 10 minutes; Serve: 2
Ingredients:
- 1/2 lb ground beef
- 1/4 tsp onion powder
- 1/4 tsp garlic powder
- 2 drops liquid smoke

- 1/2 tsp hot sauce
- 1/2 tsp dried parsley
- 1/4 tsp black pepper
- 1/2 tbsp Worcestershire sauce
- 1/4 tsp salt

Directions:
1. Spray air fryer basket with cooking spray.
2. Add all ingredients into the large mixing bowl and mix until combined.
3. Make patties from mixture and place into the air fryer basket and cook at 350 F for 10 minutes. Turn patties halfway through.
4. Serve and enjoy.

Nutritional Value (Amount per Serving):
Calories 218; Fat 7.1 g; Carbohydrates 1.5 g; Sugar 1 g; Protein 34.5 g; Cholesterol 101 mg

Meatballs

Preparation Time: 10 minutes; Cooking Time: 15 minutes; Serve: 6
Ingredients:
- 2 eggs
- 30 oz ground beef
- 1/4 cup parmesan cheese, grated
- 3 cheese sticks
- 1 tbsp Italian seasoning
- Pepper
- Salt

Directions:
1. Preheat the cosori air fryer to 375 F.
2. Spray air fryer basket with cooking spray.
3. In a bowl, mix together meat, seasoning, parmesan cheese, and egg. Cut cheese sticks into the pieces.
4. Take 2-3 tablespoons of meat mixture and place one piece of cheese stick inside and give ball shape.
5. Place meatballs into the air fryer basket and cook for 15 minutes.
6. Serve and enjoy.

Nutritional Value (Amount per Serving):
Calories 339; Fat 14.7 g; Carbohydrates 0.6 g; Sugar 0.4 g; Protein 48.3 g; Cholesterol 195 mg

Tasty Beef Patties

Preparation Time: 10 minutes; Cooking Time: 10 minutes; Serve: 2
Ingredients:
- 1/2 lb ground beef
- 1 tsp ginger, minced
- 1/2 tbsp soy sauce
- 1 tbsp gochujang
- 1/4 tsp salt
- 1 tbsp green onion, chopped
- 1/2 tbsp sesame oil

Directions:
1. In a large bowl, mix together ground beef and remaining ingredients. Place mixture in the refrigerator for 1 hour.
2. Make patties from beef mixture and place into the air fryer basket and cook at 360 F for 10 minutes.
3. Serve and enjoy.

Nutritional Value (Amount per Serving):
Calories 257; Fat 10.5 g; Carbohydrates 3.3 g; Sugar 1.5 g; Protein 35 g; Cholesterol 101 mg

Meatloaf

Preparation Time: 10 minutes; Cooking Time: 15 minutes; Serve: 2
Ingredients:
- 1 egg
- 1/2 lb ground beef
- 1/2 tsp turmeric
- 1 tsp garam masala
- 1/2 tbsp garlic, minced
- 1/2 tbsp ginger, minced
- 1 tbsp cilantro, chopped
- 1/8 tsp ground cardamom
- 1/4 tsp ground cinnamon
- 1/2 tsp cayenne
- 1/2 cup onion, chopped
- 1/2 tsp salt

Directions:
1. In a large bowl, mix together all the ingredients until well combined.
2. Place meat mixture into air fryer safe pan and place in the air fryer basket.
3. Cook at 360 F for 15 minutes.
4. Slice and serve.

Nutritional Value (Amount per Serving):
Calories 266; Fat 9.5 g; Carbohydrates 5.5 g; Sugar 1.5 g; Protein 37.9 g; Cholesterol 183 mg

Tender & Juicy Kebab

Preparation Time: 10 minutes; Cooking Time: 10 minutes; Serve: 2
Ingredients:
- 1/2 lb ground beef
- 1 tbsp parsley, chopped
- 1/2 tbsp olive oil
- 1 tbsp kabab spice mix
- 1/2 tbsp garlic, minced
- 1/2 tsp salt

Directions:
1. Add all ingredients into the stand mixer until well combined.
2. Equally, divide the meat mixture into two portions and make two sausage shapes.
3. Place kababs into the air fryer basket and cook at 370 F for 10 minutes.
4. Serve and enjoy.

Nutritional Value (Amount per Serving):
Calories 259; Fat 11.1 g; Carbohydrates 2.7 g; Sugar 1.1 g; Protein 35.2 g; Cholesterol 101 mg

Meatloaf

Preparation Time: 10 minutes; Cooking Time: 25 minutes; Serve: 2
Ingredients:
- 1/2 lb ground beef
- 1 tbsp chorizo, chopped
- 1 1/2 tbsp breadcrumbs
- 1 egg, lightly beaten
- 1 mushroom, sliced
- 1/2 tbsp fresh thyme
- 1/2 small onion, chopped
- Pepper
- Salt

Directions:
1. Preheat the cosori air fryer at 400 F.
2. In a large bowl, mix together all ingredients until well combined.
3. Transfer meat mixture into the air fryer safe pan.
4. Place pan into the air fryer basket and cook for 25 minutes.
5. Slice and serve.

Nutritional Value (Amount per Serving):
Calories 337; Fat 15.1 g; Carbohydrates 6.5 g; Sugar 1.4 g; Protein 41.8 g; Cholesterol 196 mg

Meatballs

Preparation Time: 10 minutes; Cooking Time: 20 minutes; Serve: 2
Ingredients:
- 1/2 lb ground beef
- 2 tbsp onion, chopped
- 1 1/2 tbsp mushrooms, diced
- 1 tbsp parsley, chopped
- 1/4 cup almond flour
- 1/4 tsp pepper
- 1/2 tsp salt

Directions:
1. In a mixing bowl, combine together all ingredients until well combined.
2. Make meatballs from mixture and place into the air fryer basket and cook at 350 F for 20 minutes.
3. Serve and enjoy.

Nutritional Value (Amount per Serving):
Calories 237; Fat 8.9 g; Carbohydrates 2.1 g; Sugar 0.6 g; Protein 35.5 g; Cholesterol 101 mg

Marinated Steak

Preparation Time: 10 minutes; Cooking Time: 7 minutes; Serve: 2
Ingredients:
- 12 oz steaks
- 1 tbsp Montreal steak seasoning
- 1 tsp liquid smoke
- 1 tbsp soy sauce
- 1/2 tbsp cocoa powder
- Pepper
- Salt

Directions:
1. Add steak and remaining ingredients into the large zip-lock bag. Shake well and place it in the refrigerator overnight.
2. Spray air fryer basket with cooking spray.
3. Place marinated steaks into the air fryer basket and cook at 375 F for 5 minutes.
4. Turn steak and cook for 2 minutes more.
5. Serve and enjoy.

Nutritional Value (Amount per Serving):
Calories 356; Fat 8.7 g; Carbohydrates 1.4 g; Sugar 0.2 g; Protein 62.2 g; Cholesterol 153 mg

Asian Beef

Preparation Time: 10 minutes; Cooking Time: 20 minutes; Serve: 4
Ingredients:
- 1 lb flank steak, sliced
- 1 tsp xanthan gum
- For sauce:
- 1 tsp ground ginger
- 1 tbsp chili sauce
- 1 garlic clove, crushed
- 2 tbsp white wine vinegar
- 1 tbsp water
- 1 tbsp arrowroot powder
- 1/2 tsp sesame seeds
- 1 tsp liquid stevia
- 1/2 cup soy sauce

Directions:
1. Toss sliced meat with xanthan gum.
2. Spray air fryer basket with cooking spray.
3. Add meat into the air fryer basket and cook at 390 F for 20 minutes. Turn meat halfway through.
4. Meanwhile, add remaining ingredients into the saucepan and heat over low heat until begins to boil.

5. Add cooked meat to the sauce and coat well.
6. Serve and enjoy.

Nutritional Value (Amount per Serving):
Calories 253; Fat 9.7 g; Carbohydrates 6.2 g; Sugar 0.7 g; Protein 33.8 g; Cholesterol 62 mg

Flavorful Beef Roast

Preparation Time: 10 minutes; Cooking Time: 45 minutes; Serve: 8

Ingredients:
- 2 1/2 lbs beef roast
- 1/2 tsp onion powder
- 1 tsp rosemary
- 1 tsp dill
- 2 tbsp olive oil
- 1/2 tsp black pepper
- 1/2 tsp garlic powder

Directions:
1. Preheat the cosori air fryer to 360 F.
2. Mix together black pepper, garlic powder, onion powder, rosemary, dill, and olive oil. Rub all over the beef roast.
3. Place beef roast in the air fryer basket and cook for 45 minutes.
4. Serve and enjoy.

Nutritional Value (Amount per Serving):
Calories 296; Fat 12.4 g; Carbohydrates 0.5 g; Sugar 0.1 g; Protein 43.1 g; Cholesterol 127 mg

Cheese Butter Steak

Preparation Time: 10 minutes; Cooking Time: 8 minutes; Serve: 2

Ingredients:
- 2 ribeye steaks
- 2 tbsp blue cheese butter
- 1 tsp black pepper
- 2 tsp garlic powder
- 2 tsp kosher salt

Directions:
1. Preheat the cosori air fryer to 400 F.
2. Spray air fryer basket with cooking spray.
3. Mix together garlic powder, pepper, and salt and rub all over the steaks.
4. Place steak in the air fryer basket and cook for 8 minutes. Turn steak halfway through.
5. Top with blue butter cheese and serve.

Nutritional Value (Amount per Serving):
Calories 222; Fat 15 g; Carbohydrates 4.1 g; Sugar 0.7 g; Protein 18 g; Cholesterol 6 mg

Tasty Ginger Garlic Beef

Preparation Time: 10 minutes; Cooking Time: 20 minutes; Serve: 4

Ingredients:
- 1 lb beef tips, sliced
- 1 tbsp ginger, sliced
- 2 tbsp garlic, minced
- 2 tbsp sesame oil
- 1 tbsp fish sauce
- 2 tbsp coconut aminos
- 1 tsp xanthan gum
- 1/4 cup scallion, chopped
- 2 red chili peppers, sliced
- 2 tbsp water

Directions:
1. Spray air fryer basket with cooking spray.
2. Toss beef with xanthan gum together.
3. Add beef into the air fryer basket and cook at 390F for 20 minutes. Turn halfway through.

4. Meanwhile, in a saucepan add remaining ingredients except for green onion and heat over low heat. Once it begins boiling then remove from heat.
5. Add cooked meat into the saucepan and stir to coat. Let sit in the saucepan for 5 minutes.
6. Transfer in serving dish and top with green onion and serve.

Nutritional Value (Amount per Serving):
Calories 349; Fat 21.9 g; Carbohydrates 5.7 g; Sugar 0.5 g; Protein 31.4 g; Cholesterol 93 mg

Juicy Burger Patties

Preparation Time: 10 minutes; Cooking Time: 45 minutes; Serve: 4
Ingredients:
- 10.5 oz ground beef
- 1 tsp mustard
- 1 tsp tomato puree
- 1 tsp garlic puree
- 1 oz cheddar cheese
- 1 tsp mixed herbs
- 1 tsp basil
- Pepper
- Salt

Directions:
1. Add all ingredients into the large bowl and mix until well combined.
2. Make four equal shape of patties from mixture and place into the air fryer basket.
3. Cook at 390 F for 25 minutes. Turn patties and cook at 350 F for 20 minutes more.
4. Serve and enjoy.

Nutritional Value (Amount per Serving):
Calories 173; Fat 7.2 g; Carbohydrates 0.8 g; Sugar 0.2 g; Protein 24.7 g; Cholesterol 74 mg

Meatloaf

Preparation Time: 10 minutes; Cooking Time: 25 minutes; Serve: 4
Ingredients:
- 1 lb ground beef
- 2 oz sausage, chopped
- 3 tbsp almond flour
- 1 egg, lightly beaten
- 2 mushrooms, sliced
- 1 tbsp thyme, chopped
- 1 onion, chopped
- Pepper
- Salt

Directions:
1. Preheat the cosori air fryer to 390 F.
2. Add all ingredients into the large bowl and mix until well combined.
3. Transfer bowl mixture into the air fryer safe dish and place it into the air fryer basket.
4. Cook meatloaf for 25 minutes.
5. Serve and enjoy.

Nutritional Value (Amount per Serving):
Calories 256; Fat 18.8 g; Carbohydrates 10.7 g; Sugar 2.3 g; Protein 14.4 g; Cholesterol 74 mg

Meatballs

Preparation Time: 10 minutes; Cooking Time: 8 minutes; Serve: 10
Ingredients:
- 5 oz ground beef
- 2 oz feta cheese, crumbled
- 2 tbsp almond flour
- 1/2 tbsp lemon zest, grated
- 1 tbsp fresh oregano, chopped
- Pepper
- Salt

Directions:

1. Preheat the cosori air fryer to 392 F.
2. Add all ingredients into the mixing bowl and mix until well combined.
3. Make meatballs from mixture and place into the air fryer basket and cook for 8 minutes.
4. Serve and enjoy.

Nutritional Value (Amount per Serving):
Calories 75; Fat 4.9 g; Carbohydrates 1.8 g; Sugar 0.5 g; Protein 6.4 g; Cholesterol 18 mg

Spiced Steak

Preparation Time: 10 minutes; Cooking Time: 9 minutes; Serve: 3

Ingredients:
- 1 lb ribeye steak
- 1/4 tsp onion powder
- 1/4 tsp garlic powder
- 1/4 tsp chili powder
- 1/2 tsp black pepper
- 1/8 tsp cocoa powder
- 1/8 tsp coriander powder
- 1/4 tsp chipotle powder
- 1/4 tsp paprika
- 1/2 tsp coffee powder
- 1 1/2 tsp sea salt

Directions:
1. In a small bowl, mix together all ingredients except steak.
2. Rub spice mixture all over the steak.
3. Spray air fryer basket with cooking spray.
4. Preheat the cosori air fryer to 390 F.
5. Place steak in the air fryer basket and cook for 9 minutes.
6. Serve and enjoy.

Nutritional Value (Amount per Serving):
Calories 533; Fat 36.8 g; Carbohydrates 0.8 g; Sugar 0.2 g; Protein 0.2 g; Cholesterol 0 mg

Healthy Beef & Broccoli

Preparation Time: 10 minutes; Cooking Time: 12 minutes; Serve: 5

Ingredients:
- 3/4 lb round steak, cut into strips
- 1 tsp soy sauce
- 1/3 cup sherry
- 2 tsp sesame oil
- 1/3 cup oyster sauce
- 1 tbsp olive oil
- 1 lb broccoli florets
- 1 garlic clove, minced
- 1/2 tbsp ginger, sliced
- 1 tsp arrowroot powder
- 1 tsp liquid stevia

Directions:
1. In a small bowl, combine together oyster sauce, stevia, soy sauce, sherry, arrowroot, and sesame oil.
2. Add broccoli and meat in a large mixing bowl.
3. Pour oyster sauce mixture over meat and broccoli and toss well. Place in the refrigerator for 1 hour.
4. Add marinated meat and broccoli into the air fryer basket. Top with olive oil, ginger, and garlic.
5. Cook at 360 F for 12 minutes.
6. Serve and enjoy.

Nutritional Value (Amount per Serving):
Calories 230; Fat 11.5 g; Carbohydrates 7.7 g; Sugar 1.6 g; Protein 23.3 g; Cholesterol 58 mg

Meatloaf

Preparation Time: 10 minutes; Cooking Time: 15 minutes; Serve: 4
Ingredients:
- 2 eggs
- 1 lb ground beef
- 1/2 tbsp garlic, minced
- 1/2 tbsp ginger, minced
- 1/4 cup fresh cilantro, chopped
- 1 cup onion, diced
- 1/4 tsp cinnamon
- 1 tsp cayenne
- 1/2 tsp turmeric
- 1 tsp garam masala
- 1 tsp salt

Directions:
1. Add all ingredients into the mixing bowl and mix until well combined.
2. Transfer meat mixture into the air fryer safe pan.
3. Place pan in the air fryer basket and cook at 360 F for 15 minutes.
4. Slice and serve.

Nutritional Value (Amount per Serving):
Calories 261; Fat 9.5 g; Carbohydrates 4.3 g; Sugar 1.5 g; Protein 37.7 g; Cholesterol 183 mg

Tasty Kebab

Preparation Time: 10 minutes; Cooking Time: 10 minutes; Serve: 4
Ingredients:
- 1 lb ground beef
- 1/4 tsp ground cumin
- 1/4 tsp garlic powder
- 1/4 tsp onion powder
- 1/2 tsp chili powder
- 1 tbsp garlic, minced
- 1/4 cup fresh parsley, chopped
- 1 tbsp vegetable oil
- 1 tsp salt

Directions:
1. Spray air fryer basket with cooking spray.
2. Add all ingredients into the mixing bowl and mix until well combined. Place in refrigerator for 30 minutes.
3. Divide mixture into the four equal portions and make sausage shape kebab.
4. Place kebab into the air fryer basket and cook at 370 F for 10 minutes.
5. Serve and enjoy.

Nutritional Value (Amount per Serving):
Calories 248; Fat 10.6 g; Carbohydrates 1.4 g; Sugar 0.2 g; Protein 34.8 g; Cholesterol 101 mg

Meatballs

Preparation Time: 10 minutes; Cooking Time: 20 minutes; Serve: 4
Ingredients:
- 1/2 lb ground beef
- 1/2 tsp garlic powder
- 1/2 tsp onion powder
- 1/2 lb Italian sausage
- 1/2 cup cheddar cheese, shredded
- 1/2 tsp black pepper

Directions:
1. Spray air fryer basket with cooking spray.
2. Add all ingredients into the large mixing bowl and mix until well combined.
3. Make meatballs from mixture and place into the air fryer basket and cook at 370 F for 15 minutes. Turn meatballs and cook for 5 minutes more.
4. Serve and enjoy.

Nutritional Value (Amount per Serving):

Calories 357; Fat 24.3 g; Carbohydrates 0.8 g; Sugar 0.3 g; Protein 31.9 g; Cholesterol 113 mg

Easy Beef & Broccoli

Preparation Time: 10 minutes; Cooking Time: 10 minutes; Serve: 4
Ingredients:
- 1 lb ground beef cubes
- 1 tsp garlic powder
- 1 tbsp Worcestershire sauce
- 1/2 lb broccoli florets, steamed
- 1 tsp olive oil
- 1/2 onion, diced
- 1 tsp onion powder

Directions:
1. Spray air fryer basket with cooking spray.
2. Add all ingredients except broccoli into the large bowl and toss until well combined.
3. Add meat mixture into the air fryer basket and cook at 360 F for 10 minutes.
4. Serve with broccoli and enjoy it.

Nutritional Value (Amount per Serving):
Calories 227; Fat 6 g; Carbohydrates 6.8 g; Sugar 2.7 g; Protein 35.2 g; Cholesterol 62 mg

Meatballs

Preparation Time: 10 minutes; Cooking Time: 20 minutes; Serve: 4
Ingredients:
- 1 lb ground beef
- 1/4 cup onion, chopped
- 3 tbsp mushrooms, chopped
- 2 tbsp fresh parsley, chopped
- 1/2 cup almond flour
- 1/2 tsp pepper
- 1 tsp salt

Directions:
1. Spray air fryer basket with cooking spray.
2. In a bowl, mix together ground beef, parsley, onions, and mushrooms. Add remaining ingredients and mix until well combined.
3. Make meatballs from the mixture and place it into the air fryer basket and cook at 350 F for 20 minutes.
4. Serve and enjoy.

Nutritional Value (Amount per Serving):
Calories 236; Fat 8.9 g; Carbohydrates 1.8 g; Sugar 0.5 g; Protein 35.4 g; Cholesterol 101 mg

Tender Steak

Preparation Time: 10 minutes; Cooking Time: 12 minutes; Serve: 2
Ingredients:
- 2 ribeye steak
- 1 stick butter, softened
- 1 tsp Worcestershire sauce
- 2 tsp garlic, minced
- 2 tbsp fresh parsley, chopped
- Pepper
- Salt

Directions:
1. In a bowl, mix together butter, Worcestershire sauce, garlic, parsley, and salt and place in the refrigerator.
2. Preheat the cosori air fryer to 400 F.
3. Season steak with pepper and salt.
4. Spray air-fryer basket with cooking spray.

5. Place seasoned steak into the air fryer basket and cook for 12 minutes. Turn halfway through.
6. Remove steak from the air fryer and top with butter mixture.
7. Serve and enjoy.

Nutritional Value (Amount per Serving):
Calories 893; Fat 71.6 g; Carbohydrates 1.7 g; Sugar 0.6 g; Protein 2 g; Cholesterol 53 mg

Meatballs

Preparation Time: 10 minutes; Cooking Time: 20 minutes; Serve: 6

Ingredients:
- 1 lb ground beef
- 1 egg, lightly beaten
- 1/2 small onion, minced
- 2 garlic cloves, minced
- 1/4 cup parmesan cheese, grated
- 1/2 cup almond flour
- 1 tbsp fresh basil, chopped
- 1 tbsp fresh parsley, chopped
- 1 tbsp fresh rosemary, chopped
- Pepper
- Salt

Directions:
1. Add all ingredients into the mixing bowl and mix until well combined.
2. Make meatballs from meat mixture and place it into the air fryer basket and cook at 375 F for 20 minutes. Turn meatballs halfway through.
3. Serve and enjoy.

Nutritional Value (Amount per Serving):
Calories 184; Fat 7.6 g; Carbohydrates 2 g; Sugar 0.4 g; Protein 25.9 g; Cholesterol 98 mg

Cheesy Burger Patties

Preparation Time: 10 minutes; Cooking Time: 15 minutes; Serve: 6

Ingredients:
- 2 lbs ground beef
- 1 cup mozzarella cheese, grated
- 1 tsp onion powder
- 1 tsp garlic powder
- Pepper
- Salt

Directions:
1. Line air fryer basket with parchment paper.
2. Add all ingredients into the large bowl and mix until well combined.
3. Make patties from meat mixture and place into the air fryer basket and cook at 400 F for 15 minutes.
4. Serve and enjoy.

Nutritional Value (Amount per Serving):
Calories 297; Fat 10.3 g; Carbohydrates 0.8 g; Sugar 0.3 g; Protein 47.3 g; Cholesterol 138 mg

Garlicky Beef & Broccoli

Preparation Time: 10 minutes; Cooking Time: 25 minutes; Serve: 2

Ingredients:
- 1/2 lb beef stew meat, cut into pieces
- 2 garlic cloves, minced
- 1 tbsp olive oil
- 1/2 cup broccoli florets
- 1 onion, sliced
- 1 tbsp vinegar
- Pepper
- Salt

Directions:
1. Add meat and remaining ingredients into the large bowl and toss well.

2. Add meat mixture into the air fryer basket and cook at 390 F for 25 minutes. Press start.
3. Serve and enjoy.

Nutritional Value (Amount per Serving):
Calories 307; Fat 14.2 g; Carbohydrates 7.7 g; Sugar 2.8 g; Protein 35.9 g; Cholesterol 101 mg

Lime Cumin Beef

Preparation Time: 10 minutes; Cooking Time: 25 minutes; Serve: 4

Ingredients:
- 1 lb beef stew meat, cut into strips
- 1 garlic clove, minced
- 1/2 lime juice
- 1 tbsp olive oil
- 1/2 tbsp chives, chopped
- 1/2 tbsp ground cumin
- 1 tbsp garlic powder
- Pepper
- Salt

Directions:
1. Add the meat into the mixing bowl. Add remaining ingredients over meat and mix well.
2. Transfer meat into the air fryer basket and cook at 380 F for 25 minutes. Turn meat half way through.
3. Serve and enjoy.

Nutritional Value (Amount per Serving):
Calories 253; Fat 10.8 g; Carbohydrates 2.6 g; Sugar 0.6 g; Protein 35 g; Cholesterol 101 mg

Burger Patties

Preparation Time: 10 minutes; Cooking Time: 45 minutes; Serve: 4

Ingredients:
- 10 oz ground beef
- 1 oz cheddar cheese
- 1 tsp mixed herbs
- 1 tsp garlic puree
- 1 tsp dried basil
- 1 tsp mustard
- 1 tsp tomato paste
- Pepper
- Salt

Directions:
1. Spray air fryer basket with cooking spray.
2. Add all ingredients into the large bowl and mix until combined.
3. Make patties from meat mixture and place into the air fryer basket and cook at 390 F for 25 minutes.
4. Turn patties to another side and cook at 350 F for 20 minutes more.
5. Serve and enjoy.

Nutritional Value (Amount per Serving):
Calories 168; Fat 7.3 g; Carbohydrates 0.8 g; Sugar 0.3 g; Protein 23.6 g; Cholesterol 71 mg

Meatloaf

Preparation Time: 10 minutes; Cooking Time: 25 minutes; Serve: 4

Ingredients:
- 1 lb ground beef
- 2 mushrooms, sliced
- 1/4 tsp garlic powder
- 2 oz sausage, chopped
- 3 tbsp almond flour
- 1 egg, lightly beaten
- 1 onion, chopped
- 1/2 tsp chili powder
- 1 tsp Italian seasoning
- Pepper
- Salt

Directions:
1. Preheat the cosori air fryer to 390 F.
2. Add all ingredients into the large bowl and mix until well combined.
3. Transfer meat mixture into the air fryer safe pan place into the air fryer basket.
4. Cook meatloaf for 25 minutes.
5. Serve and enjoy.

Nutritional Value (Amount per Serving):
Calories 413; Fat 23.2 g; Carbohydrates 7.9 g; Sugar 2.3 g; Protein 43.7 g; Cholesterol 155 mg

Rib Eye Steak

Preparation Time: 10 minutes; Cooking Time: 9 minutes; Serve: 3
Ingredients:
- 1 lb rib eye steak
- 1/2 tsp garlic powder
- 1 tsp chili powder
- 1/4 tsp black pepper
- 1 tsp coffee powder
- 1/8 tsp cocoa powder
- 1/2 tsp chipotle powder
- 1/4 tsp paprika
- 1/4 tsp onion powder
- 1/8 tsp coriander powder
- 1 1/2 tsp sea salt

Directions:
1. In a small bowl, mix together all ingredients except steak.
2. Rub spice mixture all over the steak and.
3. Spray air fryer basket with cooking spray.
4. Preheat the cosori air fryer to 390 F.
5. Place marinated steak in the air fryer and cook for 9 minutes.
6. Serve and enjoy.

Nutritional Value (Amount per Serving):
Calories 329; Fat 16.3 g; Carbohydrates 1.4 g; Sugar 0.3 g; Protein 41.5 g; Cholesterol 134 mg

Beef Berger Patties

Preparation Time: 10 minutes; Cooking Time: 10 minutes; Serve: 2
Ingredients:
- 1/2 lb ground beef
- 1/2 tbsp Worcestershire sauce
- 1/2 tsp dried parsley
- 1/4 tsp pepper
- 1/4 tsp onion powder
- 1/4 tsp garlic powder
- 2 drops liquid smoke
- 1/2 tsp hot sauce
- 1/4 tsp cayenne
- 1/2 tsp chili powder
- 1/4 tsp salt

Directions:
1. Spray air fryer basket with cooking spray.
2. Add all ingredients into the mixing bowl and mix until well combined.
3. Make patties from mixture and place into the air fryer basket and cook at 350 F for 10 minutes.
4. Serve and enjoy.

Nutritional Value (Amount per Serving):
Calories 220; Fat 7.2 g; Carbohydrates 1.9 g; Sugar 1 g; Protein 34.7 g; Cholesterol 101 mg

Tasty Beef Satay

Preparation Time: 10 minutes; Cooking Time: 8 minutes; Serve: 2

Ingredients:
- 1 lb beef flank steak, sliced into long strips
- 1 tbsp ginger, minced
- 1 tbsp soy sauce
- 1/2 cup cilantro, chopped
- 1 tsp ground coriander
- 1 tbsp fish sauce
- 2 tbsp olive oil
- 1 tsp hot sauce
- 1 tbsp Swerve
- 1 tbsp garlic, minced

Directions:
1. Add all ingredients into the zip-lock bag and shake well. Place into the refrigerator for 1 hour.
2. Add marinated meat into the air fryer basket and cook at 400 F for 8 minutes. Turn halfway through.
3. Serve and enjoy.

Nutritional Value (Amount per Serving):
Calories 568; Fat 28.3 g; Carbohydrates 5.4 g; Sugar 0.7 g; Protein 70.4 g; Cholesterol 203 mg

Easy Kebab

Preparation Time: 10 minutes; Cooking Time: 10 minutes; Serve: 2

Ingredients:
- 1/2 lb ground beef
- 1/2 tbsp olive oil
- 1 1/2 tbsp kabab spice mix
- 1/2 tsp salt

Directions:
1. Add all ingredients into the bowl and mix well combined.
2. Divide mixture into the two equal portions and make two kebabs.
3. Place kababs into the air fryer basket and cook at 370 F for 10 minutes.
4. Serve and enjoy.s

Nutritional Value (Amount per Serving):
Calories 277; Fat 11.8 g; Carbohydrates 4.7 g; Sugar 2.6 g; Protein 35.9 g; Cholesterol 101 mg

Beef Cheese Patties

Preparation Time: 10 minutes; Cooking Time: 20 minutes; Serve: 4

Ingredients:
- 1 1/2 lbs ground lamb
- 1 tsp oregano
- 1/3 cup feta cheese, crumbled
- 1/4 tsp pepper
- 1/2 tsp salt

Directions:
1. Preheat the cosori air fryer to 375 F.
2. Spray air fryer basket with cooking spray.
3. Add all ingredients into the bowl and mix until well combined.
4. Make four equal shape of patties from meat mixture and place into the air fryer basket.
5. Cook patties for 20 minutes. Turn patties halfway through.
6. Serve and enjoy.

Nutritional Value (Amount per Serving):
Calories 351; Fat 15.2 g; Carbohydrates 0.8 g; Sugar 0.5 g; Protein 49.6 g; Cholesterol 164 mg

Stuffed Bell Peppers

Preparation Time: 10 minutes; Cooking Time: 20 minutes; Serve: 2

Ingredients:
- 8 oz ground beef
- 2 bell peppers, remove stems and seeds
- 1 1/2 tsp Worcestershire sauce
- 1/2 cup tomato sauce
- 4 oz cheddar cheese, shredded
- 1 tsp olive oil
- 1 garlic clove, minced
- 1/2 onion, chopped
- 1/2 tsp pepper
- 1/2 tsp salt

Directions:
1. Preheat the cosori air fryer to 390 F.
2. Spray air fryer basket with cooking spray.
3. Sauté garlic and onion in the olive oil in a small pan until softened.
4. Add meat, 1/4 cup tomato sauce, Worcestershire sauce, half cheese, pepper, and salt and stir to combine.
5. Stuff meat mixture into each pepper and top with remaining cheese and tomato sauce.
6. Place stuffed peppers into the air fryer basket and cook for 15-20 minutes.
7. Serve and enjoy.

Nutritional Value (Amount per Serving):
Calories 111; Fat 6.1 g; Carbohydrates 8.8 g; Sugar 4.1 g; Protein 6.1 g; Cholesterol 7 mg

Juicy Beef Kabobs

Preparation Time: 10 minutes; Cooking Time: 10 minutes; Serve: 4

Ingredients:
- 1 lb beef, cut into chunks
- 2 tbsp soy sauce
- 1/3 cup sour cream
- 1/2 onion, cut into 1-inch pieces
- 1 bell pepper, cut into 1-inch pieces

Directions:
1. In a mixing bowl, mix together soy sauce and sour cream.
2. Add beef into the bowl and coat well and place it in the refrigerator overnight.
3. Thread marinated beef, bell peppers, and onions onto the skewers.
4. Place skewers in the air fryer basket and cook at 400 F for 10 minutes. Turn halfway through.
5. Serve and enjoy.

Nutritional Value (Amount per Serving):
Calories 271; Fat 11.2 g; Carbohydrates 5 g; Sugar 2.3 g; Protein 36 g; Cholesterol 110 mg

Sirloin Steaks

Preparation Time: 10 minutes; Cooking Time: 20 minutes; Serve: 2

Ingredients:
- 12 oz sirloin steaks
- 1/2 tbsp Worcestershire sauce
- 1 1/2 tbsp soy sauce
- 2 tbsp erythritol
- 1 tbsp garlic, minced
- 1 tbsp ginger, grated
- Pepper
- Salt

Directions:
1. Spray air fryer basket with cooking spray.
2. Add steaks in a large zip-lock bag along with the remaining ingredients. Shake well and place it in the refrigerator for 1-2 hours.
3. Place marinated steaks in the air fryer basket and cook at 400 F for 10 minutes.
4. Turn steaks and cook for 10-15 minutes more.
5. Serve and enjoy.

Nutritional Value (Amount per Serving):

Calories 342; Fat 10.8 g; Carbohydrates 5 g; Sugar 1.1 g; Protein 52.9 g; Cholesterol 152 mg

Tasty Steak Fajitas

Preparation Time: 10 minutes; Cooking Time: 15 minutes; Serve: 6

Ingredients:
- 1 lb steak, sliced
- 1/2 cup onion, sliced
- 3 bell peppers, sliced
- 1 tbsp olive oil
- 1 tbsp fajita seasoning, gluten-free

Directions:
1. Line air fryer basket with aluminum foil.
2. Add all ingredients large bowl and toss until well coated.
3. Transfer fajita mixture into the air fryer basket and cook at 390 F for 5 minutes.
4. Toss and cook for 5-10 minutes more.
5. Serve and enjoy.

Nutritional Value (Amount per Serving):
Calories 199; Fat 6.3 g; Carbohydrates 6.4 g; Sugar 3.4 g; Protein 28 g; Cholesterol 68 mg

Steak with Mushrooms

Preparation Time: 10 minutes; Cooking Time: 18 minutes; Serve: 3

Ingredients:
- 1 lb steaks, cut into 1/2-inch cubes
- 2 tbsp butter, melted
- 8 oz mushrooms, sliced
- 1/2 tsp garlic powder
- 1 tsp Worcestershire sauce
- Pepper
- Salt

Directions:
1. Spray air fryer basket with cooking spray.
2. Add all ingredients into the large mixing bowl and toss well.
3. Preheat the cosori air fryer to 400 F.
4. Add steak mushroom mixture into the air fryer basket and cook for 15-18 minutes. Shake basket twice.
5. Serve and enjoy.

Nutritional Value (Amount per Serving):
Calories 388; Fat 15.5 g; Carbohydrates 3.2 g; Sugar 1.8 g; Protein 57.1 g; Cholesterol 156 mg

Flavors Burger Patties

Preparation Time: 10 minutes; Cooking Time: 10 minutes; Serve: 8

Ingredients:
- 1 lb ground beef
- 1/4 cup ketchup
- 1/4 cup coconut flour
- 1/2 cup almond flour
- 1 garlic clove, minced
- 1/4 cup onion, chopped
- 2 eggs, lightly beaten
- 1/2 tsp dried tarragon
- 1 tsp Italian seasoning
- 1 tbsp Worcestershire sauce
- 1/4 tsp pepper
- 1/2 tsp sea salt

Directions:
1. Spray air fryer basket with cooking spray
2. Add all ingredients into the mixing bowl and mix until well combined.
3. Make 8 equal shape of patties from mixture and place on a plate. Place in refrigerator for 10 minutes.

4. Preheat the cosori air fryer to 360 F.
5. Place prepared patties in the air fryer basket and cook for 10 minutes.
6. Serve and enjoy.

Nutritional Value (Amount per Serving):
Calories 146; Fat 5.8 g; Carbohydrates 3.6 g; Sugar 2.5 g; Protein 19.2 g; Cholesterol 92 mg

Beef Fajitas

Preparation Time: 10 minutes; Cooking Time: 8 minutes; Serve: 4

Ingredients:
- 1 lb beef flank steak, sliced
- 1 tsp garlic powder
- 1 tsp paprika
- 1 1/2 tsp cumin
- 1/2 tbsp chili powder
- 3 tbsp olive oil
- 1/2 onion, sliced
- 2 bell peppers, sliced
- Pepper
- Salt

Directions:
1. Preheat the cosori air fryer to 390 F.
2. Add sliced beef and remaining ingredients into the mixing bowl and toss to coat.
3. Transfer beef mixture into the air fryer basket and cook for 5 minutes.
4. Shake basket well and cook for 2-3 minutes more.
5. Serve and enjoy.

Nutritional Value (Amount per Serving):
Calories 335; Fat 18.2 g; Carbohydrates 7.5 g; Sugar 3.9 g; Protein 35.6 g; Cholesterol 101 mg

Stuffed Peppers

Preparation Time: 10 minutes; Cooking Time: 8 minutes; Serve: 12

Ingredients:
- 6 jalapeno peppers, cut in half, remove seeds and membrane
- 1/4 cup cheddar cheese, shredded
- 1 1/2 tbsp taco seasoning
- 1/2 lb ground beef meat

Directions:
1. Browned the meat in a large pan. Drain excess grease.
2. Remove pan from heat. Add taco seasoning to the ground meat and mix well.
3. Stuff meat into each jalapeno half.
4. Place stuffed jalapeno peppers into the air fryer basket and cook at 320 F for 6 minutes.
5. Sprinkle cheese on top of peppers and cook for 2 minutes more.
6. Serve and enjoy.

Nutritional Value (Amount per Serving):
Calories 26; Fat 1.7 g; Carbohydrates 0.9 g; Sugar 0.3 g; Protein 1.9 g; Cholesterol 6 mg

Steak Pepper Kebab

Preparation Time: 10 minutes; Cooking Time: 10 minutes; Serve: 4

Ingredients:
- 1 lb sirloin steak, cut into 1-inch pieces
- 1 onion, cut into 1-inch pieces
- 1 bell pepper, cut into 1-inch pieces
- For marinade:
- 1 tsp ginger, grated
- 2 tbsp red wine vinegar
- 2 tbsp olive oil
- 1/4 cup soy sauce
- 1 tsp garlic, minced
- 1 tsp pepper

Directions:

1. Add all marinade ingredients into the zip-lock bag and mix well. Add steak pieces into the bag.
2. Seal bag and place in the refrigerator overnight.
3. Thread marinated steak pieces, onion, and bell pepper onto the skewers.
4. Place skewers into the air fryer basket and cooks at 350 F for 10 minutes. Turn halfway through.
5. Serve and enjoy.

Nutritional Value (Amount per Serving):
Calories 305; Fat 14.2 g; Carbohydrates 7 g; Sugar 3 g; Protein 36.1 g; Cholesterol 101 mg

Juicy & Tender Parmesan Steak

Preparation Time: 10 minutes; Cooking Time: 12 minutes; Serve: 4
Ingredients:
- 2 lbs flank steak
- 2 tbsp parmesan cheese, grated
- 2 tbsp olive oil
- Pepper
- Salt

Directions:
1. Preheat the cosori air fryer to 400 F.
2. Rub steak with olive oil and season with pepper and salt.
3. Sprinkle grated parmesan cheese on top of the steak.
4. Place steak into the air fryer basket and cook for 12 minutes. Turn steak halfway through.
5. Serve and enjoy.

Nutritional Value (Amount per Serving):
Calories 523; Fat 27.4 g; Carbohydrates 0.3 g; Sugar 0 g; Protein 65.4 g; Cholesterol 130 mg

Chapter 5: Pork Recipes

Spicy Pork Chops

Preparation Time: 10 minutes; Cooking Time: 10 minutes; Serve: 4

Ingredients:
- 4 pork chops
- 1 1/2 tsp olive oil
- 1/2 tsp dried sage
- 1/4 tsp chili powder
- 1/2 tsp cayenne pepper
- 1/2 tsp black pepper
- 1/2 tsp ground cumin
- 1 tsp paprika
- 1/2 tsp garlic salt

Directions:
1. Preheat the cosori air fryer to 400 F.
2. In a small bowl, mix together paprika, garlic salt, sage, pepper, chili powder, cayenne pepper, and cumin.
3. Rub pork chops with spice mixture and place into the air fryer basket. Spray pork chops from the top with cooking spray.
4. Cook for 10 minutes. Turn halfway through.
5. Serve and enjoy.

Nutritional Value (Amount per Serving):
Calories 277; Fat 21.9 g; Carbohydrates 1.1 g; Sugar 0.2 g; Protein 18.3 g; Cholesterol 69 mg

Meatballs

Preparation Time: 10 minutes; Cooking Time: 15 minutes; Serve: 2

Ingredients:
- 5 oz pork minced
- 1/2 tsp mustard
- 1/2 tsp garlic paste
- 1/2 tbsp cheddar cheese, grated
- 1/2 tbsp fresh basil
- 1/2 onion, diced
- Pepper
- Salt

Directions:
1. Add all ingredients into the large bowl and mix until well combined.
2. Make small meatballs from mixture and place in air fryer basket and cook at 390 F for 15 minutes.
3. Serve and enjoy.

Nutritional Value (Amount per Serving):
Calories 243; Fat 20.2 g; Carbohydrates 5.3 g; Sugar 1.3 g; Protein 10.4 g; Cholesterol 51 mg

Meatballs

Preparation Time: 10 minutes; Cooking Time: 15 minutes; Serve: 4

Ingredients:
- 3.5 oz pork sausage meat
- 3 tbsp almond flour
- 1 tsp sage
- 1/2 tsp garlic paste
- 1/2 onion, diced
- Pepper
- Salt

Directions:
1. Preheat the cosori air fryer to 360 F.
2. Spray air fryer basket with cooking spray.
3. Add all ingredients into the mixing bowl and mix until well combined.
4. Make meatballs from mixture and place into the air fryer basket and cook for 15 minutes.
5. Serve and enjoy.

Nutritional Value (Amount per Serving):

Calories 203; Fat 17.5 g; Carbohydrates 6 g; Sugar 1.3 g; Protein 7.3 g; Cholesterol 17 mg

BBQ Pork Chops

Preparation Time: 10 minutes; Cooking Time: 14 minutes; Serve: 2
Ingredients:
- 2 pork chops
- 1/2 tsp sesame oil
- 1/4 cup BBQ sauce, sugar-free
- 2 garlic cloves, minced
- Pepper
- Salt

Directions:
1. Spray air fryer basket with cooking spray.
2. Preheat the cosori air fryer to 350 F.
3. Add all ingredients into the mixing bowl and mix well and place in the fridge for 1 hour.
4. Place marinated pork chops into the air fryer basket and cook for 14 minutes. Turn halfway through.
5. Serve and enjoy.

Nutritional Value (Amount per Serving):
Calories 317; Fat 21.1 g; Carbohydrates 12.4 g; Sugar 8.2 g; Protein 18.2 g; Cholesterol 69 mg

Pesto Pork Chops

Preparation Time: 10 minutes; Cooking Time: 18 minutes; Serve: 5
Ingredients:
- 5 pork chops
- 1 tbsp basil pesto
- 2 tbsp almond flour
- Pepper
- Salt

Directions:
1. Spray pork chops with cooking spray.
2. Rub basil pesto on top of pork chops and coat with almond flour.
3. Place pork chops into the air fryer basket and cook at 350 F for 18 minutes.
4. Serve and enjoy.

Nutritional Value (Amount per Serving):
Calories 320; Fat 25.5 g; Carbohydrates 2.4 g; Sugar 0.4 g; Protein 20.4 g; Cholesterol 69 mg

Coconut Butter Pork Chops

Preparation Time: 10 minutes; Cooking Time: 15 minutes; Serve: 2
Ingredients:
- 4 pork chops
- 1 tbsp coconut oil
- 1 tbsp coconut butter
- 2 tsp parsley
- 2 tsp garlic, grated
- Pepper
- Salt

Directions:
1. Preheat the cosori air fryer to 350 F.
2. In a large bowl, mix together garlic, butter, coconut oil, parsley, pepper, and salt.
3. Rub garlic mixture over the pork chops. Wrap marinated pork chops into the foil and place it in the refrigerator for 1 hour.
4. Remove pork chops from foil and place into the air fryer basket and cook for 15 minutes. Turn pork chops after 7 minutes.
5. Serve and enjoy.

Nutritional Value (Amount per Serving):
Calories 686; Fat 57.1 g; Carbohydrates 5 g; Sugar 1 g; Protein 37.2 g; Cholesterol 138 mg

Crispy Pork Chops

Preparation Time: 10 minutes; Cooking Time: 20 minutes; Serve: 4
Ingredients:
- 4 pork chops, boneless
- 2 eggs, lightly beaten
- 1 cup almond flour
- 1/4 cup parmesan cheese, grated
- 1 tbsp onion powder
- 1 tbsp garlic powder
- 1/2 tbsp black pepper
- 1/2 tsp sea salt

Directions:
1. Spray air fryer basket with cooking spray.
2. Preheat the cosori air fryer to 350 F.
3. In a shallow bowl, mix together almond flour, parmesan cheese, onion powder, garlic powder, pepper, and salt.
4. Whisk eggs in a shallow dish.
5. Dip pork chops into the egg then coat with almond flour mixture.
6. Place coated pork chops into the air fryer basket and cook for 20 minutes. Turn pork chops halfway through.
7. Serve and enjoy.

Nutritional Value (Amount per Serving):
Calories 363; Fat 27 g; Carbohydrates 5.3 g; Sugar 1.6 g; Protein 24.9 g; Cholesterol 155 mg

Cheese Garlicky Pork Chops

Preparation Time: 10 minutes; Cooking Time: 20 minutes; Serve: 8
Ingredients:
- 8 pork chops, boneless
- 3/4 cup parmesan cheese
- 2 tbsp butter, melted
- 2 tbsp coconut oil
- 1 tsp thyme
- 1 tbsp parsley
- 5 garlic cloves, minced
- 1/4 tsp pepper
- 1/2 tsp sea salt

Directions:
1. Spray air fryer basket with cooking spray.
2. Preheat the cosori air fryer to 400 F.
3. In a bowl, mix together butter, spices, parmesan cheese, and coconut oil.
4. Brush butter mixture on top of pork chops and place it into the air fryer basket and cook for 20 minutes. Turn pork chops halfway through.
5. Serve and enjoy.

Nutritional Value (Amount per Serving):
Calories 344; Fat 28.2 g; Carbohydrates 1.1 g; Sugar 0 g; Protein 21.2 g; Cholesterol 83 mg

Garlic Lemon Pork Chops

Preparation Time: 10 minutes; Cooking Time: 20 minutes; Serve: 5
Ingredients:
- 2 lbs pork chops
- 2 tbsp fresh lemon juice
- 2 tbsp garlic, minced
- 1 tbsp fresh parsley
- 1 1/2 tbsp olive oil
- Pepper
- Salt

Directions:
1. In a small bowl, mix together garlic, parsley, olive oil, and lemon juice. Season pork chops with pepper and salt.
2. Pour garlic mixture over the pork chops and coat well and allow to marinate for 30 minutes.

3. Add marinated pork chops into the air fryer basket and cook at 400 F for 20 minutes. Turn pork chops halfway through.
4. Serve and enjoy.

Nutritional Value (Amount per Serving):
Calories 623; Fat 49.4 g; Carbohydrates 1.3 g; Sugar 0.2 g; Protein 41.1 g; Cholesterol 156 mg

Herb Cheese Pork Chops

Preparation Time: 10 minutes; Cooking Time: 9 minutes; Serve: 2
Ingredients:
- 2 pork chops, boneless
- 1 tsp paprika
- 3 tbsp parmesan cheese, grated
- 1/3 cup almond flour
- 1/2 tsp Cajun seasoning
- 1 tsp herb de Provence

Directions:
1. Preheat the cosori air fryer to 350 F.
2. Mix together almond flour, Cajun seasoning, herb de Provence, paprika, and parmesan cheese. Spray pork chops with cooking spray.
3. Coat pork chops with almond flour mixture and place into the air fryer basket and cook for 9 minutes.
4. Serve and enjoy.

Nutritional Value (Amount per Serving):
Calories 360; Fat 27.3 g; Carbohydrates 2.4 g; Sugar 0.3 g; Protein 26.7 g; Cholesterol 85 mg

Creole Seasoned Pork Chops

Preparation Time: 10 minutes; Cooking Time: 12 minutes; Serve: 6
Ingredients:
- 1 1/2 lbs pork chops, boneless
- 1 tsp garlic powder
- 1/4 cup parmesan cheese, grated
- 1/3 cup almond flour
- 1 tsp paprika
- 1 tsp Creole seasoning

Directions:
1. Spray air fryer basket with cooking spray.
2. Preheat the cosori air fryer to 360 F.
3. Add all ingredients except pork chops into the zip-lock bag.
4. Add pork chops into the bag. Seal bag and shake well.
5. Remove pork chops from the zip-lock bag and place it into the air fryer basket and cook for 12 minutes.
6. Serve and enjoy.

Nutritional Value (Amount per Serving):
Calories 388; Fat 29.9 g; Carbohydrates 1 g; Sugar 0.2 g; Protein 27.3 g; Cholesterol 101 mg

Tender Pork Chops

Preparation Time: 10 minutes; Cooking Time: 13 minutes; Serve: 4
Ingredients:
- 4 pork chops, boneless
- 1/2 tsp granulated garlic
- 1/2 tsp celery seeds
- 1/2 tsp parsley
- 1/2 tsp granulated onion
- 2 tsp olive oil
- 1/2 tsp salt

Directions:
1. Spray air fryer basket with cooking spray.
2. In a small bowl, mix together with seasonings and sprinkle over the pork chops.

3. Place pork chops into the air fryer basket and cook at 350 F for 5 minutes. Turn pork chops and cook for 8 minutes more.
4. Serve and enjoy.

Nutritional Value (Amount per Serving):
Calories 278; Fat 22.3 g; Carbohydrates 0.4 g; Sugar 0.1 g; Protein 18.1 g; Cholesterol 69 mg

Asian Pork Chops

Preparation Time: 10 minutes; Cooking Time: 12 minutes; Serve: 2

Ingredients:
- 2 pork chops
- 1 tsp black pepper
- 3 tbsp lemongrass, chopped
- 1 tbsp shallot, chopped
- 1 tbsp garlic, chopped
- 1 tsp liquid stevia
- 1 tbsp sesame oil
- 1 tbsp fish sauce
- 1 tsp soy sauce

Directions:
1. Add pork chops in a mixing bowl. Pour remaining ingredients over the pork chops and mix well. Place in refrigerator for 2 hours.
2. Preheat the cosori air fryer to 400 F.
3. Place marinated pork chops into the air fryer basket and cook for 12 minutes. Turn pork chops after 7 minutes.
4. Serve and enjoy.

Nutritional Value (Amount per Serving):
Calories 340; Fat 26.8 g; Carbohydrates 5.3 g; Sugar 0.4 g; Protein 19.3 g; Cholesterol 69 mg

Easy & Delicious Pork Chops

Preparation Time: 10 minutes; Cooking Time: 15 minutes; Serve: 4

Ingredients:
- 4 pork chops
- 2 tsp parsley
- 2 tsp garlic, grated
- 1/4 tsp garlic powder
- 1/4 tsp onion powder
- 1 tbsp olive oil
- 1 tbsp butter
- Pepper
- Salt

Directions:
1. Preheat the cosori air fryer to 350 F.
2. In a large bowl, mix together seasonings, garlic, butter, and oil.
3. Add pork chops to the bowl and mix well. Place in refrigerator overnight.
4. Place marinated pork chops into the air fryer basket and cook for 15 minutes. Turn pork chops after 7 minutes.
5. Serve and enjoy.

Nutritional Value (Amount per Serving):
Calories 315; Fat 26.3 g; Carbohydrates 0.8 g; Sugar 0.1 g; Protein 18.2 g; Cholesterol 76 mg

Dash Seasoned Pork Chops

Preparation Time: 10 minutes; Cooking Time: 20 minutes; Serve: 2

Ingredients:
- 2 pork chops, boneless
- 1 tbsp dash seasoning
- Pepper
- Salt

Directions:
1. Spray air fryer basket with cooking spray.
2. Rub seasoning all over the pork chops.

3. Place seasoned pork chops into the air fryer basket and cook at 360 F for 20 minutes. Turn halfway through.
4. Serve and enjoy.

Nutritional Value (Amount per Serving):
Calories 256; Fat 19.9 g; Carbohydrates 0 g; Sugar 0 g; Protein 18 g; Cholesterol 69 mg

Easy Pork Butt

Preparation Time: 10 minutes; Cooking Time: 20 minutes; Serve: 4

Ingredients:
- 1 1/2 lbs pork butt, chopped into pieces
- 1/4 cup jerk paste

Directions:
1. Spray air fryer basket with cooking spray.
2. Add meat and jerk paste into the bowl and coat well. Place in refrigerator overnight.
3. Preheat the cosori air fryer to 390 F.
4. Place marinated meat to the air fryer basket and cook for 20 minutes. Turn halfway through.
5. Serve and enjoy.

Nutritional Value (Amount per Serving):
Calories 339; Fat 12.1 g; Carbohydrates 0.8 g; Sugar 0.6 g; Protein 53 g; Cholesterol 156 mg

Spicy Pork Steak

Preparation Time: 10 minutes; Cooking Time: 15 minutes; Serve: 4

Ingredients:
- 1 lb pork steaks, boneless
- 1 tsp ground fennel
- 1 tsp garam masala
- 1 tbsp garlic, minced
- 1 tbsp ginger, sliced
- 1/2 tsp cayenne
- 1/2 tsp ground cardamom
- 1 tsp cinnamon
- 1/2 onion, diced
- 1 tsp salt

Directions:
1. Spray air fryer basket with cooking spray.
2. Add all ingredients except meat into the blender and blend until smooth paste form.
3. Add the meat into the bowl. Pour blended mixture over the meat and coat well.
4. Place meat into the fridge overnight.
5. Place marinated meat into the air fryer basket and cook at 330 F for 15 minutes. Turn halfway through.
6. Slice and serve.

Nutritional Value (Amount per Serving):
Calories 156; Fat 5.1 g; Carbohydrates 4 g; Sugar 0.7 g; Protein 22.8 g; Cholesterol 51 mg

Simple Air Fryer Pork Chops

Preparation Time: 10 minutes; Cooking Time: 25 minutes; Serve: 2

Ingredients:
- 2 pork chops
- 1 tsp paprika
- Pepper
- Salt

Directions:
1. Mix together paprika, pepper, and salt and rub all over pork chops.
2. Place pork chops into the air fryer basket and cook at 325 F for 15 minutes.
3. Turn pork chops and cook for 10 minutes more.
4. Serve and enjoy.

Nutritional Value (Amount per Serving):
Calories 259; Fat 20 g; Carbohydrates 0.6 g; Sugar 0.1 g; Protein 18.1 g; Cholesterol 69 mg

Tasty Onion Pork Chops

Preparation Time: 10 minutes; Cooking Time: 35 minutes; Serve: 2
Ingredients:
- 2 pork chops
- 2 1/2 tbsp ketchup, sugar-free
- 2 onion, sliced
- Pepper
- Salt

Directions:
1. Season pork chops with pepper and salt.
2. Place pork chops in an air fryer safe dish. Pour ketchup over pork chops.
3. Top with onion slices. Cover dish with foil.
4. Place dish into the air fryer basket and cook at 375 F for 35 minutes.
5. Serve and enjoy.

Nutritional Value (Amount per Serving):
Calories 318; Fat 20.1 g; Carbohydrates 15 g; Sugar 8.9 g; Protein 19.5 g; Cholesterol 69 mg

Juicy & Tasty Pork Chops

Preparation Time: 10 minutes; Cooking Time: 15 minutes; Serve: 4
Ingredients:
- 4 pork chops, boneless
- 1/2 tsp chili powder
- 1/4 tsp onion powder
- 1/2 tsp garlic powder
- 2 tbsp olive oil
- Pepper
- Salt

Directions:
1. Brush pork chops with olive oil.
2. In a small bowl, mix together chili powder, onion powder, garlic powder, pepper, and salt and rub all over pork chops.
3. Place pork chops into the air fryer basket and cook at 400 F for 15 minutes.
4. Serve and enjoy.

Nutritional Value (Amount per Serving):
Calories 319; Fat 26.9 g; Carbohydrates 0.6 g; Sugar 0.2 g; Protein 18.1 g; Cholesterol 69 mg

Delicious Ranch Pork Chops

Preparation Time: 10 minutes; Cooking Time: 35 minutes; Serve: 6
Ingredients:
- 6 pork chops, boneless
- 1 oz ranch seasoning
- 2 tbsp olive oil
- 1 tsp dried parsley

Directions:
1. Mix together oil, dried parsley, and ranch seasoning and rub over pork chops.
2. Place pork chops into the air fryer basket and cook at 400 F for 35 minutes.
3. Serve and enjoy.

Nutritional Value (Amount per Serving):
Calories 311; Fat 24.6 g; Carbohydrates 0 g; Sugar 0 g; Protein 18 g; Cholesterol 69 mg

Meatballs

Preparation Time: 10 minutes; Cooking Time: 15 minutes; Serve: 4
Ingredients:
- 1 lb ground pork
- 1/2 tsp dried thyme

- 1 tsp paprika
- 1 tsp garlic powder
- 1 tsp onion powder
- 1/2 tsp ground cumin
- 1/2 tsp coriander
- Pepper
- Salt

Directions:
1. Add all ingredients into the large bowl and mix until well combined.
2. Make meatballs from mixture and place into the air fryer basket and cook at 400 F for 15 minutes.
3. Serve and enjoy.

Nutritional Value (Amount per Serving):
Calories 170; Fat 4.1 g; Carbohydrates 1.5 g; Sugar 0.4 g; Protein 30 g; Cholesterol 83 mg

Easy Pork Patties

Preparation Time: 10 minutes; Cooking Time: 35 minutes; Serve: 6
Ingredients:
- 2 lbs ground pork
- 1/2 cup almond flour
- 1 egg, lightly beaten
- 1 onion, minced
- 1 carrot, minced
- 1 tsp garlic powder
- 1 tsp paprika
- Pepper
- Salt

Directions:
1. Add all ingredients into the large bowl and mix until well combined.
2. Make small patties from meat mixture and place into the air fryer basket and cook at 375 F for 20 minutes.
3. Turn pork patties and cook for 15 minutes more.
4. Serve and enjoy.

Nutritional Value (Amount per Serving):
Calories 254; Fat 7.3 g; Carbohydrates 3.8 g; Sugar 1.6 g; Protein 41.4 g; Cholesterol 138 mg

Lemon Pepper Seasoned Pork Chops

Preparation Time: 10 minutes; Cooking Time: 15 minutes; Serve: 4
Ingredients:
- 4 pork chops, boneless
- 1 tsp lemon pepper seasoning
- Salt

Directions:
1. Season pork chops with lemon pepper seasoning, and salt.
2. Place pork chops into the air fryer basket and cook at 400 F for 15 minutes.
3. Serve and enjoy.

Nutritional Value (Amount per Serving):
Calories 257; Fat 19.9 g; Carbohydrates 0.3 g; Sugar 0 g; Protein 18 g; Cholesterol 69 mg

Flavorful Pork Chops

Preparation Time: 10 minutes; Cooking Time: 16 minutes; Serve: 4
Ingredients:
- 4 pork chops, boneless
- 2 tsp olive oil
- 1/2 tsp celery seed
- 1/2 tsp parsley
- 1/2 tsp onion powder
- 1/2 tsp garlic powder
- 1/2 tsp salt

Directions:
1. Brush pork chops with olive oil.

2. Mix together celery seed, parsley, onion powder, garlic powder, and salt and sprinkle over pork chops.
3. Place pork chops into the air fryer basket and cook at 350 F for 16 minutes. Turn pork chops halfway through.
4. Serve and enjoy.

Nutritional Value (Amount per Serving):
Calories 279; Fat 22.3 g; Carbohydrates 0.6 g; Sugar 0.2 g; Protein 18.1 g; Cholesterol 69 mg

Crispy Crusted Pork Chops

Preparation Time: 10 minutes; Cooking Time: 15 minutes; Serve: 2
Ingredients:
- 2 pork chops, bone-in
- 1/2 tsp parsley
- 1 tbsp olive oil
- 1 cup pork rinds, crushed
- 1/2 tsp garlic powder
- 1/2 tsp onion powder
- 1/2 tsp paprika

Directions:
1. In a large bowl, mix together pork rinds, garlic powder, onion powder, parsley, and paprika.
2. Brush pork chops with oil and coat with pork rind mixture
3. Place coated pork chops into the air fryer basket and cook at 400 F for 10 minutes.
4. Turn pork chops and air fry for 5 minutes more.
5. Serve and enjoy.

Nutritional Value (Amount per Serving):
Calories 413; Fat 32.7 g; Carbohydrates 1.3 g; Sugar 0.4 g; Protein 28.5 g; Cholesterol 92 mg

Meatballs

Preparation Time: 10 minutes; Cooking Time: 20 minutes; Serve: 6
Ingredients:
- 8 oz ground pork
- 1 egg, lightly beaten
- 1/4 cup parmesan cheese, grated
- 1/2 cup almond flour
- 8 oz ground beef
- 1/4 cup parsley, chopped
- 1 tsp garlic, minced
- 1/2 onion, diced
- Pepper
- Salt

Directions:
1. Add all ingredients into the large bowl and mix until well combined.
2. Make meatballs from mixture and place into the air fryer basket and cook at 400 F for 20 minutes.
3. Serve and enjoy.

Nutritional Value (Amount per Serving):
Calories 167; Fat 6.5 g; Carbohydrates 1.9 g; Sugar 0.6 g; Protein 24.3 g; Cholesterol 92 mg

Meatloaf

Preparation Time: 10 minutes; Cooking Time: 20 minutes; Serve: 4
Ingredients:
- 1 lb ground pork
- 1 onion, chopped
- 1 tbsp thyme, chopped
- 1/4 tsp garlic powder
- 1 egg, lightly beaten
- 3 tbsp almond flour
- Pepper
- Salt

Directions:
1. Spray air fryer safe pan with cooking spray and set aside.

2. Add all ingredients into the mixing bowl and mix until well combined.
3. Pour meat mixture into the prepared pan.
4. Place pan into the air fryer basket and cook at 390 F for 20 minutes.
5. Serve and enjoy.

Nutritional Value (Amount per Serving):
Calories 311; Fat 15.7 g; Carbohydrates 7.7 g; Sugar 2.1 g; Protein 36 g; Cholesterol 124 mg

Herb Butter Pork Chops

Preparation Time: 10 minutes; Cooking Time: 15 minutes; Serve: 2

Ingredients:
- 2 pork chops
- 1 tbsp thyme, chopped
- 4 tbsp butter, melted
- 2 garlic cloves, minced
- Pepper
- Salt

Directions:
1. Season pork chops with pepper and salt.
2. In a small bowl, mix together butter, thyme, and garlic.
3. Brush pork chops with butter mixture and place into the air fryer basket and cook at 375 F for 15 minutes.
4. Serve and enjoy.

Nutritional Value (Amount per Serving):
Calories 468; Fat 43 g; Carbohydrates 1.9 g; Sugar 0.1 g; Protein 18.5 g; Cholesterol 130 mg

Air Fried Pork Chops

Preparation Time: 10 minutes; Cooking Time: 18 minutes; Serve: 2

Ingredients:
- 2 pork chops, boneless
- 1 tsp garlic powder
- 1 tsp onion powder
- 1/2 tbsp paprika
- 1 tbsp olive oil
- 1/2 tsp oregano
- Pepper
- Salt

Directions:
1. Coat pork chops with oil. Mix together oregano, garlic powder, onion powder, paprika, pepper, and salt and sprinkle over pork chops.
2. Place pork chops into the air fryer basket and cook at 400 F for 18 minutes.
3. Serve and enjoy.

Nutritional Value (Amount per Serving):
Calories 331; Fat 27.2 g; Carbohydrates 3.2 g; Sugar 1 g; Protein 18.7 g; Cholesterol 69 mg

Cheddar Cheese Pork Chops

Preparation Time: 10 minutes; Cooking Time: 25 minutes; Serve: 4

Ingredients:
- 1 1/2 lbs pork chops
- 1/2 cup sour cream
- 1/2 cup cheddar cheese, shredded
- 1 tsp garlic salt

Directions:
1. Spray air fryer safe dish with cooking spray and set aside.
2. Place pork chops in dish and season with garlic salt.
3. Pour sour cream over pork chops and sprinkle cheese on top of pork chops.
4. Place dish into the air fryer basket and cook at 350 F for 25 minutes.
5. Serve and enjoy.

Nutritional Value (Amount per Serving):
Calories 665; Fat 53 g; Carbohydrates 1.9 g; Sugar 0.3 g; Protein 42.8 g; Cholesterol 174 mg

Meatballs

Preparation Time: 10 minutes; Cooking Time: 20 minutes; Serve: 4
Ingredients:
- 1 lb ground pork
- 1/4 cup parmesan cheese, grated
- 1 egg, lightly beaten
- 2 garlic cloves, minced
- 1/2 tbsp dried parsley
- 3 tbsp ketchup, sugar-free
- 1/2 onion, chopped
- Pepper
- Salt

Directions:
1. Add all ingredients into the bowl and mix until well combined.
2. Make small balls from meat mixture and place it into the air fryer basket and cook at 400 F for 20 minutes.
3. Serve and enjoy.

Nutritional Value (Amount per Serving):
Calories 217; Fat 6.5 g; Carbohydrates 5 g; Sugar 3.2 g; Protein 33.5 g; Cholesterol 128 mg

Garlic Pork Chops

Preparation Time: 10 minutes; Cooking Time: 20 minutes; Serve: 4
Ingredients:
- 1 lb pork chops
- 5 garlic cloves, minced
- 2 tbsp soy sauce
- 2 tbsp olive oil
- Pepper
- Salt

Directions:
1. Coat pork chops with oil. Mix together garlic, soy sauce, pepper, and salt and rub over pork chops.
2. Place pork chops into the air fryer basket and cook at 390 F for 20 minutes.
3. Serve and enjoy.

Nutritional Value (Amount per Serving):
Calories 433; Fat 35.2 g; Carbohydrates 1.9 g; Sugar 0.2 g; Protein 26.2 g; Cholesterol 98 mg

Mustard Pork Chops

Preparation Time: 10 minutes; Cooking Time: 12 minutes; Serve: 3
Ingredients:
- 3 pork chops
- 3 tbsp mustard
- 1 tbsp garlic, minced
- Pepper
- Salt

Directions:
1. In a small bowl, mix together mustard, garlic, pepper, and salt
2. Place pork chops into the air fryer basket and cook at 350 F for 12 minutes. Turn pork chops halfway through.
3. Serve and enjoy.

Nutritional Value (Amount per Serving):
Calories 313; Fat 23.1 g; Carbohydrates 4.9 g; Sugar 0.8 g; Protein 21 g; Cholesterol 69 mg

Meatballs

Preparation Time: 10 minutes; Cooking Time: 15 minutes; Serve: 4
Ingredients:
- 4 oz pork sausage
- 3 tbsp almond flour
- 1 cup onion, chopped
- 1 tsp sage
- 1/2 tsp garlic, minced
- Pepper

- Salt

Directions:
1. Add all ingredients into the bowl and mix until well combined.
2. Make small balls from the meat mixture and place it into the air fryer basket and cook at 350 F for 15 minutes.
3. Serve and enjoy.

Nutritional Value (Amount per Serving):
Calories 229; Fat 18.6 g; Carbohydrates 7.4 g; Sugar 2 g; Protein 10.4 g; Cholesterol 24 mg

Pork & Peppers

Preparation Time: 10 minutes; Cooking Time: 20 minutes; Serve: 3
Ingredients:
- 6 oz pork tenderloin, cut into strips
- 3 bell peppers, cut into strips
- 1 onion, chopped
- 1 tbsp olive oil
- Pepper
- Salt

Directions:
1. Add all ingredients into the mixing bowl and toss well.
2. Transfer meat mixture into the air fryer basket and cook at 390 F for 20 minutes. Shake basket halfway through.
3. Serve and enjoy.

Nutritional Value (Amount per Serving):
Calories 174; Fat 7 g; Carbohydrates 12.4 g; Sugar 7.6 g; Protein 16.4 g; Cholesterol 41 mg

Simple Rosemary Pork Chops

Preparation Time: 10 minutes; Cooking Time: 15 minutes; Serve: 2
Ingredients:
- 2 pork chops
- 1 tbsp olive oil
- 1 tbsp rosemary, chopped
- Pepper
- Salt

Directions:
1. Mix together oil, rosemary, pepper, and salt and rub all over pork chops.
2. Place pork chops into the air fryer basket and cook at 400 F for 15 minutes.
3. Serve and enjoy.

Nutritional Value (Amount per Serving):
Calories 322; Fat 27.1 g; Carbohydrates 1.1 g; Sugar 0 g; Protein 18.1 g; Cholesterol 69 mg

Asian Pork ribs

Preparation Time: 10 minutes; Cooking Time: 40 minutes; Serve: 4
Ingredients:
- 1 lb baby pork ribs
- 1 tbsp olive oil
- 1 tbsp ginger, minced
- 2 garlic cloves, minced
- 1/2 tbsp soy sauce
- 1 tbsp hoisin sauce

Directions:
1. In a bowl add all ingredients and coat well. Cover and place in the refrigerator for 1 hour.
2. Place marinated ribs into the air fryer basket and cook at 320 F for 40 minutes.
3. Serve and enjoy.

Nutritional Value (Amount per Serving):
Calories 368; Fat 30.8 g; Carbohydrates 3.4 g; Sugar 1.2 g; Protein 18.5 g; Cholesterol 90 mg

Flavorful Pork Roast

Preparation Time: 10 minutes; Cooking Time: 15 minutes; Serve: 4
Ingredients:
- 1 lb pork shoulder, cut into slices
- 1/2 tsp Chinese five-spice
- 1 1/2 tsp ginger, minced
- 1 1/2 tsp garlic, minced
- 1/2 tbsp hoisin sauce
- 1 tbsp rice wine
- 1 1/2 tbsp soy sauce

Directions:
1. Add all ingredients except pork into the mixing bowl and stir well.
2. Add pork slices in a large bowl. Pour half sauce over pork slices and coat well and let it marinate for a half-hour.
3. Place marinated pork slices into the air fryer basket and cook at 390 F for 15 minutes.
4. Meanwhile, microwave half sauce for 30 seconds.
5. Brush meat with sauce and serve.

Nutritional Value (Amount per Serving):
Calories 349; Fat 24.4 g; Carbohydrates 3.9 g; Sugar 1.7 g; Protein 27 g; Cholesterol 102 mg

Spicy Pork Shoulder

Preparation Time: 10 minutes; Cooking Time: 15 minutes; Serve: 4
Ingredients:
- 1 lb pork shoulder, boneless and cut into slices
- 1 1/2 tbsp ginger garlic paste
- 1 onion, sliced
- 3 tbsp green onions, sliced
- 1/2 tbsp sesame seeds
- 2 tbsp chili paste
- 1 tbsp sesame oil
- 1 tbsp rice wine
- 1 tbsp soy sauce

Directions:
1. In a large bowl, mix together pork, sesame oil, rice wine, soy sauce, ginger garlic paste, chili paste, and onion. Cover and marinate for 30 minutes.
2. Place marinated meat slices into the air fryer basket and cook at 400 F for 15 minutes. Turn halfway through.
3. Sprinkle with sesame seeds and green onion.
4. Serve and enjoy.

Nutritional Value (Amount per Serving):
Calories 423; Fat 29.9 g; Carbohydrates 9.3 g; Sugar 4.3 g; Protein 28.1 g; Cholesterol 105 mg

Meatballs

Preparation Time: 10 minutes; Cooking Time: 15 minutes; Serve: 2
Ingredients:
- 5 oz pork minced
- 1/2 tbsp cheddar cheese, grated
- 1/2 tbsp fresh basil
- 1/2 onion, diced
- 1/2 tsp mustard
- 1/2 tsp garlic paste
- Pepper
- Salt

Directions:
1. Add all ingredients into the bowl and mix until well combined.
2. Make meatballs from mixture and place into the air fryer basket and cook at 390 F for 15 minutes.
3. Serve and enjoy.

Nutritional Value (Amount per Serving):
Calories 243; Fat 20.2 g; Carbohydrates 5.3 g; Sugar 1.3 g; Protein 10.4 g; Cholesterol 51 mg

Cheesy Pork Chops

Preparation Time: 10 minutes; Cooking Time: 12 minutes; Serve: 6

Ingredients:
- 1 1/2 lbs pork chops, boneless
- 1 tsp paprika
- 1/4 cup parmesan cheese, grated
- 1/3 cup almond flour
- 1 tsp Cajun seasoning
- 1 tsp garlic powder

Directions:
1. Preheat the cosori air fryer to 360 F.
2. Add all ingredients except pork chops in a zip-lock bag. Add pork chops in the bag. Seal bag and shake well to coat pork chops.
3. Remove pork chops from the zip-lock bag and place it in the air fryer basket and cook for 10-12 minutes.
4. Serve and enjoy.

Nutritional Value (Amount per Serving):
Calories 388; Fat 29.9 g; Carbohydrates 1 g; Sugar 0.2 g; Protein 27.3 g; Cholesterol 101 mg

Paprika Pork Chops

Preparation Time: 10 minutes; Cooking Time: 9 minutes; Serve: 4

Ingredients:
- 4 pork chops, boneless
- 1/2 cup parmesan cheese, grated
- 2 tbsp olive oil
- 1 tsp onion powder
- 1 tsp smoked paprika
- 1/2 tsp pepper
- 1 tsp kosher salt

Directions:
1. Spray air fryer basket with cooking spray.
2. Brush pork chops with olive oil.
3. In a bowl, mix together parmesan cheese and spices.
4. Coat pork chops with cheese mixture and place in the air fryer basket and cook at 375 F for 9 minutes. Turn halfway through.
5. Serve and enjoy.

Nutritional Value (Amount per Serving):
Calories 360; Fat 29.7 g; Carbohydrates 1.4 g; Sugar 0.3 g; Protein 22.2 g; Cholesterol 78 mg

Smoked Paprika Pork Chops

Preparation Time: 5 minutes; Cooking Time: 14 minutes; Serve: 3

Ingredients:
- 3 pork chops, rinsed and pat dry
- 1/2 tsp smoked paprika
- 2 tsp olive oil
- 1/2 tsp garlic powder
- Pepper
- Salt

Directions:
1. Coat pork chops with olive oil and season with paprika, garlic powder, pepper, and salt.
2. Place pork chops in the air fryer basket and cook at 380 F for 14 minutes. Turn halfway through.
3. Serve and enjoy.

Nutritional Value (Amount per Serving):
Calories 285; Fat 23 g; Carbohydrates 0.6 g; Sugar 0.2 g; Protein 18.1 g; Cholesterol 69 mg

Delicious Pork & Mushrooms

Preparation Time: 10 minutes; Cooking Time: 18 minutes; Serve: 4

Ingredients:

- 1 lb pork chops, rinsed and pat dry
- 2 tbsp butter, melted
- 8 oz mushrooms, halved
- 1/2 tsp garlic powder
- 1 tsp soy sauce
- Pepper
- Salt

Directions:
1. Preheat the cosori air fryer to 400 F.
2. Cut pork chops into the 3/4-inch cubes and place in a large bowl.
3. Add remaining ingredients into the bowl and toss well.
4. Transfer pork and mushroom mixture into the air fryer basket and cook for 18 minutes. Shake basket halfway through.
5. Serve and enjoy.

Nutritional Value (Amount per Serving):
Calories 428; Fat 34.1 g; Carbohydrates 2.2 g; Sugar 1.1 g; Protein 27.5 g; Cholesterol 113 mg

Cheesy Pork Chops

Preparation Time: 10 minutes; Cooking Time: 8 minutes; Serve: 2
Ingredients:
- 4 pork chops
- 1/4 cup pepper jack cheese, shredded
- 1/2 tsp garlic powder
- 1/2 tsp salt

Directions:
1. Preheat the cosori air fryer to 350 F.
2. Rub pork chops with garlic powder and salt and place in the air fryer basket. Cook pork chops for 4 minutes.
3. Turn pork chops and cook for 2 minutes.
4. Add cheese on top of pork chops and cook for 2 minutes more.
5. Serve and enjoy.

Nutritional Value (Amount per Serving):
Calories 528; Fat 40.9 g; Carbohydrates 0.5 g; Sugar 0.2 g; Protein 37 g; Cholesterol 141 mg

Delicious Stuffed Pork Chops

Preparation Time: 10 minutes; Cooking Time: 28 minutes; Serve: 4
Ingredients:
- 4 pork chops, boneless and thick-cut
- 1/2 cup feta cheese, crumbled
- 1 tsp garlic, minced
- 2 tbsp fresh parsley, chopped
- 2 tbsp olives, chopped
- 2 tbsp sun-dried tomatoes, chopped

Directions:
1. Preheat the cosori air fryer to 350 F.
2. In a bowl, combine together feta cheese, garlic, parsley, olives, and sun-dried tomatoes. Stuff cheese mixture all the pork chops.
3. Season pork chops with pepper and salt and place into the air fryer basket and cook for 28 minutes.
4. Serve and enjoy.

Nutritional Value (Amount per Serving):
Calories 313; Fat 24.4 g; Carbohydrates 1.6 g; Sugar 1 g; Protein 20.8 g; Cholesterol 85 mg

Simple & Tasty Pork Bites

Preparation Time: 10 minutes; Cooking Time: 21 minutes; Serve: 6
Ingredients:
- 1 lb pork tenderloin, cut into cubes
- 1/4 cup almond flour

- 2 eggs, lightly beaten
- 1/2 tsp ground coriander
- 1/2 tsp paprika
- 1/2 tsp lemon zest
- 1/2 tsp kosher salt

Directions:
1. Spray air fryer basket with cooking spray.
2. Preheat the cosori air fryer to 365 F.
3. In a shallow bowl, whisk eggs.
4. In a shallow dish, mix together almond flour, coriander, paprika, lemon zest, and salt.
5. Dip each pork cube in egg then coat with almond flour mixture.
6. Add coated pork cubes into the air fryer basket and cook for 14 minutes. Turn pork cubes and cook for 7 minutes more.
7. Serve and enjoy.

Nutritional Value (Amount per Serving):
Calories 136; Fat 4.7 g; Carbohydrates 0.5 g; Sugar 0.2 g; Protein 21.9 g; Cholesterol 110 mg

Pork Tenderloin

Preparation Time: 10 minutes; Cooking Time: 15 minutes; Serve: 3
Ingredients:
- 1 lb pork tenderloin
- 1/2 tsp onion powder
- 1/2 tsp garlic powder
- 1/2 tsp cinnamon
- 1 tsp sage
- 1/2 tsp saffron
- 1 tbsp vinegar
- 2 garlic cloves, minced
- 3 tbsp butter

Directions:
1. In a small bowl, mix together saffron, onion powder, garlic powder, cinnamon, and sage and rub over pork tenderloin.
2. Rub pork tenderloin with garlic and vinegar and let sit for 10 minutes.
3. Preheat the cosori air fryer to 320 F.
4. Place pork tenderloin into the air fryer and top with butter and cook for 15 minutes.
5. Slice and serve.

Nutritional Value (Amount per Serving):
Calories 327; Fat 16.9 g; Carbohydrates 1.9 g; Sugar 0.3 g; Protein 40 g; Cholesterol 141 mg

Pesto Pork Chops

Preparation Time: 10 minutes; Cooking Time: 18 minutes; Serve: 5
Ingredients:
- 5 pork chops
- 1 tbsp olive oil
- 3 tbsp basil pesto
- 2 tbsp almond flour
- 1/4 tsp onion powder
- 1/4 tsp garlic powder
- 1/4 tsp chili powder

Directions:
1. Spray pork chops with cooking spray.
2. In a shallow dish mix together almond flour, chili powder, garlic powder, and onion powder.
3. Coat pork chops with pesto then coat with almond flour mixture.
4. Place pork chops into the air fryer basket and cook at 350 F for 18 minutes.
5. Serve and enjoy.

Nutritional Value (Amount per Serving):
Calories 346; Fat 28.3 g; Carbohydrates 2.7 g; Sugar 0.5 g; Protein 20.5 g; Cholesterol 69 mg

Cheese Garlic Pork Chops

Preparation Time: 10 minutes; Cooking Time: 20 minutes; Serve: 8
Ingredients:
- 8 pork chops, boneless
- 6 garlic cloves, minced
- 1 tbsp parsley
- 2 tbsp olive oil
- 1 cup parmesan cheese
- 2 tbsp butter, melted
- 1 tsp thyme
- 1/4 tsp pepper
- 1/2 tsp sea salt

Directions:
1. Spray air fryer basket with cooking spray.
2. Preheat the cosori air fryer to 400 F.
3. In a bowl, mix together butter, spices, cheese, and oil.
4. Rub butter mixture on top of pork chops and place it into the air fryer basket and cook for 20 minutes. Turn pork chops halfway through.
5. Serve and enjoy.

Nutritional Value (Amount per Serving):
Calories 356; Fat 29 g; Carbohydrates 1.4 g; Sugar 0 g; Protein 22.2 g; Cholesterol 85 mg

Balsamic Pork Chops

Preparation Time: 10 minutes; Cooking Time: 10 minutes; Serve: 2
Ingredients:
- 4 pork loin chops
- 1/8 tsp ground ginger
- 1 garlic clove, chopped
- 1/2 tsp balsamic vinegar
- 1 tbsp swerve
- 1 tbsp soy sauce

Directions:
1. Season pork chops with pepper and salt.
2. In a bowl, mix together sweetener, soy sauce, and vinegar. Add ginger and garlic and set aside.
3. Add pork chops into the marinade mixture and marinate for 2 hours.
4. Preheat the cosori air fryer to 350 F.
5. Add marinated pork chops into the air fryer basket and cook for 10 minutes. Turn pork chops halfway through.
6. Serve and enjoy.

Nutritional Value (Amount per Serving):
Calories 522; Fat 39.8 g; Carbohydrates 2.2 g; Sugar 0.2 g; Protein 36.6 g; Cholesterol 138 mg

Tasty BBQ Ribs

Preparation Time: 10 minutes; Cooking Time: 30 minutes; Serve: 2
Ingredients:
- 1 lb pork ribs
- 3 garlic cloves, chopped
- 1 tsp soy sauce
- 1 tsp pepper
- 1 tsp sesame oil
- 1/2 tsp five-spice powder
- 1 tbsp swerve
- 4 tbsp BBQ sauce, sugar-free
- 1 tsp salt

Directions:
1. Preheat the cosori air fryer to 350 F.
2. Add all ingredients into the large bowl and mix well. Place into the fridge for 1 hour.
3. Add marinated ribs into the air fryer basket and cook for 30 minutes. Turn ribs halfway through.

4. Serve and enjoy.

Nutritional Value (Amount per Serving):
Calories 656; Fat 42.5 g; Carbohydrates 3.8 g; Sugar 0.1 g; Protein 60.8 g; Cholesterol 234 mg

Spicy Pork Shoulder

Preparation Time: 10 minutes; Cooking Time: 15 minutes; Serve: 2

Ingredients:
- 1/2 lb pork shoulder, cut into 1/2-inch slices
- 1 tbsp green onion, sliced
- 1/2 tbsp sesame seeds
- 1/4 tsp cayenne pepper
- 1/2 tbsp garlic, minced
- 1/2 tbsp ginger, minced
- 1/2 tsp Swerve
- 1/2 tbsp sesame oil
- 1/2 tbsp rice wine
- 1/2 tbsp soy sauce
- 1 tbsp gochujang
- 1/2 onion, sliced

Directions:
1. In a large bowl, mix together all ingredients and place in the refrigerator for 1 hour.
2. Line air fryer basket with aluminum foil.
3. Add pork mixture into the air fryer and cook at 400 F for 15 minutes. Toss halfway through.
4. Serve and enjoy.

Nutritional Value (Amount per Serving):
Calories 415; Fat 29 g; Carbohydrates 10.2 g; Sugar 3.9 g; Protein 27.9 g; Cholesterol 102 mg

Balsamic Pork Chops

Preparation Time: 10 minutes; Cooking Time: 10 minutes; Serve: 2

Ingredients:
- 2 pork loin chops
- 1/8 tsp ground ginger
- 1 tbsp soy sauce
- 1 garlic clove
- 1 tbsp swerve
- 1/2 tsp balsamic vinegar
- Pepper
- Salt

Directions:
1. Preheat the cosori air fryer to 350 F.
2. Season pork chops with pepper and salt.
3. In a bowl, mix together swerve, soy sauce, garlic, ground ginger, and vinegar.
4. Add pork chops in a bowl and coat well and place it in the refrigerator for 2 hours.
5. Place marinated pork chops in the air fryer basket and cook for 10 minutes. Turn pork chops halfway through.
6. Serve and enjoy.

Nutritional Value (Amount per Serving):
Calories 266; Fat 19.9 g; Carbohydrates 2.2 g; Sugar 0.2 g; Protein 18.6 g; Cholesterol 69 mg

Meatballs

Preparation Time: 10 minutes; Cooking Time: 15 minutes; Serve: 2

Ingredients:
- 5 oz pork minced
- 1 tbsp fresh basil, chopped
- 1/2 onion, diced
- 1/2 tsp mustard
- 1/2 tbsp parmesan cheese, grated
- 1/2 tsp Swerve
- 1/2 tsp garlic, minced
- Pepper
- Salt

Directions:
1. Add all ingredients into the large bowl and mix well to combine.
2. Make meatballs from mixture and place in the air fryer basket and cook at 390 F for 15 minutes.
3. Serve and enjoy.

Nutritional Value (Amount per Serving):
Calories 249; Fat 20.3 g; Carbohydrates 5.9 g; Sugar 1.2 g; Protein 11.1 g; Cholesterol 52 mg

Herb Butter Pork Chops

Preparation Time: 5 minutes; Cooking Time: 15 minutes; Serve: 2
Ingredients:
- 4 pork chops
- 1 tbsp fresh parsley, chopped
- 4 garlic cloves, grated
- 1 tbsp olive oil
- 1 tbsp herb butter
- Pepper
- Salt

Directions:
1. Preheat the cosori air fryer to 350 F.
2. In a small bowl, mix together herb butter, olive oil, garlic, parsley, pepper, and salt.
3. Rub herb butter mixture over pork chops and place in the refrigerator for 1 hour.
4. Place marinated pork chops into the air fryer basket and cook for 7 minutes. Turn pork chops and cook for 8 minutes.
5. Serve and enjoy.

Nutritional Value (Amount per Serving):
Calories 599; Fat 48.1 g; Carbohydrates 2.3 g; Sugar 0.1 g; Protein 37.5 g; Cholesterol 143 mg

Spicy Pork Patties

Preparation Time: 5 minutes; Cooking Time: 10 minutes; Serve: 8
Ingredients:
- 1 lb ground pork
- 1/4 tsp dried thyme
- 1/2 tsp onion powder
- 1/2 tsp dried marjoram
- 1 tsp red pepper, crushed
- 1 tsp sage
- Pepper
- Salt

Directions:
1. Add all ingredients into the mixing bowl and mix until well combined.
2. Make 8 equal shape of patties from mixture and place into the air fryer basket.
3. Cook patties at 400 F for 10 minutes. Turn patties halfway through.
4. Serve and enjoy.

Nutritional Value (Amount per Serving):
Calories 87; Fat 2 g; Carbohydrates 1.4 g; Sugar 0.8 g; Protein 15 g; Cholesterol 41 mg

Herb Pork Loin

Preparation Time: 5 minutes; Cooking Time: 40 minutes; Serve: 6
Ingredients:
- 3 lbs pork loin cut in half
- 1 1/2 tsp herbs de Provence
- 1 tbsp olive oil
- 1/2 tsp garlic salt
- 1/4 tsp pepper

Directions:
1. Brush meat with olive oil and season with pepper, garlic salt, and herb de Provence.

2. Place meat in the air fryer basket and cook at 360 F for 25 minutes. Turn meat and cook for 15 minutes more.
3. Serve and enjoy.

Nutritional Value (Amount per Serving):
Calories 572; Fat 34 g; Carbohydrates 0.2 g; Sugar 0.1 g; Protein 62.2 g; Cholesterol 181 mg

Herb Pepper Pork Tenderloin

Preparation Time: 10 minutes; Cooking Time: 15 minutes; Serve: 2

Ingredients:
- 1 pork tenderloin, cut into pieces
- 1 bell pepper, cut into strips
- 2 tsp herb de Provence
- 1/4 tsp garlic powder
- 1/4 tsp onion powder
- 1/2 tbsp mustard
- 1 onion, sliced
- 1 tbsp olive oil
- Pepper
- Salt

Directions:
1. Preheat the cosori air fryer to 390 F.
2. In a bowl, mix together bell pepper, herb de Provence, onion, pepper, and salt. Add 1/2 tbsp oil and mix well.
3. Season pork tenderloin with mustard, onion powder, garlic powder, pepper, and salt. Coat pork tenderloin with remaining oil.
4. Place pork tenderloin pieces into the air fryer pan and top with bell pepper mixture.
5. Place pan in the air fryer basket and cook for 15 minutes. Stir halfway through.
6. Serve and enjoy.

Nutritional Value (Amount per Serving):
Calories 352; Fat 14.1 g; Carbohydrates 9.4 g; Sugar 4.1 g; Protein 46.1 g; Cholesterol 122 mg

Chapter 6: Lamb Recipes

Juicy & Savory Lamb Chops

Preparation Time: 10 minutes; Cooking Time: 10 minutes; Serve: 1
Ingredients:
- 1/3 lb lamb chop
- 1 tbsp mixed fresh herbs, chopped
- 1/2 tbsp olive oil
- 1/2 tbsp Dijon mustard
- Pepper
- Salt

Directions:
1. Season lamb chop with pepper and salt.
2. In a small bowl, mix together oil, mustard, and mixed herbs.
3. Brush lamb chop from both the sides with oil mixture.
4. Place lamb chop into the air fryer basket and cook at 375 F for 10 minutes. Turn halfway through.
5. Serve and enjoy.

Nutritional Value (Amount per Serving):
Calories 350; Fat 18.5 g; Carbohydrates 1.2 g; Sugar 0.1 g; Protein 43 g; Cholesterol 136 mg

Rosemary Lamb Chops

Preparation Time: 10 minutes; Cooking Time: 12 minutes; Serve: 2
Ingredients:
- 4 lamb chops
- 2 tsp ginger garlic paste
- 2 tsp olive oil
- 1 tsp rosemary, chopped
- Pepper
- Salt

Directions:
1. Add lamb chops, ginger garlic paste, oil, rosemary, pepper, and salt into the zip-lock bag.
2. Seal bag shake well and place it in the refrigerator for 1 hour.
3. Add marinated lamb chops into the air fryer basket and cook at 360 F for 12 minutes. Turn halfway through.
4. Serve and enjoy.

Nutritional Value (Amount per Serving):
Calories 461; Fat 22.3 g; Carbohydrates 3.4 g; Sugar 0 g; Protein 64.2 g; Cholesterol 203 mg

Dijon Garlic Lamb Chops

Preparation Time: 10 minutes; Cooking Time: 17 minutes; Serve: 4
Ingredients:
- 8 lamb chops
- 1 tsp cayenne pepper
- 1 tsp cumin powder
- 1 tsp garlic, minced
- 1 tsp soy sauce
- 2 tsp olive oil
- 2 tsp Dijon mustard
- 1/4 tsp salt

Directions:
1. Add lamb chops and remaining ingredients into the zip-lock bag. Seal bag shake well and place it in the refrigerator for 30 minutes.
2. Place marinated lamb chops into the air fryer basket and cook at 350 F for 17 minutes. Turn lamb chops halfway through.
3. Serve and enjoy.

Nutritional Value (Amount per Serving):
Calories 445; Fat 19.1 g; Carbohydrates 0.9 g; Sugar 0.1 g; Protein 63.6 g; Cholesterol 203 mg

Flavorful Cumin Lamb

Preparation Time: 10 minutes; Cooking Time: 10 minutes; Serve: 4
Ingredients:
- 1 lb lamb, cut into 1/2-inch pieces
- 1/4 tsp Swerve
- 12 red chili peppers, chopped
- 1 tbsp garlic, minced
- 1 tbsp soy sauce
- 2 tbsp olive oil
- 1/2 tsp cayenne
- 1 1/2 tbsp ground cumin
- 1 tsp kosher salt

Directions:
1. Add lamb pieces and remaining ingredients into the zip-lock bag. Seal bag shake well and place it in the refrigerator for 30 minutes.
2. Place marinated lamb pieces into the air fryer basket and cook at 360 F for 10 minutes. Shake basket halfway through.
3. Serve and enjoy.

Nutritional Value (Amount per Serving):
Calories 291; Fat 16 g; Carbohydrates 3.3 g; Sugar 0.8 g; Protein 32.8 g; Cholesterol 102 mg

Juicy & Tender Lemon Mustard Lamb Chops

Preparation Time: 10 minutes; Cooking Time: 15 minutes; Serve: 4
Ingredients:
- 8 lamb chops
- 1 tbsp fresh lemon juice
- 1 tsp tarragon
- 1/2 tsp olive oil
- 2 tbsp mustard
- Pepper
- Salt

Directions:
1. Preheat the cosori air fryer to 390 F.
2. In a small bowl, mix together lemon juice, tarragon, oil, mustard, pepper, and salt.
3. Brush lamb chops from both sides with lemon juice mixture.
4. Place lamb chops into the air fryer basket and cook for 15 minutes. Turn halfway through.
5. Serve and enjoy.

Nutritional Value (Amount per Serving):
Calories 451; Fat 18.7 g; Carbohydrates 2.1 g; Sugar 0.5 g; Protein 64.6 g; Cholesterol 203 mg

Meatballs

Preparation Time: 10 minutes; Cooking Time: 12 minutes; Serve: 6
Ingredients:
- 1 lb ground lamb
- 1 lemon juice
- 1 tbsp dried dill
- 1 tbsp dried rosemary
- 1 egg, lightly beaten
- 1 lb ground beef
- Pepper
- Salt

Directions:
1. Spray air fryer basket with cooking spray.
2. Add all ingredients into the mixing bowl and mix until well combined.
3. Make 1-inch balls from mixture and place into the air fryer basket and cook at 350 F for 7 minutes.
4. Shake basket and cook for 5 minutes more.
5. Serve and enjoy.

Nutritional Value (Amount per Serving):

Calories 297; Fat 11.1 g; Carbohydrates 0.9 g; Sugar 0.2 g; Protein 45.3 g; Cholesterol 163 mg

Spicy Lamb Steak

Preparation Time: 10 minutes; Cooking Time: 15 minutes; Serve: 4

Ingredients:
- 1 lb lamb sirloin steaks, boneless
- 1 tsp cayenne pepper
- 1/2 tsp ground cardamom
- 1 tsp ground cinnamon
- 1 tsp ground fennel
- 1 tsp garam masala
- 4 garlic cloves
- 1 tbsp ginger
- 1/2 onion
- 1 tsp kosher salt

Directions:
1. Add all ingredients except lamb steaks into the blender and blend until a smooth paste is formed.
2. Add lamb steaks and blended paste into the mixing bowl and mix well. Place in refrigerator for 30 minutes.
3. Spray air fryer basket with cooking spray.
4. Place marinated lamb steaks into the air fryer basket and cook at 330 F for 15 minutes. Turn halfway through.
5. Serve and enjoy.

Nutritional Value (Amount per Serving):
Calories 76; Fat 2.3 g; Carbohydrates 4.6 g; Sugar 0.7 g; Protein 9.7 g; Cholesterol 0 mg

Lamb Roast

Preparation Time: 10 minutes; Cooking Time: 15 minutes; Serve: 2

Ingredients:
- 10 oz lamb leg roast
- 1 tsp dried thyme
- 1 tsp dried rosemary
- 1 tbsp olive oil
- Pepper
- Salt

Directions:
1. Preheat the cosori air fryer to 360 F.
2. In a small bowl, mix together oil, rosemary, thyme, pepper, and salt and rub all over lamb roast.
3. Place lamb roast into the air fryer basket and cook for 15 minutes.
4. Serve and enjoy.

Nutritional Value (Amount per Serving):
Calories 319; Fat 16.6 g; Carbohydrates 0.7 g; Sugar 0 g; Protein 40 g; Cholesterol 123 mg

Easy Greek Lamb Chops

Preparation Time: 10 minutes; Cooking Time: 10 minutes; Serve: 4

Ingredients:
- 2 lbs lamb chops
- 2 tsp garlic, minced
- 2 tsp dried oregano
- 1/4 cup fresh lemon juice
- 1/4 cup olive oil
- Pepper
- Salt

Directions:
1. In a mixing bowl, mix together lemon juice, oil, oregano, garlic, pepper, and salt. Add lamb chops to the bowl and coat well.
2. Add lamb chops into the air fryer basket and cook at 400 F for 10 minutes. Turn halfway through.

3. Serve and enjoy.

Nutritional Value (Amount per Serving):
Calories 538; Fat 29.4 g; Carbohydrates 1.3 g; Sugar 0.4 g; Protein 64 g; Cholesterol 204 mg;

Delicious Zaatar Lamb Chops

Preparation Time: 10 minutes; Cooking Time: 10 minutes; Serve: 4

Ingredients:
- 8 lamb chops, trimmed
- 1 tbsp zaatar
- 1/2 lemon
- 1 tsp olive oil
- 2 garlic cloves, crushed
- Pepper
- Salt

Directions:
1. Preheat the cosori air fryer to 400 F.
2. Rub lamb chops with garlic and oil.
3. Squeeze lemon juice over lamb chops and season with zaatar, pepper, and salt.
4. Place lamb chops into the air fryer basket and cook for 10 minutes. Turn halfway through.
5. Serve and enjoy.

Nutritional Value (Amount per Serving):
Calories 435; Fat 17.9 g; Carbohydrates 1.2 g; Sugar 0.2 g; Protein 63.4 g; Cholesterol 203 mg

Quick & Easy Lamb Chops

Preparation Time: 10 minutes; Cooking Time: 5 minutes; Serve: 2

Ingredients:
- 4 lamb chops
- 1/2 tbsp fresh oregano, chopped
- 1 1/2 tbsp olive oil
- 1 garlic clove, minced
- Pepper
- Salt

Directions:
1. Preheat the cosori air fryer to 400 F.
2. Mix together garlic, olive oil, oregano, pepper, and salt and rub all over lamb chops.
3. Place lamb chops into the air fryer basket and cook for 5 minutes.
4. Serve and enjoy.

Nutritional Value (Amount per Serving):
Calories 514; Fat 27.1 g; Carbohydrates 1.3 g; Sugar 0.1 g; Protein 63.4 g; Cholesterol 203 mg

Dried Herb Lamb Chops

Preparation Time: 10 minutes; Cooking Time: 8 minutes; Serve: 4

Ingredients:
- 1 lb lamb chops
- 1 tsp oregano
- 1 tsp thyme
- 1 tsp rosemary
- 2 tbsp fresh lemon juice
- 2 tbsp olive oil
- 1 tsp coriander
- 1 tsp salt

Directions:
1. Add all ingredients except lamb chops into the zip-lock bag. Add lamb chops to the zip-lock bag.
2. Seal bag and shake well and place it in the fridge overnight.
3. Place marinated lamb chops into the air fryer basket and cook at 390 F for 8 minutes. Turn lamb chops halfway through.
4. Serve and enjoy.

Nutritional Value (Amount per Serving):
Calories 276; Fat 15.5 g; Carbohydrates 0.8 g; Sugar 0.2 g; Protein 32 g; Cholesterol 102 mg

Moist Lamb Roast

Preparation Time: 10 minutes; Cooking Time: 1 hour 30 minutes; Serve: 4

Ingredients:
- 2.75 lbs lamb leg roast, make slits on top of the meat
- 2 garlic cloves, sliced
- 1 tbsp olive oil
- 1 tbsp dried rosemary
- Pepper
- Salt

Directions:
1. Stuff sliced garlic into the slits. Season with pepper and salt.
2. Mix together oil and rosemary and rub all over the meat.
3. Place meat into the air fryer basket and cook at 400 F for 15 minutes.
4. Turn temperature to 320 F for 1 hour 15 minutes.
5. Serve and enjoy.

Nutritional Value (Amount per Serving):
Calories 670; Fat 45 g; Carbohydrates 1.1 g; Sugar 0 g; Protein 58.1 g; Cholesterol 221 mg

Thyme Lamb Chops

Preparation Time: 10 minutes; Cooking Time: 12 minutes; Serve: 4

Ingredients:
- 4 lamb chops
- 3 tbsp olive oil
- 1 tbsp dried thyme
- 3 garlic clove, minced
- Pepper
- Salt

Directions:
1. Preheat the cosori air fryer to 390 F.
2. In a small bowl, mix together thyme, oil, and garlic.
3. Season lamb chops with pepper and salt and rubs with thyme oil mixture.
4. Place chops into the air fryer basket and cook for 12 minutes. Turn halfway through.
5. Serve and enjoy.

Nutritional Value (Amount per Serving):
Calories 305; Fat 18.8 g; Carbohydrates 1.2 g; Sugar 0 g; Protein 31.8 g; Cholesterol 101 mg

Baked Lamb Chops

Preparation Time: 10 minutes; Cooking Time: 30 minutes; Serve: 4

Ingredients:
- 4 lamb chops
- 1 1/2 tsp tarragon
- 1 1/2 tsp ginger
- 1 tsp garlic powder
- 1 tsp ground cinnamon
- Pepper
- Salt

Directions:
1. Add garlic powder, cinnamon, tarragon, ginger, pepper, and salt into the zip-lock bag and mix well. Add lamb chops in a bag.
2. Seal bag shake well and place it in the fridge for 2 hours.
3. Place marinated lamb chops into the air fryer basket and cook at 375 F for 20 minutes.
4. Turn lamb chops and cook for 10 minutes more.
5. Serve and enjoy.

Nutritional Value (Amount per Serving):
Calories 216; Fat 8.3 g; Carbohydrates 1.6 g; Sugar 0.2 g; Protein 31.8 g; Cholesterol 101 mg

Meatballs

Preparation Time: 10 minutes; Cooking Time: 15 minutes; Serve: 4; Ingredients:
- 1 lb ground lamb
- 1 tsp onion powder
- 1 tbsp garlic, minced
- 1 tsp ground coriander
- 1 tsp ground cumin
- Pepper
- Salt

Directions:
1. Add all ingredients into the large bowl and mix until well combined.
2. Make meatballs from mixture and place into the air fryer basket and cook at 400 F for 15 minutes.
3. Serve and enjoy.

Nutritional Value (Amount per Serving):
Calories 218; Fat 8.5 g; Carbohydrates 1.4 g; Sugar 0.2 g; Protein 32.1 g; Cholesterol 102 mg

Meatballs

Preparation Time: 10 minutes; Cooking Time: 12 minutes; Serve: 4
Ingredients:
- 4 oz ground lamb meat
- 1 tbsp oregano, chopped
- 1/2 tbsp lemon zest
- 1 egg, lightly beaten
- 1/4 tsp garlic powder
- 1/4 tsp onion powder
- Pepper
- Salt

Directions:
1. Line air fryer basket with parchment paper.
2. Add all ingredients into the bowl and mix until well combined.
3. Make meatballs from mixture and place into the air fryer basket and cook at 400 F for 12 minutes.
4. Serve and enjoy.

Nutritional Value (Amount per Serving):
Calories 79; Fat 5 g; Carbohydrates 1.2 g; Sugar 0.3 g; Protein 6.8 g; Cholesterol 61 mg

Meatballs

Preparation Time: 10 minutes; Cooking Time: 15 minutes; Serve: 2
Ingredients:
- 1/2 lb ground lamb
- 1 egg white
- 1/2 tbsp olive oil
- 1 garlic cloves, minced
- 1/2 tbsp coriander, chopped
- 1/2 tbsp basil, chopped
- 1 tbsp parsley, chopped
- 2 oz turkey
- 1/2 tsp salt

Directions:
1. Preheat the cosori air fryer to 320 F.
2. Add all ingredients into the mixing bowl and mix until well combined.
3. Make meatballs from mixture and place into the air fryer basket and cook for 15 minutes.
4. Serve and enjoy.

Nutritional Value (Amount per Serving):
Calories 301; Fat 13.3 g; Carbohydrates 0.8 g; Sugar 0.2 g; Protein 42.1 g; Cholesterol 124 mg

Lamb Patties

Preparation Time: 10 minutes; Cooking Time: 30 minutes; Serve: 4
Ingredients:

- 1 lb ground lamb meat
- 1 egg, lightly beaten
- 1/2 tbsp garlic, minced
- 1 spring onion, chopped
- 1/4 cup almond flour
- 1 tbsp basil, chopped
- 1 tbsp cilantro, chopped
- Pepper
- Salt

Directions:
1. Spray air fryer basket with cooking spray.
2. Add all ingredients into the bowl and mix until well combined.
3. Make small patties from meat mixture and place into the air fryer basket and cook at 390 F for 30 minutes. Turn patties halfway through.
4. Serve and enjoy.

Nutritional Value (Amount per Serving):
Calories 260; Fat 17 g; Carbohydrates 1.1 g; Sugar 0.2 g; Protein 23 g; Cholesterol 121 mg

Spicy Lamb Chops

Preparation Time: 10 minutes; Cooking Time: 24 minutes; Serve: 3
Ingredients:
- 6 lamb chops
- 1/2 tsp garlic, minced
- 1/2 green chili pepper, minced
- 1/4 cup fresh parsley, chopped
- 1 1/2 tbsp olive oil
- 1/2 lime juice
- Pepper
- Salt

Directions:
1. Spray air fryer basket with cooking spray.
2. Add lamb chops in a bowl with remaining ingredients and coat well.
3. Place lamb chops into the air fryer basket and cook at 400 F for 24 minutes. Turn lamb chops halfway through.
4. Serve and enjoy.

Nutritional Value (Amount per Serving):
Calories 468; Fat 22.9 g; Carbohydrates 1.2 g; Sugar 0.2 g; Protein 61.1 g; Cholesterol 195 mg

Lemon Basil Lamb Chops

Preparation Time: 10 minutes; Cooking Time: 24 minutes; Serve: 4
Ingredients:
- 4 lamb chops
- 1 garlic clove, minced
- 1/2 cup basil, chopped
- 1 tbsp olive oil
- 1/2 lemon juice
- Pepper
- Salt

Directions:
1. Spray air fryer basket with cooking spray.
2. Add oil, lemon juice, garlic, basil, pepper, and salt into the blender and blend until smooth.
3. Add lamb chops in a bowl. Pour blended mixture over lamb chops and rub well.
4. Place lamb chops into the air fryer basket and cook at 400 F for 24 minutes. Turn lamb chops halfway through.
5. Serve and enjoy.

Nutritional Value (Amount per Serving):
Calories 143; Fat 11.8 g; Carbohydrates 0.5 g; Sugar 0.1 g; Protein 31.8 g; Cholesterol 101 mg

Lemon Pepper Lamb

Preparation Time: 10 minutes; Cooking Time: 20 minutes; Serve: 4
Ingredients:
- 1 lb lamb meat, cubed
- 1 tbsp lemon juice
- 1/4 tsp dried rosemary
- 1/2 tbsp dried oregano
- 1/2 red bell pepper, cut into chunks
- 1/2 green bell pepper, cut into chunks
- 1/2 tbsp vinegar
- 1/2 tbsp garlic, minced
- 2 tbsp olive oil
- Pepper
- Salt

Directions:
1. Spray air fryer basket with cooking spray.
2. Add all ingredients into the large bowl and toss well.
3. Transfer meat mixture into the air fryer basket and cook at 380 F for 20 minutes.
4. Serve and enjoy.

Nutritional Value (Amount per Serving):
Calories 304; Fat 22.2 g; Carbohydrates 3.1 g; Sugar 1.5 g; Protein 21.5 g; Cholesterol 80 mg

Meatballs

Preparation Time: 10 minutes; Cooking Time: 30 minutes; Serve: 4
Ingredients:
- 1 lb ground lamb
- 2 garlic, minced
- 1/2 tbsp thyme, chopped
- 1/4 cup pine nuts, toasted and chopped
- 1 egg, lightly beaten
- 1 tbsp olive oil
- Pepper
- Salt

Directions:
1. Add all ingredients into the bowl and mix until well combined.
2. Make meatballs from meat mixture and place it into the air fryer basket and cook at 380 F for 30 minutes. Turn meatballs halfway through.
3. Serve and enjoy.

Nutritional Value (Amount per Serving):
Calories 317; Fat 18.8 g; Carbohydrates 1.9 g; Sugar 0.4 g; Protein 34.5 g; Cholesterol 143 mg

Greek Lamb Cutlets

Preparation Time: 10 minutes; Cooking Time: 30 minutes; Serve: 4
Ingredients:
- 4 lamb cutlets
- 3 garlic cloves
- 1/4 cup basil
- 2 tbsp olive oil
- 2 tbsp lemon juice
- 1/2 tbsp coriander seeds
- 1/2 tbsp ground cumin
- Pepper
- Salt

Directions:
1. Spray air fryer basket with cooking spray.
2. Add all ingredients except meat into the blender and blend until smooth.
3. Rub blended mixture over lamb cutlets.
4. Place lamb cutlets into the air fryer basket and cook at 380 F for 30 minutes. Turn lamb cutlets halfway through.
5. Serve and enjoy.

Nutritional Value (Amount per Serving):

Calories 227; Fat 13.5 g; Carbohydrates 1.3 g; Sugar 0.2 g; Protein 24.3 g; Cholesterol 77 mg

Herb Lamb Cutlets

Preparation Time: 10 minutes; Cooking Time: 30 minutes; Serve: 4
Ingredients:
- 4 lamb cutlets
- 2 garlic cloves, minced
- 1/2 tsp thyme, chopped
- 1 tbsp rosemary, chopped
- 1 tbsp olive oil
- 1/8 tsp cayenne
- Pepper
- Salt

Directions:
1. Spray air fryer basket with cooking spray.
2. Add lamb cutlets into the bowl with remaining ingredients and coat well.
3. Place lamb cutlets into the air fryer basket and cook at 380 F for 30 minutes. Turn lamb cutlets halfway through.
4. Serve and enjoy.

Nutritional Value (Amount per Serving):
Calories 194; Fat 9.9 g; Carbohydrates 1.2 g; Sugar 0 g; Protein 24 g; Cholesterol 77 mg

Meatballs

Preparation Time: 10 minutes; Cooking Time: 12 minutes; Serve: 4
Ingredients:
- 4 oz ground lamb
- 1/2 tbsp lemon zest
- 1 egg, lightly beaten
- 1 tbsp oregano, chopped
- 1/4 tsp dried thyme
- Pepper
- Salt

Directions:
1. Spray air fryer basket with cooking spray.
2. Add all ingredients into the bowl and mix until well combined.
3. Make meatballs from mixture and place into the air fryer basket and cook at 400 F for 12 minutes.
4. Serve and enjoy.

Nutritional Value (Amount per Serving):
Calories 73; Fat 3.3 g; Carbohydrates 1 g; Sugar 0.2 g; Protein 9.5 g; Cholesterol 66 mg

Garlic Herb Lamb Cutlets

Preparation Time: 10 minutes; Cooking Time: 30 minutes; Serve: 4
Ingredients:
- 4 lamb cutlets
- 1/2 tbsp chives, chopped
- 2 tbsp mustard
- 2 garlic cloves, minced
- 1/2 tbsp oregano, chopped
- 1/2 tbsp basil, chopped
- 1 tsp olive oil
- Pepper
- Salt

Directions:
1. Spray air fryer basket with cooking spray.
2. Add lamb cutlets into the bowl with remaining ingredients and coat well.
3. Place lamb cutlets into the air fryer basket and cook at 380 F for 30 minutes. Turn lamb cutlets halfway through.
4. Serve and enjoy.

Nutritional Value (Amount per Serving):
Calories 199; Fat 9.1 g; Carbohydrates 2.9 g; Sugar 0.4 g; Protein 25.5 g; Cholesterol 77 mg

Spicy Lamb Chops

Preparation Time: 10 minutes; Cooking Time: 20 minutes; Serve: 4
Ingredients:
- 4 lamb chops
- 1/2 tsp chili powder
- 1 tbsp garlic, minced
- 1 tbsp olive oil
- 1/4 tsp paprika
- 1/4 tsp cayenne
- Pepper
- Salt

Directions:
1. Add lamb chops into the bowl with remaining ingredients and coat well.
2. Place lamb chops into the air fryer basket and cook at 390 F for 20 minutes. Turn lamb chops halfway through.
3. Serve and enjoy.

Nutritional Value (Amount per Serving):
Calories 193; Fat 9.8 g; Carbohydrates 1 g; Sugar 0.1 g; Protein 24.1 g; Cholesterol 77 mg

Greek Lamb Patties

Preparation Time: 10 minutes; Cooking Time: 20 minutes; Serve: 4
Ingredients:
- 1 1/2 lbs ground lamb
- 1/3 cup feta cheese, crumbled
- 1 tsp oregano
- 1/4 tsp Italian seasoning
- 1/4 tsp pepper
- 1/2 tsp salt

Directions:
1. Preheat the cosori air fryer to 375 F.
2. Add all ingredients into the bowl and mix until well combined.
3. Make four equal shape of patties from meat mixture and place into the air fryer basket.
4. Cook patties for 20 minutes. Turn patties halfway through.
5. Serve and enjoy.

Nutritional Value (Amount per Serving):
Calories 352; Fat 15.3 g; Carbohydrates 0.9 g; Sugar 0.6 g; Protein 49.6 g; Cholesterol 164 mg

Mustard Lamb Chops

Preparation Time: 10 minutes; Cooking Time: 15 minutes; Serve: 4
Ingredients:
- 8 lamb chops
- 1/2 tsp olive oil
- 1 1/2 tbsp Dijon mustard
- 1 1/2 tbsp fresh lemon juice
- Pepper
- Salt

Directions:
1. Preheat the cosori air fryer to 390 F.
2. In a small bowl, mix together mustard, lemon juice, and olive oil.
3. Brush lamb chops with mustard mixture and place into the air fryer basket.
4. Cook lamb chops for 15 minutes. Turn halfway through.
5. Serve and enjoy.

Nutritional Value (Amount per Serving):
Calories 327; Fat 13.3 g; Carbohydrates 0.5 g; Sugar 0.2 g; Protein 48.1 g; Cholesterol 153 mg

Chapter 7: Snacks & Appetizers

Roasted Herb Olives

Preparation Time: 10 minutes; Cooking Time: 5 minutes; Serve: 4
Ingredients:
- 2 cups olives
- 1/2 tsp dried fennel seeds
- 1/2 tsp dried oregano
- 1/2 tsp crushed red pepper
- 2 tsp garlic, minced
- 2 tbsp olive oil
- Pepper
- Salt

Directions:
1. Add olives and remaining ingredients into the mixing bowl and toss to coat well.
2. Add olives into the air fryer basket and cook at 300 F for 5 minutes.
3. Serve and enjoy.

Nutritional Value (Amount per Serving):
Calories 142; Fat 14.3 g; Carbohydrates 5.1 g; Sugar 0 g; Protein 0.7 g; Cholesterol 0 mg

Cheesy Crab Dip

Preparation Time: 10 minutes; Cooking Time: 12 minutes; Serve: 8
Ingredients:
- 8 oz lump crabmeat
- 1 tbsp Italian seasoning
- 1/2 cup cheddar cheese, shredded
- 1/4 cup mayonnaise
- 1/4 cup sour cream
- 4 oz cream cheese

Directions:
1. Spray air fryer safe dish with cooking spray and set aside.
2. In a mixing bowl, mix together crabmeat, Italian seasoning, cheddar cheese, mayonnaise, sour cream, and cream cheese.
3. Pour crabmeat mixture into the prepared dish.
4. Place dish into the air fryer basket and cook at 320 F for 12 minutes.
5. Serve and enjoy.

Nutritional Value (Amount per Serving):
Calories 156; Fat 12.3 g; Carbohydrates 2.7 g; Sugar 0.7 g; Protein 8.9 g; Cholesterol 58 mg

Roasted Walnuts

Preparation Time: 10 minutes; Cooking Time: 5 minutes; Serve: 6
Ingredients:
- 2 cups walnuts
- 1/4 tsp chili powder
- 1 tsp olive oil
- Pepper
- Salt

Directions:
1. Add walnuts, chili powder, oil, pepper, and salt into the mixing bowl and toss well.
2. Add walnuts into the air fryer basket and cook at 320 F for 5 minutes.
3. Serve and enjoy.

Nutritional Value (Amount per Serving):
Calories 265; Fat 25.4 g; Carbohydrates 4.2 g; Sugar 0.5 g; Protein 10 g; Cholesterol 0 mg

Cheese Stuffed Mushrooms

Preparation Time: 10 minutes; Cooking Time: 5 minutes; Serve: 3
Ingredients:
- 12 baby mushrooms
- 1 tsp chives, minced
- 4 oz cream cheese
- 2 tbsp butter, melted

- 4 bacon slices, cooked and crumbled
- Pepper
- Salt

Directions:
1. In a small bowl, mix together cream cheese, chives, butter, bacon, pepper, and salt.
2. Stuff cream cheese mixture into the mushrooms.
3. Place mushrooms into the air fryer basket and cook at 350 F for 5 minutes.
4. Serve and enjoy.

Nutritional Value (Amount per Serving):
Calories 397; Fat 32.2 g; Carbohydrates 10.6 g; Sugar 4.9 g; Protein 21.1 g; Cholesterol 90 mg

Parmesan Carrot Fries

Preparation Time: 10 minutes; Cooking Time: 15 minutes; Serve: 4
Ingredients:
- 6 carrots, peeled and cut into fries shapes
- 2 tbsp parmesan cheese, grated
- 2 tbsp garlic, minced
- 2 tbsp olive oil
- Pepper
- Salt

Directions:
1. In a mixing bowl, toss carrot fries, parmesan cheese, garlic, oil, pepper, and salt.
2. Add carrot fries into the air fryer basket and cook at 350 F for 15 minutes. Turn fries halfway through.
3. Serve and enjoy.

Nutritional Value (Amount per Serving):
Calories 126; Fat 8.5 g; Carbohydrates 10.7 g; Sugar 4.5 g; Protein 3.3 g; Cholesterol 5 mg

Stuffed Jalapeno Poppers

Preparation Time: 10 minutes; Cooking Time: 7 minutes; Serve: 10
Ingredients:
- 10 jalapeno peppers, cut in half, remove seeds & membranes
- 1/4 tsp paprika
- 1/2 tsp chili powder
- 1 tsp ground cumin
- 1 tsp garlic powder
- 1/2 cup cheddar cheese, shredded
- 4 oz cream cheese
- 1 tsp salt

Directions:
1. In a small bowl, mix together cream cheese, cheddar cheese, garlic powder, cumin, chili powder, paprika, and salt.
2. Stuff cream cheese mixture into each jalapeno half.
3. Place stuffed jalapeno peppers into the air fryer basket and cook at 350 F for 7 minutes.
4. Serve and enjoy.

Nutritional Value (Amount per Serving):
Calories 71; Fat 6.1 g; Carbohydrates 1.8 g; Sugar 0.6 g; Protein 2.6 g; Cholesterol 18 mg

Spicy Crab Dip

Preparation Time: 10 minutes; Cooking Time: 7 minutes; Serve: 4
Ingredients:
- 1 cup crab meat
- 2 tbsp parsley, chopped
- 2 tbsp lemon juice
- 2 tbsp hot sauce
- 1/2 cup green scallions, chopped
- 2 cups jalapeno jack cheese, grated
- 1/4 cup mayonnaise
- Pepper

- Salt

Directions:
1. Spray air fryer safe dish with cooking spray and set aside.
2. In a mixing bowl, mix together crab meat, hot sauce, green scallions, cheese, mayonnaise, pepper, and salt.
3. Pour crab meat mixture into the prepared dish.
4. Place dish into the air fryer basket and cook at 400 F for 7 minutes.
5. Once done then add lemon juice and stir well.
6. Garnish with parsley and serve.

Nutritional Value (Amount per Serving):
Calories 283; Fat 22.3 g; Carbohydrates 5.5 g; Sugar 2 g; Protein 15 g; Cholesterol 58 mg

Crispy Zucchini Fries

Preparation Time: 10 minutes; Cooking Time: 10 minutes; Serve: 4

Ingredients:
- 2 medium zucchini, cut into fries shapes
- 1/2 tsp garlic powder
- 1 tsp Italian seasoning
- 1/2 cup parmesan cheese, grated
- 1/2 cup almond flour
- 1 egg, lightly beaten
- Pepper
- Salt

Directions:
1. Spray air fryer basket with cooking spray.
2. In a shallow dish, mix together almond flour, cheese, Italians seasoning, garlic powder, pepper, and salt.
3. In a shallow bowl, add the egg.
4. Dip zucchini fries into the egg and coat with almond flour mixture.
5. Place coated zucchini fries into the air fryer basket and cook at 400 F for 10 minutes.
6. Serve and enjoy.

Nutritional Value (Amount per Serving):
Calories 93; Fat 5.7 g; Carbohydrates 4.8 g; Sugar 2 g; Protein 7.4 g; Cholesterol 50 mg

Healthy Zucchini Chips

Preparation Time: 10 minutes; Cooking Time: 30 minutes; Serve: 2

Ingredients:
- 2 medium zucchini, cut into 1/4-inch thick slices
- 1/2 tsp garlic powder
- 1/2 cup parmesan cheese, grated
- 1 tbsp rosemary, chopped
- 1/4 cup olive oil
- Pepper
- Salt

Directions:
1. In a mixing bowl, toss zucchini slices with garlic powder, cheese, rosemary, oil, pepper, and salt.
2. Arrange zucchini slices into the air fryer basket and cook at 300 F for 30 minutes. turn halfway through.
3. Serve and enjoy.

Nutritional Value (Amount per Serving):
Calories 255; Fat 31.2 g; Carbohydrates 9.1 g; Sugar 3.6 g; Protein 10.6 g; Cholesterol 18 mg

Chicken Stuffed Poblanos

Preparation Time: 10 minutes; Cooking Time: 15 minutes; Serve: 6

Ingredients:

- 3 poblano peppers, cut in half & remove seeds
- 2 oz cheddar cheese, grated
- 1 1/2 cup spinach artichoke dip
- 1 cup chicken breast, cooked and chopped

Directions:
1. In a small bowl, mix together chicken, spinach artichoke dip, and half cheddar cheese.
2. Stuff chicken mixture into the poblano peppers.
3. Place stuffed poblano peppers into the air fryer basket. Sprinkle remaining cheese on top of peppers.
4. Cook at 350 F for 12-15 minutes.
5. Serve and enjoy.

Nutritional Value (Amount per Serving):
Calories 91; Fat 5.6 g; Carbohydrates 3 g; Sugar 1.5 g; Protein 7.1 g; Cholesterol 24 mg

Ranch Zucchini Chips

Preparation Time: 10 minutes; Cooking Time: 15 minutes; Serve: 2
Ingredients:
- 1 egg
- 2 medium zucchini, cut into thin slices
- 1 tsp ranch seasoning
- 1 tsp parsley
- 1 tsp dill
- Pepper
- Salt

Directions:
1. In a small bowl, mix together ranch seasoning, parsley, dill, pepper, and salt.
2. Brush zucchini slices with egg and sprinkle with ranch seasoning mix.
3. Arrange zucchini slices into the air fryer basket and cook at 380 F for 10 minutes.
4. Turn zucchini slices and cook for 5 minutes more.
5. Serve and enjoy.

Nutritional Value (Amount per Serving):
Calories 69; Fat 2.6 g; Carbohydrates 7.1 g; Sugar 3.6 g; Protein 5.3 g; Cholesterol 82 mg

Crispy Tofu

Preparation Time: 10 minutes; Cooking Time: 15 minutes; Serve: 4
Ingredients:
- 16 oz extra-firm tofu, pressed and cut into cubes
- 1 tsp sesame oil
- 1 tbsp rice vinegar
- 2 tbsp soy sauce

Directions:
1. In a mixing bowl, mix together tofu, sesame oil, vinegar, and soy sauce. Marinate for 15 minutes.
2. Spray air fryer basket with cooking spray.
3. Remove tofu from marinade and place into the air fryer basket and cook at 400 F for 15 minutes. Turn tofu after 10 minutes.
4. Serve and enjoy.

Nutritional Value (Amount per Serving):
Calories 120; Fat 7.7 g; Carbohydrates 2.9 g; Sugar 0.7 g; Protein 11.7 g; Cholesterol 0 mg

Crispy Cauliflower Florets

Preparation Time: 10 minutes; Cooking Time: 15 minutes; Serve: 5
Ingredients:
- 1 medium cauliflower head, cut into florets
- 1/2 tsp old bay seasoning
- 1/4 tsp paprika

- 1 tbsp garlic, minced
- 3 tbsp olive oil
- Pepper
- Salt

Directions:
1. In a mixing bowl, toss cauliflower with remaining ingredients.
2. Add cauliflower florets into the air fryer basket and cook at 400 F for 15 minutes. Toss after every 5 minutes.
3. Serve and enjoy.

Nutritional Value (Amount per Serving):
Calories 104; Fat 8.5 g; Carbohydrates 6.7 g; Sugar 2.8 g; Protein 2.4 g; Cholesterol 0 mg

Parmesan Asparagus

Preparation Time: 10 minutes; Cooking Time: 5 minutes; Serve: 2
Ingredients:
- 1 egg, lightly beaten
- 10 asparagus spears, trimmed and cut woody ends
- 1 tbsp heavy cream
- 1/3 cup parmesan cheese, grated
- 1/3 cup almond flour
- 1/2 tsp paprika
- 1/2 tsp salt

Directions:
1. Spray air fryer basket with cooking spray.
2. In a shallow dish, whisk together egg and cream until well mix.
3. In a separate dish, mix together almond flour, parmesan cheese, paprika, and salt.
4. Dip asparagus spear into the egg mixture then coat with almond flour mixture.
5. Place coated asparagus into the air fryer basket and cook at 350 F for 5 minutes.
6. Serve and enjoy.

Nutritional Value (Amount per Serving):
Calories 166; Fat 11.3 g; Carbohydrates 7 g; Sugar 2.7 g; Protein 12.3 g; Cholesterol 105 mg

Tasty Buffalo Cauliflower Bites

Preparation Time: 10 minutes; Cooking Time: 15 minutes; Serve: 4
Ingredients:
- 8 oz cauliflower florets
- 1 tsp cayenne pepper
- 1 tsp chili powder
- 6 tbsp almond flour
- 1 tsp olive oil
- 1 tsp garlic, minced
- 1 tomato, diced
- Pepper
- Salt

Directions:
1. Preheat the cosori air fryer to 350 F.
2. Spray air fryer basket with cooking spray.
3. Add tomato, garlic, black pepper, olive oil, cayenne pepper, and chili powder into the blender and blend until smooth.
4. Add cauliflower florets into the large bowl. Season with pepper and salt.
5. Pour blended tomato mixture over cauliflower florets and coat well.
6. Coat cauliflower florets with almond flour.
7. Place coated cauliflower florets into the air fryer basket and cook for 15 minutes. Shake basket twice.
8. Serve and enjoy.

Nutritional Value (Amount per Serving):
Calories 42; Fat 2.3 g; Carbohydrates 4.9 g; Sugar 1.9 g; Protein 1.8 g; Cholesterol 0 mg

Beetroot Chips

Preparation Time: 10 minutes; Cooking Time: 15 minutes; Serve: 4
Ingredients:
- 2 beetroot, wash, peeled, and sliced thinly
- 1 tsp olive oil
- Pepper
- Salt

Directions:
1. Season beetroot slices with pepper and salt.
2. Preheat the cosori air fryer to 300 F.
3. Arrange beetroot slices into the air fryer basket and drizzle with oil.
4. Cook for 15 minutes. Shake basket after every 5 minutes.
5. Serve and enjoy.

Nutritional Value (Amount per Serving):
Calories 32; Fat 1.3 g; Carbohydrates 5 g; Sugar 4 g; Protein 0.8 g; Cholesterol 0 mg

Parmesan Brussels sprouts

Preparation Time: 10 minutes; Cooking Time: 12 minutes; Serve: 4
Ingredients:
- 1 lb Brussels sprouts, cut stems and halved
- 1/4 cup parmesan cheese, grated
- 1 tbsp olive oil
- Pepper
- Salt

Directions:
1. Preheat the cosori air fryer to 350 F.
2. Toss Brussels sprouts with oil, pepper, and salt into the mixing bowl.
3. Transfer Brussels sprouts into the air fryer basket and cook for 12 minutes. Shake basket halfway through.
4. Top with cheese and serve.

Nutritional Value (Amount per Serving):
Calories 107; Fat 5.8 g; Carbohydrates 10.6 g; Sugar 2.5 g; Protein 6.7 g; Cholesterol 6 mg

Spicy Crab Dip

Preparation Time: 10 minutes; Cooking Time: 7 minutes; Serve: 4
Ingredients:
- 1 cup crab, cooked
- 2 tbsp fresh parsley, chopped
- 2 tbsp fresh lemon juice
- 2 cups cheddar cheese, grated
- 1/4 cup mayonnaise
- 2 tbsp hot sauce
- 1/8 tsp cayenne
- 1/2 tsp chili powder
- 1 tsp pepper
- 1/2 tsp salt

Directions:
1. Spray air fryer safe dish with cooking spray and set aside.
2. Add all ingredients except parsley and lemon juice into the mixing bowl and mix well.
3. Pour mixture into the prepared dish. Place dish into the air fryer basket and cook at 400 F for 7 minutes.
4. Add parsley and lemon juice. Stir well.
5. Serve and enjoy.

Nutritional Value (Amount per Serving):
Calories 321; Fat 24.4 g; Carbohydrates 5.2 g; Sugar 1.5 g; Protein 20.4 g; Cholesterol 93 mg

Flavors Chicken Tandoori

Preparation Time: 10 minutes; Cooking Time: 15 minutes; Serve: 4

Ingredients:
- 1 lb chicken tenders, cut in half
- 1/4 cup parsley, chopped
- 1 tbsp garlic, minced
- 1 tbsp ginger, minced
- 1 tsp paprika
- 1 tsp garam masala
- 1 tsp turmeric
- 1 tsp cayenne pepper
- 1/4 cup yogurt
- 1 tsp salt

Directions:
1. Preheat the Cosori air fryer to 350 F.
2. Add all ingredients into the large bowl and mix well. Place in refrigerator for 30 minutes.
3. Spray air fryer basket with cooking spray.
4. Add marinated chicken into the air fryer basket and cook for 15 minutes. Turn chicken after 10 minutes.
5. Serve and enjoy.

Nutritional Value (Amount per Serving):
Calories 240; Fat 8.9 g; Carbohydrates 3.9 g; Sugar 1.3 g; Protein 34.2 g; Cholesterol 102 mg

Asian Chicken Wings

Preparation Time: 10 minutes; Cooking Time: 30 minutes; Serve: 2

Ingredients:
- 4 chicken wings
- 1 tbsp soy sauce
- 1 tbsp Chinese spice
- 1 tsp mixed spice
- Pepper
- Salt

Directions:
1. Add chicken wings into the mixing bowl. Add remaining ingredients and toss well.
2. Transfer chicken wings into the air fryer basket and cook at 350 F for 30 minutes. Turn halfway through.
3. Serve and enjoy.

Nutritional Value (Amount per Serving):
Calories 392; Fat 15.2 g; Carbohydrates 0.9 g; Sugar 0.2 g; Protein 59 g; Cholesterol 178 mg

Chicken Kabab

Preparation Time: 10 minutes; Cooking Time: 6 minutes; Serve: 3

Ingredients:
- 1 lb ground chicken
- 2 green onion, chopped
- 1 egg, lightly beaten
- 1/3 cup fresh parsley, chopped
- 2 garlic cloves
- 4 oz onion, chopped
- 1/4 tsp turmeric powder
- 1/2 tsp black pepper
- 1 tbsp fresh lemon juice
- 1/4 cup almond flour

Directions:
1. Spray air fryer basket with cooking spray.
2. Add all ingredients into the food processor and process until well combined.
3. Transfer chicken mixture to the mixing bowl and place it in the refrigerator for 30 minutes.
4. Divide mixture into the 6 equal portions and roll around the skewers.
5. Place kabab into the air fryer basket and cook at 400 F for 6 minutes.
6. Serve and enjoy.

Nutritional Value (Amount per Serving):
Calories 348; Fat 14 g; Carbohydrates 6.4 g; Sugar 2.2 g; Protein 47.1 g; Cholesterol 189 mg

Meatballs

Preparation Time: 10 minutes; Cooking Time: 10 minutes; Serve: 4
Ingredients:
- 1 lb ground chicken
- 1 tbsp soy sauce
- 1 tbsp hoisin sauce
- 1/2 cup fresh cilantro, chopped
- 2 green onions, chopped
- 1/4 cup shredded coconut
- 1 tsp sesame oil
- 1 tsp sriracha
- Pepper
- Salt

Directions:
1. Spray air fryer basket with cooking spray.
2. Add all ingredients into the large mixing bowl and mix until well combined.
3. Make meatballs from mixture and place into the air fryer basket and cook at 350 F for 10 minutes. Turn halfway through.
4. Serve and enjoy.

Nutritional Value (Amount per Serving):
Calories 258; Fat 11.4 g; Carbohydrates 3.7 g; Sugar 1.7 g; Protein 33.5 g; Cholesterol 101 mg

Tasty Chicken Tenders

Preparation Time: 10 minutes; Cooking Time: 12 minutes; Serve: 4
Ingredients:
- 1 lb chicken tenders
- 1 egg, lightly beaten
- 1/2 tsp paprika
- 1 cup pecans, crushed
- 1/4 cup ground mustard
- 1 tsp pepper
- 1 tsp salt

Directions:
1. Spray air fryer basket with cooking spray.
2. Add chicken into the large bowl. Season with paprika, pepper, and salt. Add mustard mix well.
3. In a separate bowl, add egg and whisk well.
4. In a shallow dish, add crushed pecans.
5. Dip chicken into the egg then coat with crushed pecans.
6. Place coated chicken pieces into the air fryer basket and cook at 350 F for 12 minutes. Turn halfway through.
7. Serve and enjoy.

Nutritional Value (Amount per Serving):
Calories 304; Fat 14.9 g; Carbohydrates 4.5 g; Sugar 0.9 g; Protein 37.1 g; Cholesterol 142 mg

Meatballs

Preparation Time: 10 minutes; Cooking Time: 10 minutes; Serve: 6
Ingredients:
- 2 lbs ground chicken breast
- 1/2 cup ricotta cheese
- 2 eggs, lightly beaten
- 1/4 cup fresh parsley, chopped
- 1/2 cup almond flour
- 1 tsp pepper
- 2 tsp salt

Directions:
1. Spray air fryer basket with cooking spray.
2. Add all ingredients into the large mixing bowl and mix until well combined.

3. Make meatballs from mixture and place into the air fryer basket and cook at 380 F for 10 minutes. Shake basket twice.
4. Serve and enjoy.

Nutritional Value (Amount per Serving):
Calories 227; Fat 5.6 g; Carbohydrates 2.1 g; Sugar 0.3 g; Protein 42.6 g; Cholesterol 155 mg

Easy Taro Fries

Preparation Time: 10 minutes; Cooking Time: 20 minutes; Serve: 2

Ingredients:
- 8 small taro, peel and cut into fries shape
- 1 tbsp olive oil
- Pepper
- Salt

Directions:
1. Add taro fries in a mixing bowl. Drizzle with olive oil and season with pepper and salt.
2. Add taro fries into the air fryer basket and cook at 360 F for 20 minutes. Toss halfway through.
3. Serve and enjoy.

Nutritional Value (Amount per Serving):
Calories 96; Fat 7 g; Carbohydrates 8.7 g; Sugar 0.1 g; Protein 0.1 g; Cholesterol 0 mg

Broccoli Fritters

Preparation Time: 10 minutes; Cooking Time: 30 minutes; Serve: 4

Ingredients:
- 2 eggs, lightly beaten
- 2 garlic cloves, minced
- 3 cups broccoli florets, steam & chopped
- 2 cups cheddar cheese, shredded
- 1/4 cup almond flour
- Pepper
- Salt

Directions:
1. Line air fryer basket with parchment paper.
2. Add all ingredients into the large bowl and mix until well combined.
3. Make patties from the broccoli mixture and place it into the air fryer basket.
4. Cook at 375 F for 30 minutes. Turn patties halfway through.
5. Serve and enjoy.

Nutritional Value (Amount per Serving):
Calories 295; Fat 22 g; Carbohydrates 6.3 g; Sugar 1.7 g; Protein 19.2 g; Cholesterol 141 mg

Crispy Brussels sprouts

Preparation Time: 10 minutes; Cooking Time: 14 minutes; Serve: 2

Ingredients:
- 1/2 lb Brussels sprouts, trimmed and halved
- 1/2 tsp chili powder
- 1/4 tsp cayenne
- 1/2 tbsp olive oil
- Pepper
- Salt

Directions:
1. Add all ingredients into the large bowl and toss well.
2. Spread Brussels sprouts into the air fryer basket and cook at 370 F for 14 minutes. Toss halfway through.
3. Serve and enjoy.

Nutritional Value (Amount per Serving):
Calories 82; Fat 4 g; Carbohydrates 10.8 g; Sugar 2.5 g; Protein 4 g; Cholesterol 0 mg

Herb Roasted Carrots

Preparation Time: 10 minutes; Cooking Time: 20 minutes; Serve: 6
Ingredients:
- 2 lbs carrots, peeled and cut into fries shape
- 1 tsp dried thyme
- 3 tbsp olive oil
- 2 tbsp dried parsley
- 1 tsp dried oregano
- Pepper
- Salt

Directions:
1. Add carrots in a large bowl. Add remaining ingredients and toss well.
2. Add carrots fries into the air fryer basket and cook at 400 F for 20 minutes. Toss halfway through.
3. Serve and enjoy.

Nutritional Value (Amount per Serving):
Calories 124; Fat 7.1 g; Carbohydrates 15.2 g; Sugar 7.5 g; Protein 1.3 g; Cholesterol 0 mg

Simple Air Fried Vegetables

Preparation Time: 10 minutes; Cooking Time: 18 minutes; Serve: 4
Ingredients:
- 1 cup broccoli florets
- 1 cup carrots, sliced
- 1 cup cauliflower, cut into florets
- 1 tbsp olive oil
- Pepper
- Salt

Directions:
1. Add all vegetables in a large bowl. Drizzle with olive oil and season with pepper and salt.
2. Transfer vegetables to the air fryer basket and cook at 380 F for 18 minutes. Toss halfway through.
3. Serve and enjoy.

Nutritional Value (Amount per Serving):
Calories 55; Fat 3.6 g; Carbohydrates 5.6 g; Sugar 2.3 g; Protein 1.4 g; Cholesterol 0 mg

Healthy Roasted Pecans

Preparation Time: 10 minutes; Cooking Time: 6 minutes; Serve: 6
Ingredients:
- 2 cups pecan halves
- 1 tbsp butter, melted
- Pepper
- Salt

Directions:
1. Preheat the cosori air fryer to 200 F.
2. Add pecans, butter, and salt in a bowl and toss well.
3. Transfer pecans into the air fryer basket and cook for 4-6 minutes. Toss after every 2 minutes.
4. Serve and enjoy.

Nutritional Value (Amount per Serving):
Calories 307; Fat 31.7 g; Carbohydrates 6 g; Sugar 1.5 g; Protein 4.5 g; Cholesterol 5 mg

Meatballs

Preparation Time: 10 minutes; Cooking Time: 25 minutes; Serve: 6
Ingredients:
- 1 egg
- 1 lb ground turkey
- 1/4 cup almond flour
- 1/4 cup fresh parsley, chopped
- 1/4 onion, minced
- 1 garlic clove, minced
- 1/2 tsp ground cumin
- 1/2 tsp dried oregano

- 1 tsp mint, chopped
- 1/2 tsp salt

Directions:
1. Spray air fryer basket with cooking spray.
2. Add all ingredients into the large bowl and mix until well combined.
3. Make meatballs from mixture and place into the air fryer basket and cook at 375 F for 25 minutes. Shake basket halfway through.
4. Serve and enjoy.

Nutritional Value (Amount per Serving):
Calories 169; Fat 9.7 g; Carbohydrates 1.3 g; Sugar 0.3 g; Protein 22.1 g; Cholesterol 104 mg

Sausage Meatballs

Preparation Time: 10 minutes; Cooking Time: 15 minutes; Serve: 8
Ingredients:
- 4 oz ground sausage meat
- 3 tbsp almond flour
- 2 garlic cloves, minced
- 1 small onion, chopped
- Pepper
- Salt

Directions:
1. Spray air fryer basket with cooking spray.
2. Add all ingredients into the mixing bowl and mix until well combined.
3. Make meatballs from mixture and place into the air fryer basket and cook at 360 F for 15 minutes.
4. Serve and enjoy.

Nutritional Value (Amount per Serving):
Calories 101; Fat 7.4 g; Carbohydrates 5.8 g; Sugar 1 g; Protein 4.2 g; Cholesterol 5 mg

Cheesy Chicken Dip

Preparation Time: 10 minutes; Cooking Time: 25 minutes; Serve: 10
Ingredients:
- 2 cups cooked chicken, shredded
- 6 oz Monterey jack cheese, grated
- 4 scallions, chopped
- 2 tsp curry powder
- 12 oz cream cheese
- 1/2 cup almonds, sliced
- 1/4 cup cilantro, chopped
- 1 cup yogurt
- 3 tbsp butter, melted

Directions:
1. Spray air fryer safe dish with cooking spray and set aside.
2. Add all ingredients into the mixing bowl and mix until well combined.
3. Pour mixture into the prepared dish.
4. Place dish into the air fryer basket and cook at 300 F for 25 minutes.
5. Serve and enjoy.

Nutritional Value (Amount per Serving):
Calories 303; Fat 24.1 g; Carbohydrates 4.4 g; Sugar 2.2 g; Protein 17.5 g; Cholesterol 85 mg

Delicious Shrimp Dip

Preparation Time: 10 minutes; Cooking Time: 8 minutes; Serve: 6
Ingredients:
- 1 lb shrimp, peeled, deveined and chopped
- 1 cup heavy cream
- 2 tbsp olive oil
- 1 tsp chili powder
- 1 tsp turmeric powder

Directions:
1. Spray air fryer safe dish with cooking spray and set aside.

2. Add all ingredients into the mixing bowl and mix until well combined.
3. Pour mixture into the prepared dish.
4. Place dish into the air fryer basket and cook at 380 F for 8 minutes.
5. Serve and enjoy.

Nutritional Value (Amount per Serving):
Calories 201; Fat 13.5 g; Carbohydrates 2.2 g; Sugar 0.1 g; Protein 17.7 g; Cholesterol 187 mg

Quick & Easy Eggplant Fries

Preparation Time: 10 minutes; Cooking Time: 8 minutes Serve: 2
Ingredients:
- 1 eggplant, sliced
- 1 tsp olive oil
- 1 tsp soy sauce
- Salt

Directions:
1. Spray air fryer basket with cooking spray.
2. In a large bowl, mix together soy sauce, oil, and salt.
3. Add eggplant slices to the bowl, stir to coat and let sit for 5 minutes.
4. Arrange eggplant slices into the air fryer basket and cook at 400 F for 8 minutes. Turn halfway through.
5. Serve and enjoy.

Nutritional Value (Amount per Serving):
Calories 65; Fat 2.6 g; Carbohydrates 11.1 g; Sugar 4.1 g; Protein 1.2 g; Cholesterol 0 mg

Lime Radish Chips

Preparation Time: 10 minutes; Cooking Time: 12 minutes; Serve: 2
Ingredients:
- 1/2 lb radishes, sliced thinly
- 1/2 tbsp lime juice
- 1/4 tsp chili powder
- 1/2 tbsp olive oil
- Pepper
- Salt

Directions:
1. Spray air fryer basket with cooking spray.
2. Add all ingredients into the large bowl and toss well.
3. Arrange sliced radishes into the air fryer basket and cook at 380 F for 12 minutes.
4. Serve and enjoy.

Nutritional Value (Amount per Serving):
Calories 52; Fat 3.7 g; Carbohydrates 5 g; Sugar 2.3 g; Protein 0.9 g; Cholesterol 0 mg

Tasty Carrot Fries

Preparation Time: 10 minutes; Cooking Time: 15 minutes; Serve: 2
Ingredients:
- 1/2 lb carrots, peeled and cut into fries shapes
- 1/4 tsp cumin
- 1/2 tbsp olive oil
- 1/4 tsp onion powder
- 1/4 tsp paprika
- 1/4 tsp garlic powder
- 1/2 tsp kosher salt

Directions:
1. Spray air fryer basket with cooking spray.
2. In a large bowl, add all ingredients and toss until well coated.
3. Transfer carrot fries into the air fryer basket and cook at 400 F for 15 minutes. Toss halfway through.
4. Serve and enjoy.

Nutritional Value (Amount per Serving):
Calories 80; Fat 3.6 g; Carbohydrates 11.9 g; Sugar 5.8 g; Protein 1.1 g; Cholesterol 0 mg

Flavorful Herb Mushrooms

Preparation Time: 10 minutes; Cooking Time: 14 minutes; Serve: 4
Ingredients:
- 1 lb mushroom caps
- 1 tsp rosemary, chopped
- 1 tbsp basil, minced
- 1 garlic clove, minced
- 1/2 tbsp vinegar
- 1/2 tsp ground coriander
- Pepper
- Salt

Directions:
1. Spray air fryer basket with cooking spray.
2. Add all ingredients into the large bowl and toss well.
3. Add mushrooms into the air fryer basket and cook at 350 F for 14 minutes. Shake basket halfway through.
4. Serve and enjoy.

Nutritional Value (Amount per Serving):
Calories 27; Fat 0.4 g; Carbohydrates 4.2 g; Sugar 2 g; Protein 3.6 g; Cholesterol 0 mg

Turkey Dip

Preparation Time: 10 minutes; Cooking Time: 25 minutes; Serve: 6
Ingredients:
- 1 lb turkey breast, skinless, boneless, and minced
- 1 cup tomatoes, chopped
- 1 tbsp garlic, minced
- 2 shallots, chopped
- 1 tbsp olive oil
- 1/4 cup heavy cream
- Pepper
- Salt

Directions:
1. Spray air fryer safe dish with cooking spray and set aside.
2. Add all ingredients into the large bowl and mix until well combined.
3. Pour mixture into the prepared dish.
4. Place dish into the air fryer basket and cook at 380 F for 25 minutes.
5. Serve and enjoy.

Nutritional Value (Amount per Serving):
Calories 126; Fat 5.5 g; Carbohydrates 5.5 g; Sugar 3.5 g; Protein 13.4 g; Cholesterol 39 mg

Easy Zucchini Chips

Preparation Time: 10 minutes; Cooking Time: 16 minutes; Serve: 2
Ingredients:
- 1 zucchini, cut into 1/8-inch thick slices
- 1 tsp Cajun seasoning
- 1 tbsp olive oil
- Pepper
- Salt

Directions:
1. Spray air fryer basket with cooking spray.
2. Add all ingredients into the mixing bowl and toss well to coat.
3. Arrange zucchini slices into the air fryer basket and cook at 370 F for 16 minutes. Turn halfway through.
4. Serve and enjoy.

Nutritional Value (Amount per Serving):
Calories 76; Fat 7.2 g; Carbohydrates 3.3 g; Sugar 1.7 g; Protein 1.2 g; Cholesterol 0 mg

Easy Sweet Potato Fries

Preparation Time: 10 minutes; Cooking Time: 20 minutes; Serve: 2

Ingredients:
- 1 sweet potato, peeled and cut into fries shape
- 2 tsp olive oil
- 1/4 tsp chili powder
- 1/4 tsp garlic powder
- Pepper
- Salt

Directions:
1. Add all ingredients into the mixing bowl and toss well.
2. Add sweet potato fries into the air fryer basket and cook at 400 F for 20 minutes. Turn halfway through.
3. Serve and enjoy.

Nutritional Value (Amount per Serving):
Calories 94; Fat 4.8 g; Carbohydrates 12.3 g; Sugar 3.8 g; Protein 1.3 g; Cholesterol 0 mg

Healthy Jicama Fries

Preparation Time: 10 minutes; Cooking Time: 20 minutes; Serve: 2

Ingredients:
- 2 cups jicama strips
- 1/2 tsp garlic powder
- 1/2 tsp paprika
- 2 tbsp olive oil
- 1/2 tsp onion powder
- 1/8 tsp cayenne
- 1/4 tsp chili powder

Directions:
1. Spray air fryer basket with cooking spray.
2. Add all ingredients into the mixing bowl and toss well to coat.
3. Add jicama strips into the air fryer basket and cook at 400 F for 20 minutes. Shake basket halfway through.
4. Serve and enjoy.

Nutritional Value (Amount per Serving):
Calories 172; Fat 14.2 g; Carbohydrates 12.5 g; Sugar 3.5 g; Protein 1.3 g; Cholesterol 0 mg

Crispy Cauliflower Bites

Preparation Time: 10 minutes; Cooking Time: 15 minutes; Serve: 4

Ingredients:
- 1 lb cauliflower florets
- 1 tsp sesame seeds
- 1 tsp dried rosemary
- 1 1/2 tsp garlic powder
- 1 tbsp olive oil
- Pepper
- Salt

Directions:
1. Spray air fryer basket with cooking spray.
2. Add all ingredients into the bowl and toss well to coat.
3. Add cauliflower florets into the air fryer basket and cook at 400 F for 15 minutes. Shake basket halfway through.
4. Serve and enjoy.

Nutritional Value (Amount per Serving):
Calories 67; Fat 4 g; Carbohydrates 7.2 g; Sugar 3 g; Protein 2.6 g; Cholesterol 0 mg

Spicy Salmon Bites

Preparation Time: 10 minutes; Cooking Time: 12 minutes; Serve: 4

Ingredients:

- 1 lb salmon fillets, boneless and cubes
- 1/2 tsp chili powder
- 2 tsp olive oil
- 1/4 tsp cayenne pepper
- Pepper
- Salt

Directions:
1. Spray air fryer basket with cooking spray.
2. Add all ingredients into the bowl and toss well.
3. Arrange salmon cubes into the air fryer basket and cook at 350 F for 12 minutes. Turn halfway through.
4. Serve and enjoy.

Nutritional Value (Amount per Serving):
Calories 171; Fat 9.4 g; Carbohydrates 0.3 g; Sugar 0 g; Protein 22.1 g; Cholesterol 50 mg

Healthy Roasted Almonds

Preparation Time: 5 minutes; Cooking Time: 8 minutes; Serve: 8
Ingredients:
- 2 cups almonds
- 1 tbsp garlic powder
- 1 tbsp soy sauce
- 1/4 tsp pepper
- 1 tsp paprika
- Pinch of cayenne

Directions:
1. Spray air fryer basket with cooking spray.
2. Add pepper, paprika, garlic powder, cayenne, and soy sauce in a bowl and stir well. Add almonds and stir to coat.
3. Add almonds in the air fryer basket and cook at 320 F for 6-8 minutes. Shake basket after every 2 minutes.
4. Serve and enjoy.

Nutritional Value (Amount per Serving):
Calories 143; Fat 11.9 g; Carbohydrates 6.2 g; Sugar 1.3 g; Protein 5.4 g; Cholesterol 0 mg

Flavorful Eggplant Slices

Preparation Time: 5 minutes; Cooking Time: 20 minutes; Serve: 4
Ingredients:
- 1 eggplant, cut into 1-inch slices
- 1/2 tsp red pepper
- 1 tsp garlic powder
- 1/2 tsp Italian seasoning
- 1 tsp paprika
- 2 tbsp olive oil
- 1/8 tsp cayenne

Directions:
1. Add all ingredients into the large bowl and toss well.
2. Place eggplant slices into the air fryer basket and cook at 375 F for 20 minutes. Turn eggplant slices halfway through.
3. Serve and enjoy.

Nutritional Value (Amount per Serving):
Calories 99; Fat 7.5 g; Carbohydrates 8.8 g; Sugar 4.5 g; Protein 1.5 g; Cholesterol 0 mg

Easy Jalapeno Poppers

Preparation Time: 10 minutes; Cooking Time: 5 minutes; Serve: 5
Ingredients:
- 10 fresh jalapeno peppers, cut in half and remove seeds
- 1/4 cup cheddar cheese, shredded
- 6 oz cream cheese, softened
- 3 bacon slices, cooked and crumbled
- 1/4 tsp onion powder
- 1/4 tsp garlic powder

Directions:
1. Spray air fryer basket with cooking spray.
2. In a bowl, mix together bacon, cream cheese, garlic powder, onion powder, and cheddar cheese.
3. Stuff each jalapeno half with a bacon cheese mixture.
4. Place stuffed jalapeno peppers in the air fryer basket and cook at 370 F for 5 minutes.
5. Serve and enjoy.

Nutritional Value (Amount per Serving):
Calories 216; Fat 18.9 g; Carbohydrates 3.4 g; Sugar 1.1 g; Protein 8.6 g; Cholesterol 56 mg

Easy Broccoli Nuggets

Preparation Time: 10 minutes; Cooking Time: 15 minutes; Serve: 4

Ingredients:
- 2 cups broccoli florets, cooked until soft
- 1 cup cheddar cheese, shredded
- 1/4 cup almond flour
- 2 egg whites
- 1/8 tsp salt

Directions:
1. Preheat the cosori air fryer to 325 F.
2. Spray air fryer basket with cooking spray.
3. Add cooked broccoli into the mixing bowl and mash using potato masher into the small pieces. Add remaining ingredients mix well to combine.
4. Make small nuggets from the broccoli mixture.
5. Place broccoli nuggets into the air fryer basket and cook for 15 minutes. Turn halfway through.
6. Serve and enjoy.

Nutritional Value (Amount per Serving):
Calories 148; Fat 10.4 g; Carbohydrates 3.9 g; Sugar 1.1 g Protein 10.5 g; Cholesterol 30 mg

Crab Stuffed Mushrooms

Preparation Time: 10 minutes; Cooking Time: 8 minutes; Serve: 16

Ingredients:
- 16 mushrooms, clean and chop stems
- 2 oz crab meat, chopped
- 8 oz cream cheese, softened
- 2 garlic cloves, minced
- 1/2 tsp chili powder
- 1/4 tsp onion powder
- 1/4 cup cheddar cheese, shredded
- 1/4 tsp pepper

Directions:
1. In a large bowl, mix together cheese, mushroom stems, chili powder, onion powder, pepper, crabmeat, cream cheese, and garlic until well combined.
2. Stuff mushrooms with cheese mixture.
3. Place stuffed mushrooms into the air fryer basket and cook at 370 F for 8 minutes.
4. Serve and enjoy.

Nutritional Value (Amount per Serving):
Calories 65; Fat 5.7 g; Carbohydrates 1.3 g; Sugar 0.4 g; Protein 2.6 g; Cholesterol 19 mg

Delicious Chicken Dip

Preparation Time: 10 minutes; Cooking Time: 20 minutes; Serve: 6

Ingredients:
- 2 cups chicken, cooked and shredded
- 7.5 oz cream cheese, softened
- 4 tbsp hot sauce
- 1/4 tsp garlic powder
- 3/4 cup sour cream
- 1/4 tsp onion powder

Directions:
1. Preheat the cosori air fryer to 325 F.
2. Add all ingredients in a mixing bowl and mix until well combined.
3. Pour mixture in air fryer safe dish.
4. Place dish in the air fryer basket and cook for 20 minutes.
5. Serve and enjoy.

Nutritional Value (Amount per Serving):
Calories 258; Fat 19.8 g; Carbohydrates 2.5 g; Sugar 0.3 g; Protein 17.2 g; Cholesterol 88 mg

Chapter 8: Seafood Recipes

Easy Cajun Shrimp

Preparation Time: 10 minutes; Cooking Time: 6 minutes; Serve: 2
Ingredients:
- 1/2 lb shrimp, peeled and deveined
- 1 tbsp olive oil
- 1/4 tsp paprika
- 1/2 tsp old bay seasoning
- 1/2 tsp cayenne pepper
- Pinch of salt

Directions:
1. Preheat the cosori air fryer to 390 F.
2. Add shrimp and remaining ingredients into the mixing bowl and toss well to coat.
3. Add shrimp into the air fryer basket and cook for 6 minutes.
4. Serve and enjoy.

Nutritional Value (Amount per Serving):
Calories 197; Fat 9 g; Carbohydrates 2.1 g; Sugar 0.1 g; Protein 25.9 g; Cholesterol 239 mg

Tender & Juicy Salmon

Preparation Time: 10 minutes; Cooking Time: 7 minutes; Serve: 2
Ingredients:
- 2 salmon fillets
- 2 tsp paprika
- 2 tsp olive oil
- Pepper
- Salt

Directions:
1. Rub salmon fillets with oil, paprika, pepper, and salt.
2. Place fillets into the air fryer basket and cook at 390 F for 7 minutes.
3. Serve and enjoy.

Nutritional Value (Amount per Serving):
Calories 282; Fat 15.9 g; Carbohydrates 1.2 g; Sugar 0.2 g; Protein 34.9 g; Cholesterol 78 mg

Shrimp & Vegetable Dinner

Preparation Time: 10 minutes; Cooking Time: 10 minutes; Serve: 4
Ingredients:
- 1 lb jumbo shrimp, cleaned & peeled
- 2 tbsp olive oil
- 1 bell pepper, cut into 1-inch pieces
- 8 oz yellow squash, sliced into 1/4-inch half moons
- 1 medium zucchini, sliced into 1/4-inch half moons
- 6 oz sausage, cooked and sliced
- 1 tbsp Cajun seasoning
- 1/4 tsp kosher salt

Directions:
1. Add shrimp and remaining ingredients into the large mixing bowl and toss well to coat.
2. Preheat the cosori air fryer to 400 F.
3. Add shrimp mixture into the air fryer basket and cook for 10 minutes. Shake air fryer basket 3 times.
4. Serve and enjoy.

Nutritional Value (Amount per Serving):
Calories 312; Fat 19.3 g; Carbohydrates 5.8 g; Sugar 5.4 g; Protein 30.1 g; Cholesterol 269 mg

Lemon Garlic Shrimp

Preparation Time: 10 minutes; Cooking Time: 15 minutes; Serve: 3
Ingredients:

- 1 lb shrimp, peeled and deveined
- 1/4 tsp garlic powder
- 1 tbsp olive oil
- 1/2 fresh lemon
- 2 tbsp fresh parsley, chopped
- Pepper
- Salt

Directions:
1. Toss shrimp with garlic powder, olive oil, pepper, and salt.
2. Add shrimp into the air fryer basket and cook at 400 F for 12-15 minutes. Shake basket halfway through.
3. Transfer shrimp to the serving bowl.
4. Squeeze lemon juice over shrimp.
5. Garnish with parsley and serve.

Nutritional Value (Amount per Serving):
Calories 224; Fat 7.3 g; Carbohydrates 3.6 g; Sugar 0.3 g; Protein 34.7 g; Cholesterol 318 mg

Lemon Garlic White Fish

Preparation Time: 10 minutes; Cooking Time: 10 minutes; Serve: 2
Ingredients:
- 12 oz white fish fillets
- 1/2 tsp onion powder
- 1/2 tsp lemon pepper seasoning
- 1/2 tsp garlic powder
- Pepper
- Salt

Directions:
1. Preheat the cosori air fryer to 360 F.
2. Spray fish fillets with cooking spray and season with onion powder, lemon pepper seasoning, garlic powder, pepper, and salt.
3. Place parchment paper in the bottom of the air fryer basket. Place fish fillets into the air fryer basket and cook for 6-10 minutes.
4. Serve and enjoy.

Nutritional Value (Amount per Serving):
Calories 298; Fat 12.8 g; Carbohydrates 1.4 g; Sugar 0.4 g; Protein 41.9 g; Cholesterol 131 mg

Easy Coconut Shrimp

Preparation Time: 10 minutes; Cooking Time: 8 minutes; Serve: 8
Ingredients:
- 2 eggs, lightly beaten
- 1 lb large shrimp, peeled and deveined
- 1 cup unsweetened flaked coconut
- 1/4 cup coconut flour

Directions:
1. In a small bowl, add coconut flour.
2. In a shallow bowl, add eggs. In a separate shallow bowl, add flakes coconut.
3. Coat shrimp with coconut flour then dip in eggs and finally coat with flaked coconut.
4. Spray air fryer basket with cooking spray.
5. Place coated shrimp into the air fryer basket and cook at 400 F for 6-8 minutes. Turn shrimp halfway through.
6. Serve and enjoy.

Nutritional Value (Amount per Serving):
Calories 112; Fat 4.8 g; Carbohydrates 5.1 g; Sugar 0.7 g; Protein 12.9 g; Cholesterol 122 mg

Parmesan White Fish Fillets

Preparation Time: 10 minutes; Cooking Time: 10 minutes; Serve: 4
Ingredients:

- 1 lb white fish fillets
- 1/2 tsp lemon pepper seasoning
- 1/4 cup parmesan cheese
- 1/4 cup coconut flour

Directions:
1. In a shallow dish, mix together coconut flour, parmesan cheese, and lemon pepper seasoning.
2. Spray white fish fillets from both sides with cooking spray.
3. Coat fish fillets with coconut flour mixture.
4. Place coated fish fillets into the air fryer basket and cook at 400 F for 10 minutes. Turn fish fillets halfway through.
5. Serve and enjoy.

Nutritional Value (Amount per Serving):
- Calories 220; Fat 10 g; Carbohydrates 0.9 g; Sugar 0.1 g; Protein 29.9 g;

Tasty Shrimp Fajitas

Preparation Time: 10 minutes; Cooking Time: 22 minutes; Serve: 12
Ingredients:
- 1 lb shrimp, tail-off
- 2 tbsp taco seasoning
- 1/2 cup onion, diced
- 1 green bell pepper, diced
- 1 red bell pepper, diced

Directions:
1. Spray air fryer basket with cooking spray.
2. Add shrimp, taco seasoning, onion, and bell peppers into the mixing bowl and toss well.
3. Place shrimp mixture into the air fryer basket and cook at 390 F for 12 minutes.
4. Stir shrimp mixture and cook for 10 minutes more.
5. Serve and enjoy.

Nutritional Value (Amount per Serving):
Calories 55; Fat 0.8 g; Carbohydrates 2.7 g; Sugar 1.2 g; Protein 9 g; Cholesterol 80 mg

Ginger Garlic Salmon

Preparation Time: 10 minutes; Cooking Time: 10 minutes; Serve: 2
Ingredients:
- 2 salmon fillets, boneless and skinless
- 2 tbsp mirin
- 2 tbsp soy sauce
- 1 tbsp olive oil
- 2 tbsp scallions, minced
- 1 tbsp ginger, grated
- 2 garlic cloves, minced

Directions:
1. Add salmon fillets into the zip-lock bag.
2. In a small bowl, mix together mirin, soy sauce, olive oil, scallions, ginger, and garlic and pour over salmon. Seal bag shake well and place it in the refrigerator for 30 minutes.
3. Place marinated salmon fillets into the air fryer basket and cook at 360 F for 10 minutes.
4. Serve and enjoy.

Nutritional Value (Amount per Serving):
Calories 345; Fat 18.2 g; Carbohydrates 11.6 g; Sugar 4.5 g; Protein 36.1 g; Cholesterol 78 mg

Tasty Chipotle Shrimp

Preparation Time: 10 minutes; Cooking Time: 8 minutes; Serve: 4
Ingredients:
- 1 1/2 lbs shrimp, peeled and deveined
- 2 tbsp olive oil
- 4 tbsp lime juice
- 1/4 tsp ground cumin

- 2 tsp chipotle in adobo

Directions:
1. Add shrimp, oil, lime juice, cumin, and chipotle in a zip-lock bag. Seal bag shake well and place it in the refrigerator for 30 minutes.
2. Thread marinated shrimp onto skewers and place skewers into the air fryer basket.
3. Cook at 350 F for 8 minutes.
4. Serve and enjoy.

Nutritional Value (Amount per Serving):
Calories 274; Fat 10 g; Carbohydrates 6.4 g; Sugar 0.7 g; Protein 39 g; Cholesterol 359 mg

Quick & Easy Salmon

Preparation Time: 10 minutes; Cooking Time: 12 minutes; Serve: 2

Ingredients:
- 2 salmon fillets
- 1/2 tsp hot sauce
- 3 tbsp coconut aminos
- 1 garlic clove, minced
- 1 tsp ginger, grated
- 1 tsp sesame seeds, toasted

Directions:
1. Add salmon fillets into the zip-lock bag.
2. Mix together hot sauce, coconut aminos, garlic, and ginger and pour over salmon. Seal bag and place in the refrigerator for 30 minutes.
3. Place marinated salmon fillets into the air fryer basket and cook at 400 F for 6 minutes.
4. Turn salmon and brush with marinade and cook for 6 minutes more or until cooked.
5. Serve and enjoy.

Nutritional Value (Amount per Serving):
Calories 272; Fat 11.8 g; Carbohydrates 6 g; Sugar 0.1 g; Protein 35 g; Cholesterol 78 mg

Healthy Salmon Patties

Preparation Time: 10 minutes; Cooking Time: 7 minutes; Serve: 2

Ingredients:
- 8 oz salmon fillet, minced
- 1/4 tsp garlic powder
- 1 egg, lightly beaten
- 1 lemon, sliced
- 1/8 tsp salt

Directions:
1. In a bowl, mix together mince salon, garlic powder, egg, and salt until well combined.
2. Make two patties from the salmon mixture.
3. Preheat the cosori air fryer to 390 F.
4. Place lemon sliced lemon on the bottom of the air fryer basket then place salmon patties on top.
5. Cook salmon patties for 7 minutes.
6. Serve and enjoy.

Nutritional Value (Amount per Serving):
Calories 191; Fat 9.3 g; Carbohydrates 3.1 g; Sugar 1 g; Protein 25.2 g; Cholesterol 132 mg

Garlic Yogurt Salmon Fillets

Preparation Time: 10 minutes; Cooking Time: 15 minutes; Serve: 2

Ingredients:
- 2 salmon fillets
- 1/2 tsp garlic powder
- 1/4 cup Greek yogurt
- 1 tsp fresh lemon juice
- 1 tbsp fresh dill, chopped
- 1 lemon, sliced
- Pepper
- Salt

Directions:
1. Place lemon slices in the bottom of the air fryer basket.
2. Season salmon fillets with pepper and salt and place on a lemon slice in the air fryer basket.
3. Cook salmon fillets at 330 F for 15 minutes.
4. Place cooked salmon fillets on a serving plate.
5. Mix together yogurt, dill, lemon juice, and garlic powder.
6. Pour yogurt mixture overcooked salmon and serve.

Nutritional Value (Amount per Serving):
Calories 277; Fat 11.9 g; Carbohydrates 5.6 g; Sugar 2.4 g; Protein 38.8 g; Cholesterol 80 mg

Lime Garlic Shrimp Kababs

Preparation Time: 10 minutes; Cooking Time: 8 minutes; Serve: 2
Ingredients:
- 1 cup raw shrimp
- 1 lime juice
- 1 garlic cloves, minced
- Pepper
- Salt

Directions:
1. Preheat the cosori air fryer to 350 F.
2. In a mixing bowl, mix together shrimp, lime juice, garlic, pepper, and salt.
3. Thread shrimp onto the skewers and place them into the air fryer basket and cook for 8 minutes. Turn halfway through.
4. Serve and enjoy.

Nutritional Value (Amount per Serving):
Calories 201; Fat 2.8 g; Carbohydrates 4.9 g; Sugar 0.4 g; Protein 37.2 g; Cholesterol 342 mg

Healthy Crab Cakes

Preparation Time: 10 minutes; Cooking Time: 10 minutes; Serve: 4
Ingredients:
- 8 oz lump crab meat
- 2 tbsp butter, melted
- 2 tsp Dijon mustard
- 1 tbsp mayonnaise
- 1 egg, lightly beaten
- 1/2 tsp old bay seasoning
- 1 green onion, sliced
- 2 tbsp parsley, chopped
- 1/4 cup almond flour
- Pepper
- Salt

Directions:
1. Add crab meat, mustard, mayonnaise, egg, old bay seasoning, green onion, parsley, almond flour, pepper, and salt into the mixing bowl and mix until well combined.
2. Make four equal shapes of patties from mixture and place on a waxed paper-lined dish and refrigerate for 30 minutes.
3. Brush melted butter over both sides of patties and place into the air fryer basket.
4. Cook patties at 350 F for 10 minutes. Turn halfway through.
5. Serve and enjoy.

Nutritional Value (Amount per Serving):
Calories 136; Fat 13.7 g; Carbohydrates 2.8 g; Sugar 0.5 g; Protein 10.3 g; Cholesterol 89 mg

Crisp Bacon Wrapped Scallops

Preparation Time: 10 minutes; Cooking Time: 8 minutes; Serve: 4
Ingredients:

- 16 scallops, clean and pat dry with paper towels
- 8 bacon slices, cut each slice in half
- Pepper
- Salt

Directions:
1. Preheat the cosori air fryer to 400 F.
2. Place bacon slices into the air fryer basket and cook for 3 minutes. Turn halfway through.
3. Wrap each scallop in bacon slice and secure with a toothpick. Season with pepper and salt.
4. Spray wrapped scallops with cooking spray and place into the air fryer basket.
5. Cook scallops for 8 minutes. Turn halfway through.
6. Serve and enjoy.

Nutritional Value (Amount per Serving):
Calories 311; Fat 16.8 g; Carbohydrates 3.4 g; Sugar 0 g; Protein 34.2 g; Cholesterol 81 mg

Parmesan Basil Salmon

Preparation Time: 10 minutes; Cooking Time: 7 minutes; Serve: 4
Ingredients:
- 4 salmon fillets
- 3 tbsp parmesan cheese, grated
- 5 fresh basil leaves, minced
- 3 tbsp mayonnaise
- 1/2 lemon juice
- Pepper
- Salt

Directions:
1. Preheat the cosori air fryer to 400 F.
2. Spray air fryer basket with cooking spray.
3. Season salmon with pepper, lemon juice, and salt.
4. In a small bowl, mix together chasse, basil, and mayonnaise.
5. Spread cheese mixture on top of salmon fillets. Place salmon fillets into the air fryer basket and cook for 7 minutes.
6. Serve and enjoy.

Nutritional Value (Amount per Serving):
Calories 316; Fat 17.1 g; Carbohydrates 3.2 g; Sugar 0.8 g; Protein 38.3 g; Cholesterol 89 mg

Crisp & Juicy Cajun Shrimp

Preparation Time: 10 minutes; Cooking Time: 10 minutes; Serve: 4
Ingredients:
- 1 lb shrimp, peeled and deveined
- 1 tbsp olive oil
- 1/2 tsp Cajun seasoning
- 1 garlic clove, minced
- Pepper
- Salt

Directions:
1. Add shrimp, oil, cajun seasoning, garlic, pepper, and salt into the mixing bowl. Toss well and place in the refrigerator for 1 hour.
2. Add shrimp mixture into the air fryer basket and cook at 350 F for 8-10 minutes. Turn halfway through.
3. Serve and enjoy.

Nutritional Value (Amount per Serving):
Calories 166; Fat 5.4 g; Carbohydrates 2 g; Sugar 0 g; Protein 25.9 g; Cholesterol 239 mg

Flavorful Curry Cod Fillets

Preparation Time: 10 minutes; Cooking Time: 10 minutes; Serve: 2
Ingredients:

- 2 cod fillets, defrosted and pat dry with a paper towel
- 1 tbsp Thai basil, sliced
- 1/8 tsp garlic powder
- 1/8 tsp paprika
- 1/4 tsp curry powder
- 1 tbsp butter, melted
- 1/8 tsp sea salt

Directions:
1. In a small bowl, mix together curry powder, garlic powder, paprika, and salt and set aside.
2. Line air fryer basket with aluminum foil.
3. Place cod fillets into the air fryer basket. Brush fillets with butter and sprinkles with dry spice mixture.
4. Cook at 360 F for 8 minutes. Drizzle with remaining butter and cook for 2 minutes more.
5. Garnish with basil and serve.

Nutritional Value (Amount per Serving):
Calories 143; Fat 6.8 g; Carbohydrates 0.4 g; Sugar 0.1 g; Protein 20.2 g; Cholesterol 70 mg

Delicious Buttery Shrimp

Preparation Time: 10 minutes; Cooking Time: 6 minutes; Serve: 4
Ingredients:
- 12 large shrimp, peeled and deveined
- 3 garlic cloves, minced
- 3 tbsp butter, melted
- Pepper
- Salt

Directions:
1. Preheat the cosori air fryer to 360 F.
2. In a bowl, add shrimp, garlic, butter, pepper, and salt and marinate shrimp for 15 minutes.
3. Remove shrimp from marinade and place into the air fryer basket and cook for 6 minutes.
4. Pour reserved marinade over shrimp and serve.

Nutritional Value (Amount per Serving):
Calories 99; Fat 8.9 g; Carbohydrates 1 g; Sugar 0 g; Protein 4 g; Cholesterol 58 mg

Mexican Shrimp Fajitas

Preparation Time: 10 minutes; Cooking Time: 8 minutes; Serve: 4
Ingredients:
- 1 lb jumbo shrimp, peeled and deveined
- 1 tsp chili powder
- 1 tsp paprika
- 1 oz fajita seasoning
- 2 garlic cloves, minced
- 1 tbsp olive oil
- 1 onion, sliced
- 1 yellow bell pepper, sliced
- 1 red bell pepper, sliced

Directions:
1. Add shrimp and remaining ingredients into the large mixing bowl and toss well.
2. Add shrimp mixture into the air fryer basket and cook at 400 F for 8 minutes. Shake basket halfway through.
3. Serve and enjoy.

Nutritional Value (Amount per Serving):
Calories 173; Fat 3.9 g; Carbohydrates 13.6 g; Sugar 6.3 g; Protein 21.4 g; Cholesterol 233 mg

Dukkah Crusted Salmon

Preparation Time: 10 minutes; Cooking Time: 10 minutes; Serve: 2
Ingredients:
- 1 tbsp dukkah
- 12 oz salmon fillets

- Pinch of salt

Directions:
1. Preheat the cosori air fryer to 390 F.
2. Season salmon with salt and sprinkle dukkah on top of salmon fillets.
3. Place salmon fillets into the air fryer basket and cook for 10 minutes.
4. Serve and enjoy.

Nutritional Value (Amount per Serving):
Calories 248; Fat 12.3 g; Carbohydrates 0.8 g; Sugar 0 g; Protein 33.8 g; Cholesterol 75 mg

Lemon Garlic Scallops

Preparation Time: 10 minutes; Cooking Time: 8 minutes; Serve: 4

Ingredients:
- 1 lb sea scallops, pat dry with paper towels
- 1 tsp fresh thyme
- 1 garlic clove, minced
- 2 tbsp fresh lemon juice
- 1/4 cup olive oil
- Pepper
- Salt

Directions:
1. Season scallops with pepper and salt.
2. Spray air fryer basket with cooking spray.
3. Add scallops into the air fryer basket and cook at 400 F for 5-8 minutes or until the internal temperature of scallops reaches 120 F.
4. Transfer scallops to the serving bowl.
5. Heat olive oil in a pan on medium heat. Add garlic and saute until garlic softens.
6. Add lemon juice and whisk until sauce is heated through.
7. Pour olive oil mixture overcooked scallops.
8. Garnish with thyme and serve.

Nutritional Value (Amount per Serving):
Calories 212; Fat 13.5 g; Carbohydrates 3.3 g; Sugar 0.2 g; Protein 19.2 g; Cholesterol 37 mg

Lemon Caper Scallops

Preparation Time: 10 minutes; Cooking Time: 6 minutes; Serve: 2

Ingredients:
- 8 large sea scallops, clean and pat dry with a paper towel
- 1/2 tsp garlic, chopped
- 1 tsp lemon zest, grated
- 2 tsp capers, chopped
- 2 tbsp fresh parsley, chopped
- 1/4 cup olive oil
- Pepper
- Salt

Directions:
1. Season scallops with pepper and salt.
2. Spray air fryer basket with cooking spray.
3. Place scallops into the air fryer basket and cook at 400 F for 6 minutes or until the internal temperature of scallops reaches 120 F.
4. In a small bowl, mix together oil, garlic, lemon zest, capers, and parsley and drizzle over scallops and serve.

Nutritional Value (Amount per Serving):
Calories 325; Fat 26.2 g; Carbohydrates 3.7 g; Sugar 0.1 g; Protein 20.4 g; Cholesterol 40 mg

Cajun Scallops

Preparation Time: 10 minutes; Cooking Time: 6 minutes; Serve: 1

Ingredients:

- 6 scallops, clean and pat dry with a paper towel
- 1/2 tsp Cajun seasoning
- Salt

Directions:
1. Preheat the cosori air fryer to 400 F.
2. Line air fryer basket with aluminum foil and spray with cooking spray.
3. Place scallops into the air fryer basket.
4. Season scallops with Cajun seasoning and salt and cooks for 6 minutes. Turn scallops halfway through.
5. Serve and enjoy.

Nutritional Value (Amount per Serving):
Calories 158; Fat 1.4 g; Carbohydrates 4.3 g; Sugar 0 g; Protein 30.2 g; Cholesterol 59 mg

Flavorful Crab Cakes

Preparation Time: 10 minutes; Cooking Time: 10 minutes; Serve: 4
Ingredients:
- 8 oz lump crab
- 1 tsp old bay seasoning
- 1 tbsp Dijon mustard
- 2 tbsp almond flour
- 2 tbsp mayonnaise
- 2 tbsp green onion, chopped
- 1/4 cup bell pepper, chopped
- Pepper
- Salt

Directions:
1. Add lump crab and remaining ingredients into the mixing bowl and mix until well combined.
2. Make four equal shapes of patties from mixture and place into the air fryer basket.
3. Spray top of patties with cooking spray.
4. Cook at 370 F for 10 minutes.
5. Serve and enjoy.

Nutritional Value (Amount per Serving):
Calories 156; Fat 14.2 g; Carbohydrates 6.7 g; Sugar 1.5 g; Protein 11.6 g; Cholesterol 34 mg

Herbed Salmon

Preparation Time: 10 minutes; Cooking Time: 5 minutes; Serve: 2
Ingredients:
- 8 oz salmon fillets
- 2 tbsp olive oil
- 1 tbsp lemon herb butter
- 1/4 tsp paprika
- 1 tsp Herb de Provence
- Pepper
- Salt

Directions:
1. In a small bowl, mix together paprika, Herb de Provence, pepper, and salt.
2. Rub salmon fillets with oil and spice mixture.
3. Place salmon fillets into the air fryer basket and cook at 390 F for 5-8 minutes.
4. Melt lemon herb butter and pour over salmon just before serving.

Nutritional Value (Amount per Serving):
Calories 305; Fat 24.2 g; Carbohydrates 1.2 g; Sugar 0 g; Protein 22.5 g; Cholesterol 58 mg

Quick & Easy Salmon Patties

Preparation Time: 10 minutes; Cooking Time: 8 minutes; Serve: 6
Ingredients:
- 14 oz can salmon, drain, remove bones, & mince
- 1 egg, lightly beaten
- 2 tbsp green onion, minced

- 3 tbsp fresh cilantro, chopped
- Pepper
- Salt

Directions:
1. Preheat the cosori air fryer to 360 F.
2. Add all ingredients into the mixing bowl and mix until well combined.
3. Lightly spray air fryer basket with cooking spray.
4. Make six equal shapes of patties from mixture and place into the air fryer basket.
5. Cook patties for 6-8 minutes. Turn halfway through.
6. Serve and enjoy.

Nutritional Value (Amount per Serving):
Calories 103; Fat 4.7 g; Carbohydrates 0.2 g; Sugar 0.1 g; Protein 14.1 g; Cholesterol 64 mg

Shrimp with Vegetables

Preparation Time: 10 minutes; Cooking Time: 10 minutes; Serve: 4

Ingredients:
- 1 lb shrimp, peeled and deveined
- 1 tsp ginger, minced
- 1 tsp garlic, minced
- 2 tsp sesame oil
- 2 tbsp olive oil
- 4 tbsp soy sauce
- 1 lb mushrooms, quartered
- 1 green bell pepper, sliced
- 1 lb zucchini, cut into quarter-inch pieces

Directions:
1. Preheat the cosori air fryer to 400 F.
2. Add shrimp and remaining ingredients into the mixing bowl and toss well.
3. Add shrimp mixture into the air fryer basket and cook for 10 minutes. Shake basket halfway through.
4. Serve and enjoy.

Nutritional Value (Amount per Serving):
Calories 278; Fat 11.8 g; Carbohydrates 13.3 g; Sugar 5.7 g; Protein 32.1 g; Cholesterol 239 mg

Nutritious Salmon Fillets

Preparation Time: 10 minutes; Cooking Time: 10 minutes; Serve: 2

Ingredients:
- 2 salmon fillets
- 1/2 tsp paprika
- Pinch of ground cardamom
- Pepper
- Salt

Directions:
1. Preheat the cosori air fryer to 350 F.
2. Spray salmon fillets with cooking spray and season with paprika, cardamom, pepper, and salt.
3. Place salmon fillets into the air fryer basket and cook for 8-10 minutes or until cooked. Turn salmon fillets halfway through.
4. Serve and enjoy.

Nutritional Value (Amount per Serving):
Calories 238; Fat 11.1 g; Carbohydrates 0.4 g; Sugar 0.1 g; Protein 34.6 g; Cholesterol 78 mg

Onion Pepper Shrimp

Preparation Time: 10 minutes; Cooking Time: 12 minutes; Serve: 4

Ingredients:

- 1 lb shrimp, peeled, deveined, & tails removed
- 1/8 tsp cayenne pepper
- 1/2 tsp garlic powder
- 1 tsp chili powder
- 1 tbsp olive oil
- 1/2 onion, cut into 1-inch chunks
- 1 red bell pepper, cut into 1-inch chunks
- Pepper
- Salt

Directions:
1. Add shrimp and remaining ingredients into the mixing bowl and toss well.
2. Add shrimp mixture into the air fryer basket and cook at 330 F for 10-12 minutes. Shake air fryer basket halfway through.
3. Serve and enjoy.

Nutritional Value (Amount per Serving):
Calories 183; Fat 5.6 g; Carbohydrates 5.9 g; Sugar 2.2 g; Protein 26.4 g; Cholesterol 239 mg

Old Bay Shrimp

Preparation Time: 10 minutes; Cooking Time: 10 minutes; Serve: 4
Ingredients:
- 12 oz shrimp, peeled
- 3.25 oz pork rind, crushed
- 1 1/2 tsp old bay seasoning
- 1/4 cup mayonnaise

Directions:
1. Spray air fryer basket with cooking spray.
2. In a shallow bowl, mix together crushed pork rind and old bay seasoning.
3. Add shrimp and mayonnaise into the mixing bowl and toss well.
4. Coat shrimp with pork rind mixture and place it into the air fryer basket.
5. Cook shrimp at 380 F for 10 minutes.
6. Serve and enjoy.

Nutritional Value (Amount per Serving):
Calories 290; Fat 14.6 g; Carbohydrates 4.8 g; Sugar 0.9 g; Protein 34.3 g; Cholesterol 216 mg

Crunchy Fish Sticks

Preparation Time: 10 minutes; Cooking Time: 15 minutes; Serve: 4
Ingredients:
- 12 oz tilapia fillets, cut into fish sticks
- 1/2 cup parmesan cheese, grated
- 3.25 oz pork rind, crushed
- 1 tsp paprika
- 1 tsp garlic powder
- 1/4 cup mayonnaise

Directions:
1. In a shallow bowl, mix together crushed pork rind, garlic powder, paprika, and parmesan cheese.
2. In a mixing bowl, mix together fish sticks and mayonnaise.
3. Coat fish sticks with pork rind mixture and place into the air fryer basket.
4. Cook fish sticks at 380 F for 15 minutes.
5. Serve and enjoy.

Nutritional Value (Amount per Serving):
Calories 303; Fat 16.7 g; Carbohydrates 4.8 g; Sugar 1.2 g; Protein 35 g; Cholesterol 87 mg

Juicy & Tender Cod Fillets

Preparation Time: 10 minutes; Cooking Time: 12 minutes; Serve: 2
Ingredients:
- 1 lb cod fillets
- 1/4 cup butter, melted

- 1 lemon, sliced
- 1 tsp salt

Directions:
1. Brush cod fillets with melted butter and season with salt.
2. Place cod fillets into the air fryer basket and top with sliced lemon.
3. Cook at 400 F for 10-12 minutes or until the internal temperature of fish fillets reaches 145 F.
4. Serve and enjoy.

Nutritional Value (Amount per Serving):
Calories 394; Fat 25.1 g; Carbohydrates 2.7 g; Sugar 0.8 g; Protein 41.1 g; Cholesterol 172 mg

Flavorful Parmesan Shrimp

Preparation Time: 10 minutes; Cooking Time: 10 minutes; Serve: 6

Ingredients:
- 2 lbs jumbo shrimp, peeled and deveined
- 2 tbsp olive oil
- 1 tsp onion powder
- 1 tsp basil
- 1/2 tsp oregano
- 2/3 cup parmesan cheese, grated
- 1 tbsp garlic, minced
- Pepper
- Salt

Directions:
1. Spray air fryer basket with cooking spray.
2. In a mixing bowl, mix together parmesan cheese, garlic, oregano, basil, onion powder, oil, pepper, and salt.
3. Add shrimp into the bowl and toss well to coat.
4. Place shrimp into the air fryer basket and cook at 350 F for 10 minutes.
5. Serve and enjoy.

Nutritional Value (Amount per Serving):
Calories 187; Fat 7 g; Carbohydrates 1.3 g; Sugar 2.9 g; Protein 30.6 g; Cholesterol 318 mg

Perfectly Tender Frozen Fish Fillets

Preparation Time: 10 minutes; Cooking Time: 12 minutes; Serve: 4

Ingredients:
- 4 tilapia fish fillets, frozen
- 1 lemon, sliced
- 1/2 tsp onion powder
- 1/2 tsp garlic powder
- 1/2 tsp lemon pepper seasoning
- 1/2 tsp salt

Directions:
1. Spray air fryer basket with cooking spray.
2. Season tilapia fillets with onion powder, garlic powder, lemon pepper seasoning, and salt.
3. Place tilapia fillets into the air fryer basket and top with lemon slices.
4. Cook at 390 F for 12 minutes.
5. Serve and enjoy.

Nutritional Value (Amount per Serving):
Calories 116; Fat 2 g; Carbohydrates 2 g; Sugar 0.6 g; Protein 22.9 g; Cholesterol 56 mg

Old Bay Seasoned Crab Cakes

Preparation Time: 10 minutes; Cooking Time: 10 minutes; Serve: 5

Ingredients:
- 2 eggs
- 1/4 cup almond flour
- 2 tsp dried parsley
- 1 tbsp dried celery
- 1 tsp old bay seasoning
- 1 1/2 tbsp Dijon mustard

- 2 1/2 tbsp mayonnaise
- 18 oz can lump crab meat, drained
- 1/2 tsp salt

Directions:
1. Line air fryer basket with aluminum foil.
2. Add all ingredients into the mixing bowl and mix until well combined. Place mixture in the refrigerator for 10 minutes.
3. Make five equal shapes of patties from mixture and place onto the aluminum foil in the air fryer basket.
4. Cook at 320 F for 10 minutes. Turn patties halfway through.
5. Serve and enjoy.

Nutritional Value (Amount per Serving):
Calories 139; Fat 13.3 g; Carbohydrates 4.2 g; Sugar 0.7 g; Protein 17.6 g; Cholesterol 125 mg

Simple & Perfect Shrimp

Preparation Time: 10 minutes; Cooking Time: 8 minutes; Serve: 4

Ingredients:
- 1 lb large shrimp, peeled, deveined, and tails removed
- 2 tbsp parmesan cheese, grated
- 1/2 tsp garlic granules
- 1 tsp fresh lemon juice
- 1 tbsp butter, melted
- Pepper
- Salt

Directions:
1. Line air fryer basket with parchment paper.
2. In a mixing bowl, mix together garlic, lemon juice, butter, pepper, and salt. Add shrimp and toss to coat.
3. Add shrimp into the air fryer basket and top with parmesan cheese.
4. Cook shrimp at 400 F for 8 minutes.
5. Serve and enjoy.

Nutritional Value (Amount per Serving):
Calories 140; Fat 4.4 g; Carbohydrates 2.5 g; Sugar 0 g; Protein 23.6 g; Cholesterol 175 mg

Asian Salmon Steak

Preparation Time: 10 minutes; Cooking Time: 18 minutes; Serve: 2

Ingredients:
- 2 salmon steaks
- 2 tbsp sesame oil
- 3 tbsp garlic paste
- 2 tbsp rice vinegar
- 3 tbsp Worcestershire sauce
- 1/2 tsp kosher salt

Directions:
1. Add salmon steaks into the zip-lock bag.
2. In a small bowl, mix together sesame oil, garlic paste, vinegar, Worcestershire sauce, and salt and pour over salmon steaks.
3. Seal ziplock bag and place in the refrigerator for 1 hour.
4. Spray air fryer basket with cooking spray.
5. Remove salmon steaks from marinade and place it into the air fryer basket.
6. Cook at 400 F for 15 minutes. Turn salmon steaks and brush with reserved marinade and cook for 3 minutes more.
7. Serve and enjoy.

Nutritional Value (Amount per Serving):
Calories 343; Fat 21.7 g; Carbohydrates 8.7 g; Sugar 4.6 g; Protein 26 g; Cholesterol 57 mg

Delicious Fish Bites

Preparation Time: 10 minutes; Cooking Time: 10 minutes; Serve: 4

Ingredients:
- 10 oz haddock
- 1 tsp paprika
- 1 tsp onion powder
- 1 tbsp dill pickle relish
- 1 tbsp mayonnaise
- 1/4 cup coconut flour
- 2 eggs, lightly beaten
- Pepper
- Salt

Directions:
1. Add fish fillet into the food processor and process until a paste is formed.
2. Add remaining ingredients and process for 1 minute.
3. Place mixture into the refrigerator for 10 minutes.
4. Make small balls from mixture and place into the air fryer basket. Spray the top of fish balls.
5. Cook at 350 F for 10 minutes. Turn halfway through.
6. Serve and enjoy.

Nutritional Value (Amount per Serving):
Calories 138; Fat 4.3 g; Carbohydrates 3.7 g; Sugar 1.8 g; Protein 20.3 g; Cholesterol 135 mg

Chili Lime Cod

Preparation Time: 10 minutes; Cooking Time: 13 minutes; Serve: 2

Ingredients:
- 2 cod fillets
- 1 lime zest
- 1 tbsp olive oil
- 1/8 tsp cayenne pepper
- 1/4 tsp ground cumin
- 1/2 tsp garlic powder
- 1/2 tsp chili powder
- 1/2 tsp dried oregano
- 1 tsp dried parsley
- 1 tsp paprika
- 1/4 tsp pepper

Directions:
1. Line air fryer basket with parchment paper.
2. In a small bowl, mix together cayenne pepper, cumin, garlic powder, chili powder, oregano, parsley, paprika, and pepper.
3. Brush cod fillets with oil and rub with spice mixture and place in the refrigerator for 30 minutes.
4. Preheat the cosori air fryer to 380 F.
5. Place cod fillets in the air fryer basket and cook for 8-13 minutes or until the internal temperature of fish fillet reaches 145 F.
6. Garnish fish fillets with lime zest and serve.

Nutritional Value (Amount per Serving):
Calories 161; Fat 8.4 g; Carbohydrates 2.3 g; Sugar 0.4 g; Protein 20.5 g; Cholesterol 55 mg

Savory Fish Sticks

Preparation Time: 10 minutes; Cooking Time: 15 minutes; Serve: 4

Ingredients:
- 1 lb tilapia fish fillets, cut into fish stick shape
- 1/2 tsp old bay seasoning
- 1 egg, lightly beaten
- 2 oz pork rind, crushed
- 1/2 cup almond flour
- Pepper
- Salt

Directions:
1. Preheat the cosori air fryer to 350 F.

2. Add almond flour in a shallow dish.
3. In a shallow bowl, add the egg. In a separate shallow bowl, add crushed pork rind.
4. Season fish stick with old bay seasoning, pepper, and salt.
5. Coat fish stick with almond flour then dip in egg and finally coat with pork rind.
6. Place coated fish sticks into the air fryer basket and cook for 12-15 minutes.
7. Serve and enjoy.

Nutritional Value (Amount per Serving):
Calories 217; Fat 10.4 g; Carbohydrates 0.9 g; Sugar 0.2 g; Protein 31.2 g; Cholesterol 101 mg

Garlic Herb Tilapia

Preparation Time: 10 minutes; Cooking Time: 10 minutes; Serve: 2

Ingredients:
- 12 oz tilapia fillets
- 1 tsp garlic, minced
- 2 tsp fresh parsley, chopped
- 2 tsp fresh chives, chopped
- 2 tsp olive oil
- Pepper
- Salt

Directions:
1. Preheat the cosori air fryer to 400 F.
2. In a small bowl, mix together oil, chives, parsley, garlic, pepper, and salt.
3. Brush oil mixture over tilapia fillets.
4. Place tilapia fillets into the air fryer basket and cook for 8-10 minutes.
5. Serve and enjoy.

Nutritional Value (Amount per Serving):
Calories 183; Fat 6.2 g; Carbohydrates 0.6 g; Sugar 0 g; Protein 31.8 g; Cholesterol 83 mg

Parmesan Salmon

Preparation Time: 10 minutes; Cooking Time: 8 minutes; Serve: 4

Ingredients:
- 4 salmon fillets
- 1 tsp herb garlic seasoning
- 1/4 cup parmesan cheese, shredded
- 1/4 cup mayonnaise

Directions:
1. Brush top of salmon fillets with mayonnaise and season with herb garlic seasoning. Top with shredded parmesan cheese.
2. Place salmon fillets into the air fryer basket and cook at 380 F for 8 minutes.
3. Serve and enjoy.

Nutritional Value (Amount per Serving):
Calories 318; Fat 17.2 g; Carbohydrates 4.7 g; Sugar 0.9 g; Protein 37.7 g; Cholesterol 87 mg

Easy Bacon Wrapped Shrimp

Preparation Time: 10 minutes; Cooking Time: 8 minutes; Serve: 6

Ingredients:
- 8 oz shrimp, thawed, peeled, deveined & tail off
- 8 bacon slices, cut in half
- 1 tsp Cajun seasoning
- 1 tbsp olive oil

Directions:
1. Add shrimp, Cajun seasoning, and oil into the mixing bowl and toss well.
2. Wrap one bacon slice around each shrimp and place into the air fryer basket.
3. Cook at 370 F for 6-8 minutes. Turn halfway through.
4. Serve and enjoy.

Nutritional Value (Amount per Serving):
 Calories 202; Fat 13.6 g; Carbohydrates 0.9 g; Sugar 0 g; Protein 18 g; Cholesterol 107 mg

Cajun Tilapia

Preparation Time: 10 minutes; Cooking Time: 12 minutes; Serve: 4
Ingredients:
- 4 tilapia fillets
- 1/2 lemon
- 1 tbsp olive oil
- 1 tbsp Cajun seasoning

Directions:
1. Brush both sides of fish fillets with oil and season with Cajun seasoning.
2. Preheat the cosori air fryer to 400 F.
3. Spray air fryer basket with cooking spray.
4. Place fish fillets into the air fryer basket and cook for 8-12 minutes. Turn fish fillets halfway through.
5. Squeeze lemon juice over fish fillets and serve.

Nutritional Value (Amount per Serving):
 Calories 125; Fat 4.5 g; Carbohydrates 0.7 g; Sugar 0.2 g; Protein 21.1 g; Cholesterol 55 mg

Easy Tuna Steaks

Preparation Time: 10 minutes; Cooking Time: 10 minutes; Serve: 2
Ingredients:
- 1 lb tuna steaks
- 6 garlic cloves, chopped
- 4 tbsp olive oil
- 1 tbsp garlic powder
- 1 tsp thyme
- Pepper
- Salt

Directions:
1. Marinate tuna steaks with garlic, oil, garlic powder, thyme, pepper, and salt and place in the refrigerator for 15 minutes.
2. Place marinated tuna steaks into the air fryer basket and cook at 400 F for 8-10 minutes.
3. Serve and enjoy.

Nutritional Value (Amount per Serving):
 Calories 686; Fat 42.4 g; Carbohydrates 6.4 g; Sugar 1.1 g; Protein 69.2 g; Cholesterol 111 mg

Healthy Tuna Patties

Preparation Time: 10 minutes; Cooking Time: 10 minutes; Serve: 2
Ingredients:
- 2 cans tuna, packed in water
- 1/2 lemon juice
- 1/2 tsp onion powder
- 1 tsp dried dill
- 1 1/2 tbsp mayonnaise
- 1 1/2 tbsp almond flour
- Pepper
- Salt

Directions:
1. Add all ingredients into the mixing bowl and mix until well combined.
2. Make four equal shapes of patties from mixture and place into the air fryer basket.
3. Preheat the cosori air fryer to 400 F.
4. Place tuna patties into the air fryer basket and cook for 10 minutes.
5. Serve and enjoy.

Nutritional Value (Amount per Serving):
 Calories 500; Fat 28.7 g; Carbohydrates 8.2 g; Sugar 1.9 g; Protein 52.1 g; Cholesterol 58 mg

Tuna Zucchini Cakes

Preparation Time: 10 minutes; Cooking Time: 20 minutes; Serve: 8
Ingredients:
- 12 oz can tuna, drained
- 1 medium zucchini, shredded and squeeze out all liquid
- 1 tsp garlic powder
- 1 tsp onion powder
- 3 egg yolks
- 1/3 cup almond flour
- Salt

Directions:
1. Add all ingredients into the mixing bowl and mix until well combined.
2. Preheat the cosori air fryer to 350 F.
3. Make small patties from mixture and place into the air fryer basket and cook for 20 minutes or until done. Turn patties halfway through.
4. Serve and enjoy.

Nutritional Value (Amount per Serving):
Calories 82; Fat 2.7 g; Carbohydrates 1.8 g; Sugar 0.7 g; Protein 12.5 g; Cholesterol 91 mg

Pesto Scallops

Preparation Time: 10 minutes; Cooking Time: 8 minutes; Serve: 4
Ingredients:
- 1 lb sea scallops
- 2 tsp garlic, minced
- 3 tbsp heavy cream
- 1/4 cup basil pesto
- 1 tbsp olive oil
- Pepper
- Salt

Directions:
1. In a small pan, mix together oil, heavy cream, garlic, basil pesto, pepper, and salt, and simmer for 2-3 minutes.
2. Add scallops into the air fryer basket and cook at 320 F for 5 minutes.
3. Turn scallops and cook for 3 minutes more.
4. Transfer scallops into the mixing bowl. Pour sauce over the scallops and toss to coat.
5. Serve and enjoy.

Nutritional Value (Amount per Serving):
Calories 171; Fat 8.5 g; Carbohydrates 3.5 g; Sugar 0 g; Protein 19.4 g; Cholesterol 53 mg

Pesto Shrimp Kebabs

Preparation Time: 10 minutes; Cooking Time: 5 minutes; Serve: 6
Ingredients:
- 1 lb shrimp, defrosted
- 16 oz basil pesto
- Pepper
- Salt

Directions:
1. Spray air fryer basket into the cooking spray.
2. In a mixing bowl, mix together shrimp, pesto, pepper, and salt.
3. Thread shrimp onto the skewers and place skewers into the air fryer basket.
4. Cook at 400 F for 5 minutes.
5. Serve and enjoy.

Nutritional Value (Amount per Serving):
Calories 107; Fat 1.8 g; Carbohydrates 3.2 g; Sugar 0.2 g; Protein 19.6 g; Cholesterol 159 mg

Flavorful Horseradish Salmon

Preparation Time: 10 minutes; Cooking Time: 7 minutes; Serve: 4
Ingredients:

- 4 salmon fillets
- 1/4 cup almond flour
- 2 tbsp olive oil
- 1 tbsp horseradish
- Pepper
- salt

Directions:
1. In a small bowl, mix together almond flour, oil, horseradish, pepper, and salt and spread on top of salmon fillets.
2. Place salmon fillets into the air fryer basket and cook at 400 F for 5-7 minutes or until cooked.
3. Serve and enjoy.

Nutritional Value (Amount per Serving):
Calories 307; Fat 18.9 g; Carbohydrates 0.8 g; Sugar 0.4 g; Protein 35 g; Cholesterol 78 mg

Lemon Garlic Herb Salmon

Preparation Time: 10 minutes; Cooking Time: 10 minutes; Serve: 2

Ingredients:
- 2 salmon fillets
- 1 tsp lemon zest
- 1 tbsp lemon juice
- 1/2 tsp red pepper flakes
- 1 tsp Italian seasoning
- 2 tsp garlic, minced
- 2 tbsp butter, melted
- Pepper
- Salt

Directions:
1. In a small bowl, mix together butter, garlic, Italian seasoning, red pepper flakes, lemon juice, lemon zest, pepper, and salt.
2. Brush salmon fillets with melted butter and place into the air fryer basket.
3. Cook at 400 F for 10 minutes.
4. Serve and enjoy.

Nutritional Value (Amount per Serving):
Calories 353; Fat 23.4 g; Carbohydrates 1.9 g; Sugar 0.5 g; Protein 35 g; Cholesterol 111 mg

Spicy Scallops

Preparation Time: 10 minutes; Cooking Time: 8 minutes; Serve: 4

Ingredients:
- 1 lb scallops, thawed, washed, and pat dry with a paper towel
- 1 tsp garlic powder
- 1 tbsp chili powder
- 1 tbsp paprika
- 2 tbsp onion flakes
- Pepper
- Salt

Directions:
1. Spray air fryer basket with cooking spray.
2. In a mixing bowl, add scallops and remaining ingredients and toss well.
3. Add scallops into the air fryer basket and cook at 340 F for 8 minutes. Shake basket halfway through.
4. Serve and enjoy.

Nutritional Value (Amount per Serving):
Calories 122; Fat 1.4 g; Carbohydrates 7.3 g; Sugar 1.4 g; Protein 19.9 g; Cholesterol 37 mg

Spicy & Tasty Shrimp

Preparation Time: 10 minutes; Cooking Time: 5 minutes; Serve: 6

Ingredients:
- 2 lbs shrimp
- 4 tbsp olive oil
- 1 tsp paprika
- 1 tsp cayenne pepper

- 2 tsp old bay seasoning
- Salt

Directions:
1. Add all ingredients into the mixing bowl and toss well.
2. Preheat the cosori air fryer to 390 F.
3. Spray air fryer basket with cooking spray.
4. Add shrimp into the air fryer basket and cook for 5 minutes.
5. Serve and enjoy.

Nutritional Value (Amount per Serving):
Calories 262; Fat 12 g; Carbohydrates 2.7 g; Sugar 0.1 g; Protein 34.5 g; Cholesterol 318 mg

Thai Shrimp

Preparation Time: 10 minutes; Cooking Time: 10 minutes; Serve: 4

Ingredients:
- 1 lb shrimp, peeled and deveined
- 2 garlic cloves, minced
- 2 tbsp soy sauce
- 2 tbsp Thai chili sauce
- 1 tbsp arrowroot
- 1 tsp sesame seeds
- 1 tbsp green onion, sliced
- 1/8 tsp ginger, minced

Directions:
1. Spray air fryer basket with cooking spray.
2. Toss shrimp with arrowroot and place into the air fryer basket.
3. Cook at 370 F for 5 minutes. Shake basket well and cook for 5 minutes more.
4. Meanwhile, in a mixing bowl, mix together soy sauce, ginger, garlic, and chili sauce. Add shrimp and toss well to coat.
5. Garnish with green onions and sesame seeds.
6. Serve and enjoy.

Nutritional Value (Amount per Serving):
Calories 157; Fat 2.3 g; Carbohydrates 5.9 g; Sugar 2.2 g; Protein 26.7 g; Cholesterol 239 mg

Chili Garlic Shrimp

Preparation Time: 10 minutes; Cooking Time: 7 minutes; Serve: 4

Ingredients:
- 1 lb shrimp, peeled and deveined
- 1 tbsp olive oil
- 1 lemon, sliced
- 1 red chili, sliced
- 1 tsp garlic powder
- Pepper
- Salt

Directions:
1. Preheat the cosori air fryer to 400 F.
2. Spray air fryer basket with cooking spray.
3. Add all ingredients into the large bowl and toss well.
4. Add shrimp mixture into the air fryer basket and cook for 5 minutes. Shake basket and cook for 2 minutes more.
5. Serve and enjoy.

Nutritional Value (Amount per Serving):
Calories 172; Fat 5.5 g; Carbohydrates 3.7 g; Sugar 0.6 g; Protein 26.1 g; Cholesterol 239 mg

Creamy Shrimp

Preparation Time: 10 minutes; Cooking Time: 8 minutes; Serve: 4

Ingredients:
- 1 lb shrimp, peeled
- 1 tbsp tomato ketchup, sugar-free
- 3 tbsp mayonnaise
- 1/2 tsp paprika

- 1 tsp sriracha
- 1 tbsp garlic, minced
- 1/2 tsp salt

Directions:
1. In a bowl, mix together mayonnaise, paprika, sriracha, garlic, ketchup, and salt. Add shrimp and stir well.
2. Spray air fryer basket with cooking spray.
3. Add shrimp into the air fryer basket and cook at 325 F for 8 minutes. Shake halfway through.
4. Serve and enjoy.

Nutritional Value (Amount per Serving):
Calories 187; Fat 5.7 g; Carbohydrates 6.4 g; Sugar 1.6 g; Protein 26.2 g; Cholesterol 242 mg

Simple Catfish Fillets

Preparation Time: 10 minutes; Cooking Time: 20 minutes; Serve: 4

Ingredients:
- 4 catfish fillets
- 1 tbsp olive oil
- 1 tbsp fish seasoning
- 1 tbsp fresh parsley, chopped

Directions:
1. Preheat the cosori air fryer to 400 F.
2. Brush fish fillets with oil and season with fish seasoning.
3. Place fish fillets into the air fryer basket and cook for 20 minutes. Turn halfway through.
4. Garnish with parsley and serve.

Nutritional Value (Amount per Serving):
Calories 252; Fat 15.7 g; Carbohydrates 1.2 g; Sugar 0 g; Protein 24.9 g; Cholesterol 75 mg

Salmon Avocado Patties

Preparation Time: 10 minutes; Cooking Time: 10 minutes; Serve: 4

Ingredients:
- 14 oz can salmon
- 2 eggs, lightly beaten
- 1/2 cup almond flour
- 1/2 onion, minced
- 1/4 cup butter
- 1/2 tsp pepper
- 1 avocado, diced
- 1 tsp salt

Directions:
1. Preheat the cosori air fryer at 400 F.
2. Spray air fryer basket with cooking spray.
3. Add all ingredients into the mixing bowl and mix until well combined.
4. Make four equal shapes of patties from mixture and place into the air fryer basket.
5. Cook patties for 10 minutes. Turn patties halfway through.
6. Serve and enjoy.

Nutritional Value (Amount per Serving):
Calories 400; Fat 31.3 g; Carbohydrates 6.7 g; Sugar 1.1 g; Protein 24.4 g; Cholesterol 167 mg

Chapter 9: Meatless Meals

Healthy Mixed Vegetables

Preparation Time: 10 minutes; Cooking Time: 10 minutes; Serve: 6
Ingredients:
- 2 cups mushrooms, cut in half
- 2 yellow squash, sliced
- 2 medium zucchini, sliced
- 3/4 tsp Italian seasoning
- 1/2 onion, sliced
- 1/2 cup olive oil
- 1/2 tsp garlic salt

Directions:
1. Add vegetables and remaining ingredients into the mixing bowl and toss well.
2. Add vegetables into the air fryer basket and cook at 400 F for 10 minutes. Shake basket halfway through.
3. Serve and enjoy.

Nutritional Value (Amount per Serving):
Calories 176; Fat 17.3 g; Carbohydrates 6.2 g; Sugar 3.2 g; Protein 2.5 g; Cholesterol 0 mg

=Easy Roasted Vegetables

Preparation Time: 10 minutes; Cooking Time: 18 minutes; Serve: 6
Ingredients:
- 1/2 cup mushrooms, sliced
- 1/2 cup zucchini, sliced
- 1/2 cup yellow squash, sliced
- 1/2 cup baby carrots
- 1 cup cauliflower florets
- 1 cup broccoli florets
- 1/4 cup parmesan cheese, grated
- 1 tsp red pepper flakes
- 1 tbsp garlic, minced
- 1 tbsp olive oil
- 1/4 cup balsamic vinegar
- 1 small onion, sliced
- 1 tsp sea salt

Directions:
1. Preheat the cosori air fryer to 400 F.
2. In a large mixing bowl, mix together olive oil, garlic, vinegar, red pepper flakes, pepper, and salt.
3. Add vegetables and toss until well coated.
4. Add vegetables into the air fryer basket and cook for 8 minutes. Shake basket and cook for 8 minutes more.
5. Add parmesan cheese and cook for 2 minutes more.
6. Serve and enjoy.

Nutritional Value (Amount per Serving):
Calories 59; Fat 3.4 g; Carbohydrates 5.3 g; Sugar 2 g; Protein 2.8 g; Cholesterol 3 mg

Easy & Crisp Brussels Sprouts

Preparation Time: 10 minutes; Cooking Time: 15 minutes; Serve: 4
Ingredients:
- 2 cups Brussels sprouts
- 2 tbsp everything bagel seasoning
- 1/4 cup almonds, crushed
- 1/4 cup parmesan cheese, grated
- 2 tbsp olive oil
- Salt

Directions:
1. Add Brussels sprouts into the saucepan with 2 cups of water. Cover and cook for 8-10 minutes.
2. Drain well and allow to cool completely. Sliced each Brussels sprouts in half.
3. Add Brussels sprouts and remaining ingredients into the mixing bowl and toss to coat.

4. Add Brussels sprouts mixture into the air fryer basket and cook at 375 F for 12-15 minutes.
5. Serve and enjoy.

Nutritional Value (Amount per Serving):
Calories 144; Fat 11.5 g; Carbohydrates 7.6 g; Sugar 1.4 g; Protein 5.1 g; Cholesterol 4 mg

Garlic Green Beans

Preparation Time: 10 minutes; Cooking Time: 8 minutes; Serve: 4

Ingredients:
- 1 lb fresh green beans, trimmed
- 1 tsp garlic powder
- 1 tbsp olive oil
- Pepper
- Salt

Directions:
1. Drizzle green beans with oil and season with garlic powder, pepper, and salt.
2. Place green beans into the air fryer basket and cook at 370 F for 8 minutes. Toss halfway through.
3. Serve and enjoy.

Nutritional Value (Amount per Serving):
Calories 68; Fat 3.7 g; Carbohydrates 8.6 g; Sugar 1.8 g; Protein 2.2 g; Cholesterol 0 mg

Simple Vegan Broccoli

Preparation Time: 10 minutes; Cooking Time: 5 minutes; Serve: 2

Ingredients:
- 4 cups broccoli florets
- 1 tbsp nutritional yeast
- 2 tbsp olive oil
- Pepper
- Salt

Directions:
1. In a medium bowl, mix together broccoli, nutritional yeast, oil, pepper, and salt.
2. Add broccoli florets into the air fryer basket and cook at 370 F for 5 minutes.
3. Serve and enjoy.

Nutritional Value (Amount per Serving):
Calories 158; Fat 14.3 g; Carbohydrates 6.3 g; Sugar 1 g; Protein 4.3 g; Cholesterol 0 mg

Sesame Carrots

Preparation Time: 10 minutes; Cooking Time: 7 minutes; Serve: 4

Ingredients:
- 2 cups carrots, sliced
- 1 tsp sesame seeds
- 1 tbsp scallions, chopped
- 1 tsp garlic, minced
- 1 tbsp soy sauce
- 1 tbsp ginger, minced
- 2 tbsp sesame oil

Directions:
1. In a medium bowl, mix together carrots, garlic, soy sauce, ginger, and sesame oil.
2. Add carrots mixture into the air fryer basket and cook at 375 for 7 minutes. Shake basket halfway through.
3. Garnish with scallions and sesame seeds and serve.

Nutritional Value (Amount per Serving):
Calories 95; Fat 7.3 g; Carbohydrates 7.2 g; Sugar 2.9 g; Protein 1 g; Cholesterol 0 mg

Asparagus with Almonds

Preparation Time: 10 minutes; Cooking Time: 5 minutes; Serve: 4

Ingredients:
- 12 asparagus spears
- 1/3 cup sliced almonds
- 2 tbsp olive oil
- 2 tbsp balsamic vinegar
- Pepper
- Salt

Directions:
1. Drizzle asparagus spears with oil and vinegar.
2. Arrange asparagus spears into the air fryer basket and season with pepper and salt.
3. Sprinkle sliced almond over asparagus spears.
4. Cook asparagus at 350 F for 5 minutes. Shake basket halfway through.
5. Serve and enjoy.

Nutritional Value (Amount per Serving):
Calories 122; Fat 11.1 g; Carbohydrates 4.6 g; Sugar 1.7 g; Protein 3.3 g; Cholesterol 0 mg

Easy Roasted Carrots

Preparation Time: 10 minutes; Cooking Time: 18 minutes; Serve: 4

Ingredients:
- 16 oz carrots, peeled and cut into 2-inch chunks
- 1 tsp olive oil
- Pepper
- Salt

Directions:
1. Preheat the cosori air fryer to 360 F.
2. Toss carrots with oil and season with pepper and salt.
3. Add carrots into the air fryer basket and cook for 15-18 minutes. Shake basket 3-4 times.
4. Serve and enjoy.

Nutritional Value (Amount per Serving):
Calories 57; Fat 1.2 g; Carbohydrates 11.2 g; Sugar 5.6 g; Protein 0.9 g; Cholesterol 0 mg

Asian Broccoli

Preparation Time: 10 minutes; Cooking Time: 20 minutes; Serve: 4

Ingredients:
- 1 lb broccoli florets
- 1 tsp rice vinegar
- 2 tsp sriracha
- 2 tbsp soy sauce
- 1 tbsp garlic, minced
- 1 1/2 tbsp sesame oil
- Salt

Directions:
1. Toss broccoli florets with garlic, sesame oil, and salt.
2. Add broccoli florets into the air fryer basket and cook at 400 F for 15-20 minutes. Shake basket halfway through.
3. In a mixing bowl, mix together rice vinegar, sriracha, and soy sauce. Add broccoli and toss well.
4. Serve and enjoy.

Nutritional Value (Amount per Serving):
Calories 94; Fat 5.5 g; Carbohydrates 9.3 g; Sugar 2.1 g; Protein 3.8 g Cholesterol 0 mg

Healthy Squash & Zucchini

Preparation Time: 10 minutes; Cooking Time: 25 minutes; Serve: 4

Ingredients:
- 1 lb zucchini, cut into 1/2-inch half-moons
- 1 lb yellow squash, cut into 1/2-inch half-moons
- 1 tbsp olive oil

- Pepper
- Salt

Directions:
1. In a mixing bowl, add zucchini, squash, oil, pepper, and salt and toss well.
2. Add zucchini and squash mixture into the air fryer basket and cook at 400 F for 20 minutes. Shake basket halfway through.
3. Shake basket well and cook for 5 minutes more.
4. Serve and enjoy.

Nutritional Value (Amount per Serving):
Calories 66; Fat 3.9 g; Carbohydrates 7.6 g; Sugar 3.9 g; Protein 2.7 g; Cholesterol 0 mg

Crunchy Fried Cabbage

Preparation Time: 10 minutes; Cooking Time: 10 minutes; Serve: 2
Ingredients:
- 1/2 cabbage head, sliced into 2-inch slices
- 1 tbsp olive oil
- Pepper
- Salt

Directions:
1. Drizzle cabbage with olive oil and season with pepper and salt.
2. Add cabbage slices into the air fryer basket and cook at 375 F for 5 minutes.
3. Toss cabbage well and cook for 5 minutes more.
4. Serve and enjoy.

Nutritional Value (Amount per Serving):
Calories 105; Fat 7.2 g; Carbohydrates 10.4 g; Sugar 5.7 g; Protein 2.3 g; Cholesterol 0 mg

Balsamic Brussels Sprouts

Preparation Time: 10 minutes; Cooking Time: 10 minutes; Serve: 5
Ingredients:
- 2 cups Brussels sprouts, cut in half
- 1 tbsp olive oil
- 1 tbsp balsamic vinegar
- 1/2 cup onion, sliced
- Pepper
- Salt

Directions:
1. Add brussels sprouts, oil, vinegar, onion, pepper, and salt into the mixing bowl and toss well.
2. Add brussels sprouts mixture into the air fryer basket and cook at 350 F for 5 minutes.
3. Shake basket well and cook for 5 minutes more.
4. Serve and enjoy.

Nutritional Value (Amount per Serving):
Calories 44; Fat 2.9 g; Carbohydrates 4.3 g; Sugar 1.3 g; Protein 1.3 g; Cholesterol 0 mg

Quick Vegetable Kebabs

Preparation Time: 10 minutes; Cooking Time: 10 minutes; Serve: 4
Ingredients:
- 2 bell peppers, cut into 1-inch pieces
- 1/2 onion, cut into 1-inch pieces
- 1 zucchini, cut into 1-inch pieces
- 1 eggplant, cut into 1-inch pieces
- Pepper
- Salt

Directions:
1. Thread vegetables onto the skewers and spray them with cooking spray. Season with pepper and salt.
2. Preheat the cosori air fryer to 390 F.
3. Place skewers into the air fryer basket and cooks for 10 minutes. Turn halfway through.

4. Serve and enjoy.

Nutritional Value (Amount per Serving):
Calories 48; Fat 0.3 g; Carbohydrates 11.2 g; Sugar 5.9 g; Protein 2.1 g; Cholesterol 0 mg

Easy Soy Garlic Mushrooms

Preparation Time: 10 minutes; Cooking Time: 12 minutes; Serve: 2

Ingredients:
- 8 oz mushrooms, cleaned
- 1 tbsp fresh parsley, chopped
- 1 tsp soy sauce
- 1/2 tsp garlic powder
- 1 tbsp olive oil
- Pepper
- Salt

Directions:
1. Toss mushrooms with soy sauce, garlic powder, oil, pepper, and salt.
2. Add mushrooms into the air fryer basket and cook at 380 F for 10-12 minutes.
3. Garnish with parsley and serve.

Nutritional Value (Amount per Serving):
Calories 89; Fat 7.4 g; Carbohydrates 4.6 g; Sugar 2.2 g; Protein 3.9 g; Cholesterol 0 mg

Spicy Edamame

Preparation Time: 10 minutes; Cooking Time: 18 minutes; Serve: 4

Ingredients:
- 16 oz frozen edamame in shell, defrosted
- 1 lemon juice
- 1 lemon zest
- 1 tbsp garlic, sliced
- 2 tsp olive oil
- 1/2 tsp chili powder
- 1/2 tsp paprika
- Salt

Directions:
1. Toss edamame with lemon zest, garlic, oil, chili powder, paprika, and salt.
2. Add edamame into the air fryer basket and cook at 400 F for 18 minutes. Shake basket twice.
3. Drizzle lemon juice over edamame and serve.

Nutritional Value (Amount per Serving):
Calories 172; Fat 8.5 g; Carbohydrates 12.2 g; Sugar 2.7 g; Protein 12.3 g; Cholesterol 0 mg

Balsamic Mushrooms

Preparation Time: 10 minutes; Cooking Time: 8 minutes; Serve: 3

Ingredients:
- 8 oz mushrooms
- 1 tsp fresh parsley, chopped
- 2 tsp balsamic vinegar
- 1/2 tsp granulated garlic
- 1 tsp olive oil
- Pepper
- Salt

Directions:
1. Toss mushrooms with garlic, oil, pepper, and salt.
2. Add mushrooms into the air fryer basket and cook at 375 F for 8 minutes. Toss halfway through.
3. Toss mushrooms with parsley and balsamic vinegar.
4. Serve and enjoy.

Nutritional Value (Amount per Serving):
Calories 32; Fat 1.8 g; Carbohydrates 2.9 g; Sugar 1.4 g; Protein 2.5 g Cholesterol 0 mg

Mediterranean Vegetables

Preparation Time: 10 minutes; Cooking Time: 15 minutes; Serve: 2

Ingredients:
- 6 cherry tomatoes, cut in half
- 1 eggplant, diced
- 1 zucchini, diced
- 1 green bell pepper, diced
- 1 tsp thyme
- 1 tsp oregano
- Pepper
- Salt

Directions:
1. In a bowl, toss eggplant, zucchini, bell pepper, thyme, oregano, pepper, and salt.
2. Add vegetable mixture into the air fryer basket and cook at 360 F for 12 minutes.
3. Add cherry tomatoes and shake basket well and cook for 3 minutes more.
4. Serve and enjoy.

Nutritional Value (Amount per Serving):
Calories 61; Fat 0.3 g; Carbohydrates 13.8 g; Sugar 7.6 g; Protein 2.8 g; Cholesterol 0 mg

Simple Roasted Okra

Preparation Time: 10 minutes; Cooking Time: 12 minutes; Serve: 1

Ingredients:
- 1/2 lb okra, trimmed and sliced
- 1 tsp olive oil
- Pepper
- Salt

Directions:
1. Preheat the cosori air fryer to 350 F.
2. Mix together okra, oil, pepper, and salt.
3. Add okra into the air fryer basket and cook for 10 minutes. Toss halfway through.
4. Toss well and cook for 2 minutes more.
5. Serve and enjoy.

Nutritional Value (Amount per Serving):
Calories 176; Fat 17.3 g; Carbohydrates 6.2 g; Sugar 3.2 g; Protein 2.5 g; Cholesterol 0 mg

Greek Vegetables

Preparation Time: 10 minutes; Cooking Time: 20 minutes; Serve: 4

Ingredients:
- 1 carrot, sliced
- 1 parsnip, sliced
- 1 green bell pepper, chopped
- 1 courgette, chopped
- 1/4 cup cherry tomatoes, cut in half
- 6 tbsp olive oil
- 2 tsp garlic puree
- 1 tsp mustard
- 1 tsp mixed herbs
- Pepper
- Salt

Directions:
1. Add cherry tomatoes, carrot, parsnip, bell pepper, and courgette into the air fryer basket.
2. Drizzle olive oil over vegetables and cook at 350 F for 15 minutes.
3. In a mixing bowl, mix together the remaining ingredients. Add vegetables into the mixing bowl and toss well.
4. Return vegetables to the air fryer basket and cook at 400 F for 5 minutes more.
5. Serve and enjoy.

Nutritional Value (Amount per Serving):
Calories 66; Fat 1.5 g; Carbohydrates 12.7 g; Sugar 5.3 g; Protein 1.8 g; Cholesterol 1 mg

Lemon Garlic Cauliflower

Preparation Time: 10 minutes; Cooking Time: 10 minutes; Serve: 2

Ingredients:
- 3 cups cauliflower
- 1 tbsp fresh parsley, chopped
- 1/2 tsp lemon juice
- 1 tbsp pine nuts
- 1/2 tsp dried oregano
- 1 1/2 tsp olive oil
- Pepper
- Salt

Directions:
1. Add cauliflower, oregano, oil, pepper, and salt into the mixing bowl and toss well.
2. Add cauliflower into the air fryer basket and cook at 375 F for 10 minutes.
3. Transfer cauliflower into the serving bowl. Add pine nuts, parsley, and lemon juice and toss well.
4. Serve and enjoy.

Nutritional Value (Amount per Serving):
Calories 99; Fat 6.7 g; Carbohydrates 8.9 g; Sugar 3.8 g; Protein 3.7 g; Cholesterol 0 mg

Balsamic Brussels Sprouts

Preparation Time: 10 minutes; Cooking Time: 20 minutes; Serve: 4

Ingredients:
- 1 lb brussels sprouts, remove ends and cut in half
- 1 tbsp balsamic vinegar
- 2 tbsp olive oil
- Pepper
- Salt

Directions:
1. Add brussels sprouts, vinegar, oil, pepper, and salt into the mixing bowl and toss well.
2. Add brussels sprouts into the air fryer basket and cook at 360 F for 15-20 minutes. Toss halfway through.
3. Serve and enjoy.

Nutritional Value (Amount per Serving):
Calories 110; Fat 7.4 g; Carbohydrates 10.4 g; Sugar 2.5 g; Protein 3.9 g; Cholesterol 0 mg

Flavorful Butternut Squash

Preparation Time: 10 minutes; Cooking Time: 15 minutes; Serve: 4

Ingredients:
- 4 cups butternut squash, cut into 1-inch pieces
- 1 tsp Chinese five-spice powder
- 1 tbsp truvia
- 2 tbsp olive oil

Directions:
1. Add butternut squash and remaining ingredients into the mixing bowl and mix well.
2. Add butternut squash into the air fryer basket and cook at 400 F for 15 minutes. Shake basket halfway through.
3. Serve and enjoy.

Nutritional Value (Amount per Serving):
Calories 83; Fat 7.1 g; Carbohydrates 6.7 g; Sugar 2.2 g; Protein 0.6 g; Cholesterol 0 mg

Crispy Green Beans

Preparation Time: 10 minutes; Cooking Time: 10 minutes; Serve: 4

Ingredients:
- 2 cups green beans, ends trimmed
- 2 tbsp parmesan cheese, shredded
- 1 tbsp fresh lemon juice
- 1 tsp Italian seasoning
- 2 tsp olive oil
- 1/4 tsp salt

Directions:
1. Preheat the cosori air fryer to 400 F.

2. Brush green beans with olive oil and season with Italian seasoning and salt.
3. Place green beans into the air fryer basket and cook for 8-10 minutes. Shake basket 2-3 times.
4. Transfer green beans on a serving plate.
5. Pour lemon juice over beans and sprinkle shredded cheese on top of beans.
6. Serve and enjoy.

Nutritional Value (Amount per Serving):
Calories 64; Fat 4.3 g; Carbohydrates 4.4 g; Sugar 1 g; Protein 3.3 g; Cholesterol 6 mg

Roasted Zucchini

Preparation Time: 10 minutes; Cooking Time: 10 minutes; Serve: 4
Ingredients:
- 2 medium zucchini, cut into 1-inch slices
- 1 tsp lemon zest
- 1 tbsp olive oil
- Pepper
- Salt

Directions:
1. Toss zucchini with lemon zest, oil, pepper, and salt.
2. Arrange zucchini slices into the air fryer basket and cook at 350 F for 10 minutes. Turn halfway through.
3. Serve and enjoy.

Nutritional Value (Amount per Serving):
Calories 46; Fat 3.7 g; Carbohydrates 3.4 g; Sugar 1.7 g; Protein 1.2 g; Cholesterol 0 mg

Air Fried Carrots, Zucchini & Squash

Preparation Time: 10 minutes; Cooking Time: 35 minutes; Serve: 2
Ingredients:
- 1 lb yellow squash, cut into 3/4-inch half-moons
- 1 lb zucchini, cut into 3/4-inch half-moons
- 1/2 lb carrots, peeled and cut into 1-inch pieces
- 6 tsp olive oil
- 1 tbsp tarragon, chopped
- Pepper
- Salt

Directions:
1. In a bowl, toss carrots with 2 tsp oil. Add carrots into the air fryer basket and cook at 400 F for 5 minutes.
2. In a mixing bowl, toss squash, zucchini, remaining oil, pepper, and salt.
3. Add squash and zucchini mixture into the air fryer basket with carrots and cook for 30 minutes. Shake basket 2-3 times.
4. Sprinkle with tarragon and serve.

Nutritional Value (Amount per Serving):
Calories 176; Fat 17.3 g; Carbohydrates 6.2 g; Sugar 3.2 g; Protein 2.5 g; Cholesterol 0 mg

Crispy & Spicy Eggplant

Preparation Time: 10 minutes; Cooking Time: 20 minutes; Serve: 4
Ingredients:
- 1 eggplant, cut into 1-inch pieces
- 1/2 tsp Italian seasoning
- 1 tsp paprika
- 1/2 tsp red pepper
- 1 tsp garlic powder
- 2 tbsp olive oil

Directions:
1. Add eggplant and remaining ingredients into the bowl and toss well.

2. Spray air fryer basket with cooking spray.
3. Add eggplant into the air fryer basket and cook at 375 F for 20 minutes. Shake basket halfway through.
4. Serve and enjoy.

Nutritional Value (Amount per Serving):
Calories 99; Fat 7.5 g; Carbohydrates 8.7 g; Sugar 4.5 g; Protein 1.5 g; Cholesterol 0 mg

Curried Eggplant Slices

Preparation Time: 10 minutes; Cooking Time: 10 minutes; Serve: 4

Ingredients:
- 1 large eggplant, cut into 1/2-inch slices
- 1 garlic clove, minced
- 1 tbsp olive oil
- 1/2 tsp curry powder
- 1/8 tsp turmeric
- Salt

Directions:
1. Preheat the cosori air fryer to 300 F.
2. In a small bowl, mix together oil, garlic, curry powder, turmeric, and salt and rub all over eggplant slices.
3. Add eggplant slices into the air fryer basket and cook for 10 minutes or until lightly browned.
4. Serve and enjoy.

Nutritional Value (Amount per Serving):
Calories 61; Fat 3.8 g; Carbohydrates 7.2 g; Sugar 3.5 g; Protein 1.2 g; Cholesterol 0 mg

Spiced Green Beans

Preparation Time: 10 minutes; Cooking Time: 10 minutes; Serve: 2

Ingredients:
- 2 cups green beans
- 1/8 tsp ground allspice
- 1/4 tsp ground cinnamon
- 1/2 tsp dried oregano
- 2 tbsp olive oil
- 1/4 tsp ground coriander
- 1/4 tsp ground cumin
- 1/8 tsp cayenne pepper
- 1/2 tsp salt

Directions:
1. Add all ingredients into the medium bowl and toss well.
2. Spray air fryer basket with cooking spray.
3. Add green beans into the air fryer basket and cook at 370 F for 10 minutes. Shake basket halfway through
4. Serve and enjoy.

Nutritional Value (Amount per Serving):
Calories 158; Fat 14.3 g; Carbohydrates 8.6 g; Sugar 1.6 g; Protein 2.1 g; Cholesterol 0 mg

Air Fryer Basil Tomatoes

Preparation Time: 10 minutes; Cooking Time: 25 minutes; Serve: 4

Ingredients:
- 4 large tomatoes, halved
- 1 garlic clove, minced
- 1 tbsp vinegar
- 1 tbsp olive oil
- 2 tbsp parmesan cheese, grated
- 1/2 tsp fresh parsley, chopped
- 1 tsp fresh basil, minced
- Pepper
- Salt

Directions:

1. Preheat the cosori air fryer to 320 F.
2. In a bowl, mix together oil, basil, garlic, vinegar, pepper, and salt. Add tomatoes and stir to coat.
3. Place tomato halves into the air fryer basket and cook for 20 minutes.
4. Sprinkle parmesan cheese over tomatoes and cook for 5 minutes more.
5. Serve and enjoy.

Nutritional Value (Amount per Serving):
Calories 87; Fat 5.4 g; Carbohydrates 7.7 g; Sugar 4.8 g; Protein 3.9 g; Cholesterol 5 mg

Air Fryer Ratatouille

Preparation Time: 10 minutes; Cooking Time: 15 minutes; Serve: 6
Ingredients:
- 1 eggplant, diced
- 1 onion, diced
- 3 tomatoes, diced
- 1 red bell pepper, diced
- 1 green bell pepper, diced
- 1 tbsp vinegar
- 2 tbsp olive oil
- 2 tbsp herb de Provence
- 2 garlic cloves, chopped
- Pepper
- Salt

Directions:
1. Preheat the cosori air fryer to 400 F.
2. Add all ingredients into the bowl and toss well and transfer into the air fryer safe dish.
3. Place dish into the air fryer basket and cook for 15 minutes. Stir halfway through.
4. Serve and enjoy.

Nutritional Value (Amount per Serving):
Calories 91; Fat 5 g; Carbohydrates 11.6 g; Sugar 6.4 g; Protein 1.9 g; Cholesterol 0 mg

Garlicky Cauliflower Florets

Preparation Time: 10 minutes; Cooking Time: 20 minutes; Serve: 4
Ingredients:
- 5 cups cauliflower florets
- 1/2 tsp cumin powder
- 1/2 tsp ground coriander
- 6 garlic cloves, chopped
- 4 tablespoons olive oil
- 1/2 tsp salt

Directions:
1. Add cauliflower florets and remaining ingredients into the large mixing bowl and toss well.
2. Add cauliflower florets into the air fryer basket and cook at 400 F for 20 minutes. Shake basket halfway through.
3. Serve and enjoy.

Nutritional Value (Amount per Serving):
Calories 159; Fat 14.2 g; Carbohydrates 8.2 g; Sugar 3.1 g; Protein 2.8 g; Cholesterol 0 mg

Parmesan Brussels sprouts

Preparation Time: 10 minutes; Cooking Time: 12 minutes; Serve: 4
Ingredients:
- 1 lb Brussels sprouts, remove stems and halved
- 1/4 cup parmesan cheese, grated
- 2 tbsp olive oil
- Pepper
- Salt

Directions:
1. Preheat the cosori air fryer to 350 F.
2. In a mixing bowl, toss Brussels sprouts with oil, pepper, and salt.

3. Transfer Brussels sprouts into the air fryer basket and cook for 12 minutes. Shake basket halfway through.
4. Sprinkle with parmesan cheese and serve.

Nutritional Value (Amount per Serving):
Calories 129; Fat 8.7 g; Carbohydrates 10.6 g; Sugar 2.5 g; Protein 5.9 g; Cholesterol 4 mg

Flavorful Tomatoes

Preparation Time: 10 minutes; Cooking Time: 15 minutes; Serve: 4

Ingredients:
- 4 Roma tomatoes, sliced, remove seeds pithy portion
- 1 tbsp olive oil
- 1/2 tsp dried thyme
- 2 garlic cloves, minced
- Pepper
- Salt

Directions:
1. Preheat the cosori air fryer to 390 F.
2. Toss sliced tomatoes with oil, thyme, garlic, pepper, and salt.
3. Arrange sliced tomatoes into the air fryer basket and cook for 15 minutes.
4. Serve and enjoy.

Nutritional Value (Amount per Serving):
Calories 55; Fat 3.8 g; Carbohydrates 5.4 g; Sugar 3.3 g; Protein 1.2 g; Cholesterol 0 mg

Healthy Roasted Carrots

Preparation Time: 10 minutes; Cooking Time: 12 minutes; Serve: 4

Ingredients:
- 2 cups carrots, peeled and chopped
- 1 tsp cumin
- 1 tbsp olive oil
- 1/4 fresh coriander, chopped

Directions:
1. Toss carrots with cumin and oil and place them into the air fryer basket.
2. Cook at 390 F for 12 minutes.
3. Garnish with fresh coriander and serve.

Nutritional Value (Amount per Serving):
Calories 55; Fat 3.6 g; Carbohydrates 5.7 g; Sugar 2.7 g; Protein 0.6 g; Cholesterol 0 mg

Curried Cauliflower with Pine Nuts

Preparation Time: 10 minutes; Cooking Time: 10 minutes; Serve: 4

Ingredients:
- 1 small cauliflower head, cut into florets
- 2 tbsp olive oil
- 1/4 cup pine nuts, toasted
- 1 tbsp curry powder
- 1/4 tsp salt

Directions:
1. Preheat the cosori air fryer to 350 F.
2. In a mixing bowl, toss cauliflower florets with oil, curry powder, and salt.
3. Add cauliflower florets into the air fryer basket and cook for 10 minutes. Shake basket halfway through.
4. Transfer cauliflower into the serving bowl. Add pine nuts and toss well.
5. Serve and enjoy.

Nutritional Value (Amount per Serving):
Calories 139; Fat 13.1 g; Carbohydrates 5.5 g; Sugar 1.9 g; Protein 2.7 g; Cholesterol 0 mg

Thyme Sage Butternut Squash

Preparation Time: 10 minutes; Cooking Time: 12 minutes; Serve: 4
Ingredients:
- 2 lbs butternut squash, cut into chunks
- 1 tsp fresh thyme, chopped
- 1 tbsp fresh sage, chopped
- 1 tbsp olive oil
- Pepper
- Salt

Directions:
1. Preheat the cosori air fryer to 390 F.
2. In a mixing bowl, toss butternut squash with thyme, sage, oil, pepper, and salt.
3. Add butternut squash into the air fryer basket and cook for 10 minutes. Shake basket well and cook for 2 minutes more.
4. Serve and enjoy.

Nutritional Value (Amount per Serving):
Calories 50; Fat 3.8 g; Carbohydrates 4.2 g; Sugar 2.5 g; Protein 1.4 g; Cholesterol 0 mg

Green Beans with Onion

Preparation Time: 10 minutes; Cooking Time: 6 minutes; Serve: 4
Ingredients:
- 1 lb green beans, trimmed
- 2 tbsp olive oil
- 1/2 cup onion, sliced
- Pepper
- Salt

Directions:
1. In a bowl, toss green beans with oil, sliced onion, pepper, and salt.
2. Add green beans into the air fryer basket and cook at 330 F for 5 minutes. Shake basket well and cook for 1 minute more.
3. Serve and enjoy.

Nutritional Value (Amount per Serving):
Calories 101; Fat 7.2 g; Carbohydrates 9.5 g; Sugar 2.2 g; Protein 2.2 g; Cholesterol 0 mg

Easy Wild Mushrooms

Preparation Time: 10 minutes; Cooking Time: 12 minutes; Serve: 4
Ingredients:
- 1 lb wild mushrooms, cleaned
- 1 tbsp olive oil
- 1 garlic clove, minced
- 1 tsp fresh thyme
- Pepper
- Salt

Directions:
1. In a bowl, add mushrooms and remaining ingredients and toss well.
2. Add mushrooms into the air fryer basket and cook at 350 F for 12 minutes. Shake basket halfway through.
3. Serve and enjoy.

Nutritional Value (Amount per Serving):
Calories 56; Fat 3.8 g; Carbohydrates 4.2 g; Sugar 2 g; Protein 3.6 g; Cholesterol 0 mg

Delicious Lemon Cheese Asparagus

Preparation Time: 10 minutes; Cooking Time: 10 minutes; Serve: 4
Ingredients:
- 1 lb asparagus, cut woody ends and trimmed
- 1 oz feta cheese, crumbled
- 1 tbsp fresh lemon juice
- 1 tsp olive oil
- Pepper

- Salt

Directions:
1. Toss asparagus with lemon juice, olive oil, half feta cheese, pepper, and salt in a mixing bowl.
2. Add asparagus into the air fryer basket and top with remaining feta cheese.
3. Cook at 400 F for 10 minutes.
4. Serve and enjoy.

Nutritional Value (Amount per Serving):
Calories 52; Fat 2.9 g; Carbohydrates 4.8 g; Sugar 2.5 g; Protein 3.5 g; Cholesterol 6 mg

Garlic Butter Mushrooms

Preparation Time: 10 minutes; Cooking Time: 15 minutes; Serve: 4

Ingredients:
- 16 oz baby portobello mushrooms, halved
- 2 tsp coconut aminos
- 2 tsp garlic, minced
- 2 tbsp butter, melted

Directions:
1. In a mixing bowl, toss mushrooms with coconut aminos, garlic, and butter.
2. Add mushrooms into the air fryer basket and cook at 400 F for 12-15 minutes. Shake basket halfway through.
3. Serve and enjoy.

Nutritional Value (Amount per Serving):
Calories 131; Fat 8.3 g; Carbohydrates 12 g; Sugar 8.4 g; Protein 1.9 g; Cholesterol 15 mg

Chapter 10: Desserts

Cinnamon Pecan Muffins

Preparation Time: 10 minutes; Cooking Time: 15 minutes; Serve: 12

Ingredients:
- 4 eggs
- 1 tbsp baking powder
- 1 1/2 cups almond flour
- 1 tsp vanilla
- 1/4 cup unsweetened almond milk
- 1/2 cup pecans, chopped
- 1/2 tsp ground cinnamon
- 2 tsp allspice
- 2 tbsp butter, melted
- 1/2 cup Swerve
- 1 tsp psyllium husk

Directions:
1. Preheat the cosori air fryer to 400 F.
2. Beat eggs, almond milk, vanilla, sweetener, and butter in a mixing bowl using a hand mixer until smooth.
3. Add remaining ingredients and mix until well combined.
4. Pour batter into silicone muffin molds and place in the air fryer basket. In batches.
5. Cook for 15 minutes.
6. Serve and enjoy.

Nutritional Value (Amount per Serving):
Calories 101; Fat 8.9 g; Carbohydrates 3.6 g; Sugar 0.5 g; Protein 3.2 g; Cholesterol 60 mg

Strawberry Almond Muffins

Preparation Time: 10 minutes; Cooking Time: 20 minutes; Serve: 12

Ingredients:
- 3 eggs
- 2 1/2 cups almond flour
- 1/2 cup Swerve
- 5 tbsp butter, melted
- 1 tsp cinnamon
- 2 tsp baking powder
- 2/3 cup strawberries, diced
- 1/3 cup heavy cream
- 1 tsp vanilla
- 1/4 tsp Himalayan salt

Directions:
1. Preheat the cosori air fryer to 350 F.
2. In a bowl, beat together butter and swerve. Add eggs, cream, and vanilla and beat until frothy.
3. Sift together almond flour, cinnamon, baking powder, and salt.
4. Add almond flour mixture to the wet ingredients and mix until combined. Add strawberries and fold well.
5. Pour batter into the silicone muffin molds and place in the air fryer basket. In batches.
6. Cook for 20 minutes.
7. Serve and enjoy.

Nutritional Value (Amount per Serving):
Calories 108; Fat 10.1 g; Carbohydrates 2.7 g; Sugar 0.7 g; Protein 2.8 g; Cholesterol 58 mg

Cinnamon Cream Cheese Muffins

Preparation Time: 10 minutes; Cooking Time: 20 minutes; Serve: 10

Ingredients:
- 2 eggs
- 1/2 tsp vanilla extract
- 1/2 cup Swerve
- 8 oz cream cheese
- 1 tsp ground cinnamon

Directions:

1. Preheat the cosori air fryer to 350 F.
2. In a bowl, mix together cream cheese, vanilla, Swerve, and eggs until soft.
3. Pour batter into the silicone muffin mold and sprinkle cinnamon on the tops.
4. Place muffin mold in the air fryer basket. In batches.
5. Cook for 20 minutes.
6. Serve and enjoy.

Nutritional Value (Amount per Serving):
Calories 93; Fat 8.8 g; Carbohydrates 1 g; Sugar 0.2 g; Protein 2.8 g; Cholesterol 58 mg

Moist Almond Muffins

Preparation Time: 10 minutes; Cooking Time: 15 minutes; Serve: 20
Ingredients:
- 1/2 cup coconut oil
- 1/2 cup almond flour
- 1/2 cup pumpkin puree
- 1/2 cup almond butter
- 1 tbsp cinnamon
- 1 tsp baking powder
- 2 scoops vanilla protein powder

Directions:
1. Preheat the cosori air fryer to 350 F.
2. In a large bowl, mix together all dry ingredients.
3. Add wet ingredients into the dry ingredients and mix until well combined.
4. Pour batter into the silicone muffin molds and place in the air fryer basket. In batches.
5. Cook for 15 minutes.
6. Serve and enjoy.

Nutritional Value (Amount per Serving):
Calories 68; Fat 6.1 g; Carbohydrates 1.2 g; Sugar 0.3 g; Protein 3 g; Cholesterol 0 mg

Lemon Cheese Muffins

Preparation Time: 10 minutes; Cooking Time: 14 minutes; Serve: 12
Ingredients:
- 3 eggs
- 1/4 cup coconut oil
- 1/4 cup ricotta cheese
- 1 cup almond flour
- 1 tsp lemon extract
- 1/4 cup heavy cream
- 4 true lemon packets
- 2 tbsp poppy seeds
- 1 tsp baking powder
- 1/3 cup Swerve

Directions:
1. Add all ingredients into the large mixing bowl and beat until fluffy.
2. Pour batter into the silicone muffin molds and place in the air fryer basket. In batches.
3. Cook at 320 F for 14 minutes or until cooked.
4. Serve and enjoy.

Nutritional Value (Amount per Serving):
Calories 93; Fat 8.8 g; Carbohydrates 1.6 g; Sugar 0.4 g; Protein 2.8 g; Cholesterol 46 mg

Easy Mug Brownie

Preparation Time: 10 minutes; Cooking Time: 10 minutes; Serve: 1
Ingredients:
- 1/4 cup unsweetened coconut milk
- 1 tbsp cocoa powder
- 1 scoop chocolate protein powder
- 1/2 tsp baking powder

Directions:
1. In a heat-safe mug blend together baking powder, protein powder, and cocoa powder. Add milk and stir well.

2. Place the mug in the air fryer basket and cook at 390 F for 10 minutes.
3. Serve and enjoy.

Nutritional Value (Amount per Serving):
Calories 207; Fat 15.8 g; Carbohydrates 9.5 g; Sugar 3.1 g; Protein 12.4 g; Cholesterol 20 mg

Delicious Chocó Cookies

Preparation Time: 10 minutes; Cooking Time: 10 minutes; Serve: 20

Ingredients:
- 1 cup almond flour
- 1 cup almond butter
- 2 tbsp chocolate protein powder
- 3 tbsp ground chia

Directions:
1. Line air fryer basket with foil.
2. Preheat the cosori air fryer to 350 F.
3. In a large bowl, add all ingredients and mix until well combined.
4. Make small balls from the mixture. Place some balls on foil in the air fryer basket. Press lightly down using the back of a fork.
5. Cook for 10 minutes. Cook remaining cookies in batches.
6. Allow to cool completely.
7. Serve and enjoy.

Nutritional Value (Amount per Serving):
Calories 21; Fat 1.3 g; Carbohydrates 0.7 g; Sugar 0.1 g; Protein 1.9 g; Cholesterol 0 mg

Almond Butter Fudge Brownies

Preparation Time: 10 minutes; Cooking Time: 10 minutes; Serve: 4

Ingredients:
- 2 tbsp cocoa powder
- 1/4 tsp baking powder
- 1/2 tsp baking soda
- 2 tbsp unsweetened applesauce
- 15 drops liquid stevia
- 3 tbsp almond flour
- 1/2 tsp vanilla
- 1 tbsp unsweetened almond milk
- 1/2 cup almond butter
- 1 tbsp coconut oil, melted
- 1/4 tsp sea salt

Directions:
1. Preheat the cosori air fryer to 350 F.
2. Grease air fryer baking dish with cooking spray and set aside.
3. In a small bowl, mix together almond flour, baking powder, baking soda, cocoa powder, and salt. Set aside.
4. In a microwave-safe bowl, gently warm coconut oil and almond butter until melted.
5. Add stevia, vanilla, milk, and applesauce in the coconut oil mixture and stir well.
6. Add dry ingredients to the wet ingredients and stir to combine.
7. Pour batter into prepared dish.
8. Place dish into the air fryer basket and cook for 10 minutes.
9. Slice and serve.

Nutritional Value (Amount per Serving):
Calories 173; Fat 15.4 g; Carbohydrates 7.5 g; Sugar 1.7 g; Protein 5.5 g; Cholesterol 0 mg

Vanilla Mug Cake

Preparation Time: 10 minutes; Cooking Time: 10 minutes; Serve: 1

Ingredients:
- 1/4 cup unsweetened almond milk
- 1 scoop vanilla protein powder
- 1/2 tsp cinnamon
- 1/4 tsp vanilla

- 1 tsp Swerve
- 1 tbsp almond flour
- 1/2 tsp baking powder

Directions:
1. Add protein powder, Swerve, cinnamon, almond flour, and baking powder into the heat-safe mug and mix well.
2. Add vanilla and almond milk and stir well.
3. Place the mug in air fryer basket and cook at 390 F for 10 minutes
4. Serve and enjoy.

Nutritional Value (Amount per Serving):
Calories 294; Fat 15 g; Carbohydrates 11.2 g; Sugar 1.5 g; Protein 33.3 g; Cholesterol 2 mg

Moist Chocolate Brownies

Preparation Time: 10 minutes; Cooking Time: 30 minutes; Serve: 8
Ingredients:
- 3 eggs
- 1/2 cup unsweetened chocolate chips
- 1 tsp vanilla
- 1/4 cup Swerve
- 1/2 cup butter

Directions:
1. Add chocolate chips and butter into the microwave-safe bowl and microwave for 1 minute. Remove from microwave and stir well.
2. In a bowl, add eggs, vanilla, and Swerve and blend until frothy.
3. Pour melted chocolate and butter into the bowl and beat until combined.
4. Pour batter into the greased air fryer pan.
5. Place pan in the air fryer basket and cook at 350 F for 30 minutes.
6. Slice and serve.

Nutritional Value (Amount per Serving):
Calories 227; Fat 21.2 g; Carbohydrates 4.3 g; Sugar 0.2 g; Protein 4.2 g; Cholesterol 92 mg

Chocolate Brownies

Preparation Time: 10 minutes; Cooking Time: 25 minutes; Serve: 16
Ingredients:
- 3 eggs
- 1/3 cup unsweetened chocolate chips
- 3/4 cup Swerve
- 1 cup unsweetened peanut butter
- 1 cup almond flour

Directions:
1. In a bowl, whisk eggs, sweetener, and peanut butter.
2. Add almond flour and cocoa powder and blend until smooth.
3. Add chocolate chips and fold well.
4. Pour batter into the air fryer safe dish.
5. Place dish into the air fryer basket and cook at 300 F for 25 minutes.
6. Serve and enjoy.

Nutritional Value (Amount per Serving):
Calories 145; Fat 12.4 g; Carbohydrates 4.9 g; Sugar 1.1 g; Protein 5.1 g; Cholesterol 31 mg

Super Easy Keto Brownies

Preparation Time: 10 minutes; Cooking Time: 10 minutes; Serve: 2
Ingredients:
- 1 egg
- 2 tbsp pecans, chopped
- 2 tbsp unsweetened chocolate chips
- 4 tbsp butter, melted
- 2 tbsp unsweetened cocoa powder
- 3 tbsp Swerve

- 1/3 cup almond flour

Directions:
1. Preheat the cosori air fryer to 350 F.
2. Spray two ramekins with cooking spray and set aside.
3. In a mixing bowl, mix together almond flour, swerve, cocoa powder, and baking powder. Add melted butter and egg and mix until smooth.
4. Add chocolate chips and pecans and fold well.
5. Pour batter into the prepared ramekins. Place ramekins into the air fryer basket and cook for 10 minutes.
6. Serve and enjoy.

Nutritional Value (Amount per Serving):
Calories 451; Fat 43.4 g; Carbohydrates 12.6 g; Sugar 0.8 g; Protein 8.1 g; Cholesterol 143 mg

Moist Chocolate Cake

Preparation Time: 10 minutes; Cooking Time: 30 minutes ; Serve: 12
Ingredients:
- 6 eggs
- 1 1/4 cup Swerve
- 1/2 cup almond flour
- 10 oz butter, melted
- 10 oz unsweetened chocolate, melted
- Pinch of salt

Directions:
1. Preheat the cosori air fryer to 350 F.
2. Spray a baking dish with cooking spray and set aside.
3. Add eggs into the large bowl and beat until foamy. Add sweetener and stir well.
4. Add melted butter, chocolate, almond flour, and salt and stir to combine.
5. Pour batter into the dish.
6. Place dish into the air fryer basket and cook for 30 minutes.
7. Slice and serve.

Nutritional Value (Amount per Serving):
Calories 326; Fat 34.3 g; Carbohydrates 7.7 g; Sugar 0.4 g; Protein 6.3 g; Cholesterol 133 mg

Delicious Chocolate Muffins

Preparation Time: 10 minutes; Cooking Time: 30 minutes ; Serve: 10
Ingredients:
- 2 eggs, lightly beaten
- 1 tbsp baking powder, gluten-free
- 4 tbsp Swerve
- 1/2 cup unsweetened cocoa powder
- 1/2 cup cream
- 1/2 tsp vanilla
- 1 cup almond flour
- Pinch of salt

Directions:
1. Preheat the cosori air fryer to 375 F.
2. In a mixing bowl, mix together almond flour, baking powder, swerve, cocoa powder, and salt.
3. In a separate bowl, beat eggs with cream, and vanilla.
4. Pour egg mixture into the almond flour mixture and mix well.
5. Pour batter into the Silicone muffin molds.
6. Place molds into the air fryer basket and cook for 30 minutes. Cook in batches.
7. Serve and enjoy.

Nutritional Value (Amount per Serving):
Calories 50; Fat 3.5 g; Carbohydrates 4.9 g; Sugar 0.5 g; Protein 2.7 g; Cholesterol 35 mg

Choco Almond Butter Brownie

Preparation Time: 10 minutes; Cooking Time: 20 minutes ; Serve: 4

Ingredients:
- 1 cup banana, overripe & mashed
- 1 scoop vanilla protein powder
- 1/2 tsp vanilla
- 2 tbsp unsweetened cocoa powder
- 1/2 cup almond butter, melted

Directions:
1. Preheat the cosori air fryer to 350 F.
2. Line baking dish with parchment paper and set aside.
3. Add all ingredients into the blender and blend until smooth.
4. Pour batter into the prepared dish.
5. Place dish into the air fryer basket and cook for 20 minutes.
6. Slice and serve.

Nutritional Value (Amount per Serving):
Calories 81; Fat 1.6 g; Carbohydrates 10.6 g; Sugar 4.9 g; Protein 8.1 g; Cholesterol 0 mg

Yummy Brownie Muffins

Preparation Time: 10 minutes; Cooking Time: 15 minutes; Serve: 6

Ingredients:
- 3 eggs
- 1/3 cup unsweetened cocoa powder
- 1/2 cup Swerve
- 1 cup almond flour
- 1 tbsp gelatin
- 1/3 cup butter, melted

Directions:
1. Add all ingredients into the mixing bowl and stir until well combined.
2. Pour mixture into the mini silicone muffin molds.
3. Place molds into the air fryer basket and cook at 350 F for 10-15 minutes.
4. Serve and enjoy.

Nutritional Value (Amount per Serving):
Calories 164; Fat 15.4 g; Carbohydrates 4 g; Sugar 0.4 g; Protein 5.8 g; Cholesterol 109 mg

Cheesecake Muffins

Preparation Time: 10 minutes; Cooking Time: 20 minutes; Serve: 12

Ingredients:
- 2 eggs
- 16 oz cream cheese
- 1/2 tsp vanilla
- 1/2 cup Swerve
- 6 tbsp unsweetened cocoa powder

Directions:
1. Preheat the cosori air fryer to 350 F.
2. In a mixing bowl, beat cream cheese until smooth.
3. Add remaining ingredients and beat until well combined.
4. Spoon mixture into the silicone muffin molds.
5. Place molds in the air fryer basket and cook for 18-20 minutes. Cook in batches.
6. Serve and enjoy.

Nutritional Value (Amount per Serving):
Calories 149; Fat 14.3 g; Carbohydrates 2.6 g; Sugar 0.2 g; Protein 4.3 g; Cholesterol 69 mg

Blueberry Muffins

Preparation Time: 10 minutes; Cooking Time: 20 minutes; Serve: 12

Ingredients:
- 2 eggs
- 1/2 tsp vanilla

- 1/2 cups Swerve
- 16 oz cream cheese
- 1/4 cup almonds, sliced
- 1/4 cup blueberries

Directions:
1. Preheat the cosori air fryer to 350 F.
2. In a mixing bowl, beat cream cheese until smooth.
3. Add eggs, vanilla, and sweetener and beat until well combined.
4. Add almonds and blueberries and fold well.
5. Spoon mixture into the silicone muffin molds.
6. Place molds in the air fryer basket and cook for 20 minutes. Cook in batches.
7. Serve and enjoy.

Nutritional Value (Amount per Serving):
Calories 156; Fat 14.9 g; Carbohydrates 2 g; Sugar 0.5 g; Protein 4.2 g; Cholesterol 69 mg

Butter Cookies

Preparation Time: 10 minutes; Cooking Time: 10 minutes; Serve: 10

Ingredients:
- 3 tbsp butter, softened
- 1/4 cup Swerve
- 1/2 tsp vanilla
- 1 cup almond flour

Directions:
1. Preheat the cosori air fryer to 350 F.
2. Line air fryer basket with parchment paper.
3. Add all ingredients into the mixing bowl and mix until well combined.
4. Make 1-inch balls from mixture and place in an air fryer basket. In batches.
5. Using a fork flatten each ball and cook for 10 minutes.
6. Serve and enjoy.

Nutritional Value (Amount per Serving):
Calories 47; Fat 4.9 g; Carbohydrates 0.7 g; Sugar 0.1 g; Protein 0.6 g; Cholesterol 9 mg

Almond Cookies

Preparation Time: 10 minutes; Cooking Time: 12 minutes; Serve: 12

Ingredients:
- 1 cup almond flour
- 2 1/2 tbsp Swerve
- 1 tbsp water
- 2 tbsp coconut oil, melted
- Pinch of salt

Directions:
1. Preheat the cosori air fryer to 350 F.
2. Line air fryer basket with parchment paper.
3. Add all ingredients into the mixing bowl and mix until well combined.
4. Make 1-inch balls from mixture and place in an air fryer basket. In batches.
5. Using a fork flatten each ball and cook for 10-12 minutes.
6. Serve and enjoy.

Nutritional Value (Amount per Serving):
Calories 34; Fat 3.4 g; Carbohydrates 0.9 g; Sugar 0.1 g; Protein 0.5 g; Cholesterol 0 mg

Cream Cheese Brownies

Preparation Time: 10 minutes; Cooking Time: 20 minutes; Serve: 12

Ingredients:
- 6 eggs
- 2 tsp vanilla
- 1/2 tsp baking powder
- 2/3 cup unsweetened cocoa powder
- 1 1/2 sticks butter, melted
- 4 tbsp Swerve

- 4 oz cream cheese, softened

Directions:
1. Add all ingredients into the large bowl and beat until smooth using a hand mixer.
2. Pour mixture into the greased air fryer baking dish.
3. Place dish into the air fryer basket and cook at 350 F for 20 minutes.
4. Slice and serve.

Nutritional Value (Amount per Serving):
Calories 181; Fat 17.6 g; Carbohydrates 3.9 g; Sugar 0.4 g; Protein 4.5 g; Cholesterol 123 mg

Chocolate Protein Brownie

Preparation Time: 10 minutes; Cooking Time: 15 minutes; Serve: 8

Ingredients:
- 1/2 tsp vanilla
- 3 tbsp coconut butter, melted
- 4 egg whites
- 2 scoops chocolate protein powder
- 3 tbsp unsweetened cocoa powder
- 1/4 cup Swerve
- 1/4 cup almond flour
- 1/4 tsp salt

Directions:
1. Preheat the cosori air fryer to 300 F.
2. Grease air fryer baking dish and set aside.
3. In a medium bowl, mix together all dry ingredients.
4. Add egg whites, vanilla, and melted coconut butter into the mixing bowl and beat until smooth.
5. Add dry mixture into the egg white mixture and mix until well combined.
6. Pour batter into the prepared dish.
7. Place dish into the air fryer basket and cook for 15 minutes.
8. Slice and serve.

Nutritional Value (Amount per Serving):
Calories 70; Fat 4.5 g; Carbohydrates 3.3 g; Sugar 0.8 g; Protein 5.2 g; Cholesterol 5 mg

Brownie Bites

Preparation Time: 10 minutes; Cooking Time: 20 minutes; Serve: 12

Ingredients:
- 6 eggs
- 4 oz cream cheese
- 2 tsp vanilla
- 1/2 tsp baking powder
- 2 oz unsweetened cocoa powder
- 5 oz butter, melted
- 1/2 cup walnuts, chopped
- 4 tbsp Swerve

Directions:
1. Add all ingredients except walnuts into the mixing bowl and beat until smooth.
2. Add walnuts and fold well.
3. Pour batter into the greased air fryer baking dish.
4. Place dish into the air fryer basket and cook at 350 F for 20-25 minutes.
5. Slice and serve.

Nutritional Value (Amount per Serving):
Calories 196; Fat 18.8 g; Carbohydrates 4.4 g; Sugar 0.4 g; Protein 5.8 g; Cholesterol 118 mg

Zucchini Brownies

Preparation Time: 10 minutes; Cooking Time: 20 minutes; Serve: 6

Ingredients:
- 2 eggs, lightly beaten
- 1/4 cup Swerve
- 1 cup sun butter
- 1/2 cup unsweetened cocoa powder

- 1/4 cup unsweetened coconut milk
- 1 zucchini, shredded and squeeze out all liquid
- 1/4 cup coconut flour

Directions:
1. Preheat the cosori air fryer to 350 F.
2. Line air fryer baking dish with parchment paper and set aside.
3. In a large bowl, mix together sun butter, milk, and eggs.
4. Add coconut flour, sweetener, zucchini, and cocoa powder and stir to combine.
5. Pour mixture in prepare dish.
6. Place dish into the air fryer basket and cook for 20 minutes.
7. Slice and serve.

Nutritional Value (Amount per Serving):
Calories 109; Fat 6.2 g; Carbohydrates 12.4 g; Sugar 1.8 g; Protein 5.1 g; Cholesterol 55 mg

Chocolate Almond Butter Brownies

Preparation Time: 10 minutes; Cooking Time: 20 minutes; Serve: 4
Ingredients:
- 1/2 cup almond butter, melted
- 2 tbsp unsweetened cocoa powder
- 2 tbsp walnuts, chopped
- 1 cup bananas, overripe
- 1 scoop whey protein powder

Directions:
1. Preheat the cosori air fryer to 350 F.
2. Spray air fryer baking dish with cooking spray.
3. Add all ingredients except walnut into the blender and blend until smooth.
4. Pour batter into the prepared dish. Add walnuts into the batter and stir well.
5. Place dish into the air fryer basket and cook for 20 minutes.
6. Serve and enjoy.

Nutritional Value (Amount per Serving):
Calories 106; Fat 4.4 g; Carbohydrates 11.7 g; Sugar 5 g; Protein 7.9 g; Cholesterol 16 mg

Choco Lava Cake

Preparation Time: 10 minutes; Cooking Time: 9 minutes; Serve: 2
Ingredients:
- 1 egg
- 2 tbsp water
- 2 tbsp unsweetened cocoa powder
- 1/2 tsp baking powder
- 1 tbsp flax meal
- 2 tbsp Swerve
- 1 tbsp coconut oil, melted
- Pinch of salt

Directions:
1. Whisk all ingredients into the bowl and pour in two ramekins.
2. Preheat the cosori air fryer to 350 F.
3. Place ramekins in the air fryer basket and cook for 8-9 minutes.
4. Serve and enjoy.

Nutritional Value (Amount per Serving):
Calories 124; Fat 11 g; Carbohydrates 6.7 g; Sugar 0.3 g; Protein 4.6 g; Cholesterol 82 mg

Delicious Coffee Cake

Preparation Time: 10 minutes; Cooking Time: 20 minutes; Serve: 6
Ingredients:
- 4 eggs
- 1/4 cup Swerve
- 1 cup butter, softened
- 2/3 cup dried cranberries

- 1 1/2 cups almond flour
- 1 tsp vanilla
- 1 tsp orange zest
- 2 tsp mixed spice
- 2 tsp cinnamon

Directions:
1. Preheat the cosori air fryer to 350 F.
2. In a bowl, add swerve and melted butter and beat until fluffy.
3. Add cinnamon, vanilla, and mixed spice and stir well.
4. Add egg one by one and stir to combine. Add almond flour, orange zest, and cranberries and mix until well combined.
5. Pour batter into the greased air fryer cake pan.
6. Place cake pan into the air fryer basket and cook for 20 minutes.
7. Slice and serve.

Nutritional Value (Amount per Serving):
- Calories 364; Fat 37.1 g; Carbohydrates 3.7 g; Sugar 1.1 g; ; Cholesterol 190 mg

Vanilla Cake

Preparation Time: 10 minutes; Cooking Time: 35 minutes; Serve: 9
Ingredients:
- 5 eggs
- 1 tsp vanilla
- 1 tsp baking powder
- 6 oz almond flour
- 1/2 cup butter, softened
- 1 cup Erythritol
- 4 oz cream cheese, softened

Directions:
1. Preheat the cosori air fryer to 350 F.
2. Grease air fryer cake pan and set aside.
3. Add all ingredients into the mixing bowl and whisk until fluffy.
4. Pour batter into the prepared pan.
5. Place pan into the air fryer basket and cook for 35-40 minutes.
6. Slice and serve.

Nutritional Value (Amount per Serving):
- Calories 278; Fat 26.4 g; Carbohydrates 4.9 g; Sugar 1 g; Protein 8.1 g;

Apple Chips

Preparation Time: 10 minutes; Cooking Time: 8 minutes; Serve: 6
Ingredients:
- 3 apples, wash, core and thinly slice
- 1 tsp ground cinnamon
- Pinch of salt

Directions:
1. Rub apple slices with cinnamon and salt and place it into the air fryer basket.
2. Cook at 390 F for 8 minutes. Turn halfway through.
3. Serve and enjoy.

Nutritional Value (Amount per Serving):
Calories 11; Fat 0 g; Carbohydrates 3 g; Sugar 2.2 g; Protein 0.1 g; Cholesterol 0 mg

Spiced Apples

Preparation Time: 10 minutes; Cooking Time: 10 minutes; Serve: 6
Ingredients:
- 4 small apples, sliced
- 2 tbsp coconut oil, melted
- 1 tsp apple pie spice
- 1/2 cup erythritol

Directions:

1. Add apple slices in a mixing bowl and sprinkle sweetener, apple pie spice, and coconut oil over apple and toss to coat.
2. Transfer apple slices in the air fryer dish.
3. Place dish in the air fryer basket and cook at 350 F for 10 minutes.
4. Serve and enjoy.

Nutritional Value (Amount per Serving):
Calories 117; Fat 4.8 g; Carbohydrates 20.7 g; Sugar 15.5 g; Protein 0.4 g; Cholesterol 0 mg

Delicious Pumpkin Muffins

Preparation Time: 10 minutes; Cooking Time: 20 minutes; Serve: 10
Ingredients:
- 4 large eggs
- 2/3 cup erythritol
- 1 tsp vanilla
- 1/3 cup coconut oil, melted
- 1/2 cup almond flour
- 1/2 cup pumpkin puree
- 1 tbsp pumpkin pie spice
- 1 tbsp baking powder, gluten-free
- 1/2 cup coconut flour
- 1/2 tsp sea salt

Directions:
1. Preheat the cosori air fryer to 325 F.
2. In a large bowl, mix together coconut flour, pumpkin pie spice, baking powder, erythritol, almond flour, and sea salt.
3. Stir in eggs, vanilla, coconut oil, and pumpkin puree until well combined.
4. Pour batter into the silicone muffin molds.
5. Place molds into the air fryer basket and cook for 20 minutes. In batches.
6. Serve and enjoy.

Nutritional Value (Amount per Serving):
Calories 135; Fat 12.3 g; Carbohydrates 14 g; Sugar 0.9 g; Protein 4 g; Cholesterol 74 mg

Cheese Cake

Preparation Time: 10 minutes; Cooking Time: 30 minutes; Serve: 8
Ingredients:
- 3 eggs, lightly beaten
- 1 tsp baking powder
- 1/2 cup ghee, melted
- 1 cup almond flour
- 1/3 cup Swerve
- 1 cup ricotta cheese, soft

Directions:
1. Add all ingredients into the bowl and mix until well combined.
2. Pour batter into the greased air fryer baking dish.
3. Place dish into the air fryer basket and cook at 350 F for 30 minutes.
4. Slice and serve.

Nutritional Value (Amount per Serving):
Calories 259; Fat 23.8 g; Carbohydrates 5.1 g; Sugar 0.7 g; Protein 8.7 g; Cholesterol 104 mg

Air Fried Pineapple Slices

Preparation Time: 5 minutes; Cooking Time: 20 minutes; Serve: 4
Ingredients:
- 4 pineapple slices
- 2 tbsp erythritol
- 1 tsp cinnamon

Directions:
1. Add pineapple slices, sweetener, and cinnamon into the zip-lock bag. Shake well and place into the fridge for 30 minutes.
2. Preheat the cosori air fryer to 350 F.

3. Place pineapples slices into the air fryer basket and cook for 20 minutes. Turn halfway through.
4. Serve and enjoy.

Nutritional Value (Amount per Serving):
Calories 11; Fat 0 g; Carbohydrates 11.7 g; Sugar 11 g; Protein 0 g; Cholesterol 0 mg

Vanilla Custard

Preparation Time: 10 minutes; Cooking Time: 20 minutes; Serve: 2

Ingredients:
- 5 eggs
- 1/2 cup unsweetened almond milk
- 1/2 cup cream cheese
- 2 tbsp swerve
- 1 tsp vanilla

Directions:
1. Add eggs in a bowl and beat using a hand mixer.
2. Add cream cheese, sweetener, vanilla, and almond milk and beat for 2 minutes.
3. Spray two ramekins with cooking spray.
4. Pour batter into the prepared ramekins.
5. Preheat the cosori air fryer to 350 F.
6. Place ramekins into the air fryer basket and cook for 20 minutes.
7. Serve and enjoy.

Nutritional Value (Amount per Serving):
Calories 381; Fat 32 g; Carbohydrates 5.2 g; Sugar 1.2 g; Protein 18.5 g; Cholesterol 473 mg

Mozzarella Cheese Butter Cookies

Preparation Time: 10 minutes; Cooking Time: 12 minutes; Serve: 8

Ingredients:
- 2 eggs
- 1/3 cup mozzarella cheese, shredded
- 1 1/4 cup almond flour
- 5 tbsp butter, melted
- 1/3 cup sour cream
- 1/2 tsp baking powder
- 1/2 tsp salt

Directions:
1. Preheat the cosori air fryer to 370 F.
2. Add all ingredients into a large bowl and mix using a hand mixer.
3. Spoon batter into the mini silicone muffin molds.
4. Place molds into the air fryer basket and cook for 12 minutes.
5. Serve and enjoy.

Nutritional Value (Amount per Serving):
Calories 204; Fat 19.3 g; Carbohydrates 4.4 g; Sugar 0.7 g; Protein 5.8 g; Cholesterol 65 mg

Vanilla Almond Cinnamon Mug Cake

Preparation Time: 5 minutes; Cooking Time: 10 minutes; Serve: 1

Ingredients:
- 1 scoop vanilla protein powder
- 1/2 tsp baking powder
- 1/4 tsp vanilla
- 1/4 cup unsweetened almond milk
- 1/2 tsp cinnamon
- 1 tsp Swerve
- 1 tbsp almond flour

Directions:
1. Add protein powder, cinnamon, almond flour, sweetener, and baking powder into the mug and mix well.
2. Add vanilla and milk and stir well.

3. Place the mug in the air fryer basket and cook at 390 F for 10 minutes
4. Serve and enjoy.

Nutritional Value (Amount per Serving):
Calories 174; Fat 4.5 g; Carbohydrates 6.7 g; Sugar 0.7 g; Protein 28.8 g; Cholesterol 2 mg

Choco Mug Brownie

Preparation Time: 5 minutes; Cooking Time: 10 minutes; Serve: 1

Ingredients:
- 1 scoop chocolate protein powder
- 1/2 tsp baking powder
- 1/4 cup unsweetened almond milk
- 1 tbsp cocoa powder

Directions:
1. Add baking powder, protein powder, and cocoa powder in a heat-safe mug and mix well.
2. Add milk and stir well.
3. Place the mug in the air fryer basket and cook at 390 F for 10 minutes.
4. Serve and enjoy.

Nutritional Value (Amount per Serving):
Calories 79; Fat 2.4 g; Carbohydrates 6.6 g; Sugar 1.1 g; Protein 11.2 g; Cholesterol 20 mg

Lemon Ricotta Cake

Preparation Time: 10 minutes; Cooking Time: 40 minutes; Serve: 8

Ingredients:
- 4 eggs
- 1 lemon juice
- 1 lb ricotta
- 1 lemon zest
- 1/4 cup Swerve

Directions:
1. Preheat the cosori air fryer to 325 F.
2. Spray air fryer baking dish with cooking spray.
3. In a bowl, beat ricotta cheese until smooth. Whisk in the eggs one by one.
4. Whisk in lemon juice and zest. Pour batter into the prepared baking dish.
5. Place dish into the air fryer basket and cook for 40 minutes.
6. Slice and serve.

Nutritional Value (Amount per Serving):
Calories 110; Fat 6.7 g; Carbohydrates 3.1 g; Sugar 0.4 g; Protein 9.2 g; Cholesterol 99 m

Cinnamon Cappuccino Muffins

Preparation Time: 10 minutes; Cooking Time: 25 minutes; Serve: 12

Ingredients:
- 4 eggs
- 1 tsp espresso powder
- 1 tsp cinnamon
- 2 tsp baking powder
- 1/4 cup coconut flour
- 1/2 cup Swerve
- 2 cups almond flour
- 1/2 tsp vanilla
- 1/2 cup sour cream
- 1/4 tsp salt

Directions:
1. Preheat the cosori air fryer to 350 F.
2. Add sour cream, vanilla, espresso powder, and eggs in a blender and blend until smooth.
3. Add almond flour, cinnamon, baking powder, coconut flour, Swerve, and salt and blend to combine.
4. Pour mixture into the silicone muffin molds.
5. Place molds into the air fryer basket and cook for 25 minutes. Cook in batches.
6. Serve and enjoy.

Nutritional Value (Amount per Serving):
Calories 151; Fat 12.9 g; Carbohydrates 5.3 g; Sugar 0.8 g; Protein 6.2 g; Cholesterol 59 mg

Moist Pumpkin Muffins

Preparation Time: 10 minutes; Cooking Time: 25 minutes; Serve: 10

Ingredients:
- 4 large eggs
- 1/2 cup almond flour
- 1 tsp vanilla
- 1/3 cup coconut oil, melted
- 1/2 cup pumpkin puree
- 1 tbsp pumpkin pie spice
- 1 tbsp baking powder, gluten-free
- 2/3 cup Swerve
- 1/2 cup coconut flour
- 1/2 tsp sea salt

Directions:
1. Preheat the cosori air fryer to 350 F.
2. In a large bowl, stir together coconut flour, pumpkin pie spice, baking powder, erythritol, almond flour, and sea salt.
3. Stir in eggs, vanilla, coconut oil, and pumpkin puree until well combined.
4. Pour mixture into the silicone muffin molds.
5. Place molds into the air fryer basket and cook for 25 minutes. Cook in batches.
6. Serve and enjoy.

Nutritional Value (Amount per Serving):
Calories 135; Fat 12.3 g; Carbohydrates 4 g; Sugar 0.9 g; Protein 4 g; Cholesterol 74 mg

Chapter 11: 30-Day Meal Plan

Day 1
Breakfast-Cheese Vegetable Frittata
Lunch-Delicious Chicken Fajita
Dinner-Mustard Pork Chops

Day 2
Breakfast-Sausage Egg Scramble
Lunch-Classic Greek Chicken
Dinner-Garlic Pork Chops

Day 3
Breakfast-Cheese Egg Breakfast Muffins
Lunch-Juicy Chicken Breasts
Dinner-Cheddar Cheese Pork Chops

Day 4
Breakfast-Classic Sweet Potato Hash
Lunch-Flavors Dijon Chicken
Dinner-Air Fried Pork Chops

Day 5
Breakfast-Easy Cheesy Breakfast Eggs
Lunch-Jerk Chicken Legs
Dinner-Herb Butter Pork Chops

Day 6
Breakfast-Cheese Egg Frittata
Lunch-Flavors & Crisp Chicken Thighs
Dinner-Crispy Crusted Pork Chops

Day 7
Breakfast-Cheese Ham Egg Cups
Lunch-Quick & Easy Lemon Pepper Chicken
Dinner-Lemon Pepper Seasoned Pork Chops

Day 8
Breakfast-Healthy Spinach Omelet
Lunch-Spicy Jalapeno Hassel-back Chicken
Dinner-Delicious Ranch Pork Chops

Day 9
Breakfast-Cheese Mushroom Egg Bake
Lunch-Healthy Greek Chicken
Dinner-Juicy & Tasty Pork Chops

Day 10
Breakfast-Breakfast Radish Hash Browns
Lunch-Delicious Chicken Meatballs
Dinner-Tasty Onion Pork Chops

Day 11
Breakfast-Cheese Omelet
Lunch-Easy Cajun Shrimp
Dinner-Simple Air Fryer Pork Chops

Day 12
Breakfast-Cheese Sausage Egg Muffins
Lunch-Tender & Juicy Salmon
Dinner-Spicy Pork Steak

Day 13
Breakfast-Easy Breakfast Frittata
Lunch-Shrimp & Vegetable Dinner
Dinner-Easy Pork Butt

Day 14
Breakfast-Bell Pepper Broccoli Frittata
Lunch-Lemon Garlic Shrimp
Dinner-Dash Seasoned Pork Chops

Day 15
Breakfast-Sausage Cheese Breakfast Frittata
Lunch-Lemon Garlic White Fish
Dinner-Easy & Delicious Pork Chops

Day 16
Breakfast-Sausage Spinach Egg Cups
Lunch-Easy Coconut Shrimp
Dinner-Tender Pork Chops

Day 17
Breakfast-Spinach Garlic Egg Muffins
Lunch-Parmesan White Fish Fillets
Dinner-Marinated Steak
Day 18
Breakfast-Veggie Frittata
Lunch-Tasty Shrimp Fajitas
Dinner-Asian Beef
Day 19
Breakfast-Kale Egg Muffins
Lunch-Ginger Garlic Salmon
Dinner-Flavorful Beef Roast
Day 20
Breakfast-Cheese Mushroom Frittata
Lunch-Tasty Chipotle Shrimp
Dinner-Cheese Butter Steak
Day 21
Breakfast-Cottage Cheese Egg Cups
Lunch-Tuna Patties
Dinner-Rosemary Thyme Beef Roast
Day 22
Breakfast-Tasty Herb Egg Cups
Lunch-Cheesy Chicken Fritters
Dinner-Tender & Juicy Kebab
Day 23
Breakfast-Tomato Basil Egg Muffins
Lunch-Delicious Chicken Burger Patties
Dinner-Tasty Ginger Garlic Beef

Day 24
Breakfast-Pepper Feta Egg Muffins
Lunch-Cheddar Cheese Omelet
Dinner-Spiced Steak
Day 25
Breakfast-Garlic Cheese Quiche
Lunch-Lemon Chicken Breasts
Dinner-Healthy Beef & Broccoli
Day 26
Breakfast-Zucchini Breakfast Patties
Lunch-Sausage Swiss Cheese Egg Bite
Dinner-Garlicky Beef & Broccoli
Day 27
Breakfast-Broccoli Quiche
Lunch-Gruyere Cheese Egg Bite
Dinner-Beef Berger Patties
Day 28
Breakfast-Cheese Sausage Pepper Frittata
Lunch-Broccoli Quiche
Dinner-Tasty Beef Satay
Day 29
Breakfast-Mushroom Frittata
Lunch-Garlic Cheese Quiche
Dinner- Rib Eye Steak
Day 30
Breakfast-Broccoli Bell Pepper Frittata
Lunch-Cheese Sausage Pepper Frittata
Dinner- Steak with Mushrooms

Conclusion

Keto diet and Cosori air fryer are one of the unique combinations of healthy and nutritious diet plan and a modern healthy cooking appliance. Keto diet is one of the world-famous healthy diet which is low in carb and high in fat. Most of the peoples worldwide use this diet for rapid weight loss purpose. Keto diet has various health benefits, in this book we have seen various health benefits of keto diet.

The book contains healthy keto diet recipes like breakfast and brunch, poultry, beef, pork, lamb, snacks and appetizer, seafood, meatless meal and desserts. All the recipes in this book are unique and written in easily understandable form. The recipes written in this book are given its exact preparation and cooking time.

www.ingramcontent.com/pod-product-compliance
Lightning Source LLC
Chambersburg PA
CBHW081345070526
44578CB00005B/734